THE FROZEN REVOLUTION

Books by Frank Gibney

FIVE GENTLEMEN OF JAPAN

THE FROZEN REVOLUTION

THE

FROZEN REVOLUTION

POLAND: A STUDY IN COMMUNIST DECAY

BY FRANK GIBNEY

FARRAR, STRAUS AND CUDAHY · NEW YORK

Contents

Author's Note		ix
Introduction		xi
1.	The Makings of an October Day	3
2.	The Contrary Communist and How He Grew	32
3.	The Party on the Operating Table	56
4.	The Intellectuals' Revolt	88
5.	The Cardinal's Country	122
6.	Taming the Wild West	169
7.	The Pond at Oswiecim	185
8.	Pillage and Patriots	195
9.	The Plan and the Jungle	215
	Epilogue	256
	Index	265

For Harri

Author's Note

When I arrived in Poland, in May 1957, I had planned to write little more than a short travel diary about my trip there. On reflection I decided to attempt what resulted: a more ambitious study of Poland's experience under Communism. This was partly because of my instant attraction to the Polish people and their country, but principally because of the importance of their experience before and after October, 1956, and its clear relevance to the conflict between Communism and the free society.

I have written this book with diffidence. Although both in Poland and in the United States I have consulted books, articles and people *ad infinitum* on the subject, I lay no claim whatsoever to be an expert on Polish problems. I went to Poland as a reporter, who felt an urgent need to tell what he saw. To make my account more comprehensive, I did a great deal of amateur scholarship on the subject after my return. If reporters object that I have too many footnotes, and scholars that I have too few, I shall be content.

Except for part of chapters 7 and 8, where I felt some personal narrative was useful, I have tried to discuss the country without intruding my own personal experiences.

Although I have indicated most written sources in the text, the nature of the subject prevents me from extending personal acknowledgment to the many Poles and foreigners, either resident in Poland or conversant with its problems, with whom I talked. They were unfailingly patient with my questions. I would like to thank the representatives of the Polish government whom I encountered, also, for their kindness in helping with my travel arrangements. I found that travel through Poland was indeed free of any restriction, nor was I subjected to any form of censorship while I was there. They will doubtless disagree with many of my conclusions, but their courtesy helped one stranger to a lasting admiration of their nation.

Members of the foreign press corps in Warsaw, an intelligent and necessarily mercurial brotherhood, were universally hospitable and helpful during my stay in Poland. So were other authorities elsewhere in Europe and the United States. In particular I would like to thank Mr. William E. Griffith, now of the Massachusetts Institute of Technology, and his former associates for their invaluable counsel and assistance. Above all, I shall always remember the help of my friend and traveling companion on my trip through the Polish countryside, the late Dan Weiner. His untimely death early this year robbed American journalism of a great photographer, who was at the same time a sensitive and perceptive reporter.

New York
April, 1959

Introduction

Europe had two revolutions in October, 1956. They were the first popular revolutions against established authority in the world since the anti-colonial revolts in Asia immediately after World War II, and the first in Europe since the Russian Revolution of 1917. One, the Hungarian revolution, began in Budapest on October 23 and was suppressed by Russian troops after the first week in November. The street battle of the Hungarian freedom-fighters will go down in history as a Thermopylae of civilized people resisting animal force. It resulted in the deaths of most of its leaders and years of reprisal against the people of the country.

The other, the Polish revolution, was encompassed within 48 hours—October 19–20—in which the formal and actual government was transferred from a Soviet Russian viceroyalty to a Polish government overwhelmingly supported by the country. Although the country stood ready to defend its revolution, a military defense was not necessary. Power passed bloodlessly and the fact was acclaimed as almost miraculous—like the feat of extracting an egg's yolk without breaking the shell.

Both revolutions came from the same source, the Soviet Russian colonization of Eastern Europe. Both tore the steel lid, temporarily, from a system of oppressive oligarchic government masquerading as a revolutionary philosophy. They proved to any who still doubted that the honest revolutionary impulses in the Bolshevik Revolution had indeed been slaughtered in its first few years (along with hundreds of thousands of Russians). "A nation which suppresses another," Marx's friend Frederick Engels had said prophetically, "cannot emancipate itself."

As absolute rebellions against the power of Soviet imperialism, both revolutions, judged absolutely, failed. Yet each achieved something of what it was fighting for, in a striking and peculiar way.

The Hungarian revolt—unplanned, unorganized, uncompromising—was the explosion of a brutalized people against tyranny. Like the Czar's troops who crushed the Hungarian revolt of 1848, the Soviet divisions stamped out every trace of resistance. All that the Hungarian rebels left to the world was their example, which was as clear and uncompromising as their act. The small war in Budapest forever destroyed the pretensions of the Russian leadership to morality, decency or justice; the same oligarchy which had attacked the crimes of Stalin showed itself to be equally criminal, when occasion demanded. In a world often deluded by Soviet pretensions, this example counted for much.

The fighting in Budapest did something equally important to the leaders of world Communism, something which had been suggested, but not thoroughly defined by the earlier 1953 rising in East Germany. It put the taste of fear in their mouths. 1956 became to the Communist leadership the same kind of calendar warning that 1848 was to the emperors of Europe. And in a world where history moves far faster, it must have been clear to this century's despots that they could not count on the seventy years of grace given to the Hapsburgs and the Romanovs.

The October Revolution in Poland was more lasting, more complicated to describe, more deadly to Communism. Where the Hungarian revolt failed, the Polish half-succeeded. The Poles were able to control, but not to extirpate the abuses of Soviet domination. They were able to gain an unprecedented independence in domestic self-government, while preserving the form of the obedient Communist satellite Poland had been before October. They accepted loans from the United States, the enemy of Communism, for an economy that inevitably remained largely dependent on Soviet materials. The leader of this revolution not only pledged his loyalty to Communism, but worked hard to rebuild the Party which the same revolution had shattered. Yet his policies were denounced as heresy by every other Communist regime—except Tito's—at the top of its mobilized lung-power. The Poles regained freedom of speech and freedom of religion, only to have both these restored privileges subjected to constant sawing tension.

The Polish Revolution, in short, was frozen in its tracks. The factors that froze it were many, and not all of them worked consciously. There was geography, which had played so many cruel tricks in Poland's history, seeing to it that Poland had no boundary with the non-Communist world, but was surrounded everywhere by Soviet force. There was a complex of self-neutralizing forces in the revolution itself—anti-Russian Communists, non-Communist Marxists, anticlerical liberals, liberal Catholics, Socialist workers, conservative peasantry.

There was, most importantly, the world stalemate between the Soviet Union and the United States, with their near parity of atomic weapons. That the United States government did not intervene quickly enough in Hungary—diplomatically, economically, or even in the form of threatened military force—was one of the great lost opportunities of post-war history, and a tragic, complete failure of American leadership. But the fact that the United States existed, and possessed force, was enough of a deterrent to save the half-revolution in Poland in 1956. For the moment a badly scared Russian leadership shrank from further open coercion. The Russians, like the Americans, thus showed their consciousness of living on an international political glass sea, where the slightest disturbing ripple makes itself felt over the whole surface, and the idlest chance wave may cause a generally destroying flood.

As the rickety stop-gap of hasty political compromise became, *faute de mieux,* the working mechanism for a country of 28,500,-000 people, it seemed to many, through the months that followed, that the Polish half-revolution was a whole failure. The heroic clarity of decision which was reached in Hungary became ever more blurred in Poland. Waverings between revolutionary hope and oppressive reality were translated into a curious national policy, which seemed logical only in the sense that it was disappointing to everyone.

All this was wrong. For the Poles in carrying out their Frozen Revolution had in fact gone far beyond the Hungarians in their destructive effect on the imperial Communist system. As Poland's "humane socialism," relatively unmarred by police terror, tried to work out its destinies by the public practice of Communism, the fallacy of this System was unroofed as a gigantic laboratory of confusion, with a completeness not thought possible. The crimes of past Communist regimes were laid out in awesome clarity. Even when trying hardest to correct them, by their own methods, Poland's national Communist leaders gave a lesson in the decay of this system as a political or economic, not to say moral—way of life. The conflicting freedoms and repressions inside their country gave the world another unique lesson—that Gresham's Law is not true of political coinage—for the customs of a free society, wherever the Poles reintroduced them, began forthwith to drive Communist methods out.

By the very existence of the Frozen Revolution, Poland opened a door to democracy's peaceful reinvasion of the world of Communism. Its half-freedom infected the rest of the Communist world. It stirred a cycle of thinking, disturbance, and resentment. There is no better witness to this than the constant efforts of the Soviet leaders to smother the Frozen Revolution and wall it up within their own broad glacier. For Russians as well as Czechs, Bulgarians and Chinese, have taken serious note of the freedoms which a stubborn people can carve out for themselves, even within the form of a Communist state, which by definition restricts liberty whenever it sees it.

In 1959 Communism is in retreat ideologically, at the moment of its greatest physical triumphs. We cannot underestimate the importance of the country which has forecast the direction of this retreat. As Ernst Halperin, a shrewd Swiss commentator on Eastern Europe, put it: "For more than 20 years, since the Comintern laid down the Popular Front strategy at the twelfth World Congress, Communist totalitarianism has again and again used democracy as camouflage. Today one encounters for the first time here in Poland an experience where democracy camouflages itself under the cloak of totalitarianism."

THE FROZEN REVOLUTION

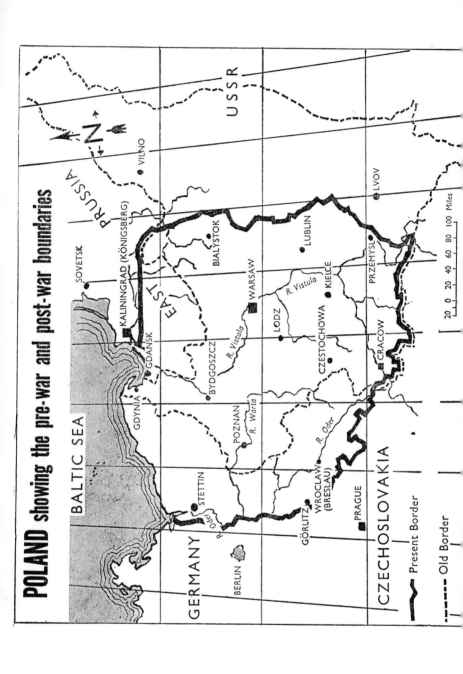

POLAND showing the pre-war and post-war boundaries

1

The Makings of an October Day

> "There is a tremendous difference between simply
> repairing a bridge and building a new one . . ."
>
> —*Nikolai I. Bukharin*

IN THE FIRST hours of October 20, 1956, the Communist satellite government of Poland announced to the leading members of the Soviet Politburo its decision to seek Poland's own course as a nation, after ten years as a Russian satellite. Given a slightly different set of circumstances—a weaker Russia, notably, or a more watchful and powerful United States, the announcement might have changed the course of history then and there. At another moment it might have resulted in complete suppression, sending the members of Wladyslaw Gomulka's Central Committee off to join the liquidated leaders of the 1938 Polish Communist party, the massacred officers of Katyn, and generations of Poles before them, in fertilizing the soil of Russian cemeteries. As things turned out, the result was tantalizingly in the middle. But in the beginning the men who cheered the Committee's decision saw their first glimpse in many decades of a future stretched clear before them, banishing clouds or compromise.

The ten days surrounding Poland's half-successful defiance were for the people who lived them as fateful as the Ten Days That Shook the World, in the words of the Soviet Revolution's Harvard biographer, in October, 1917. They had their masses of cheering and angry crowds, their barrages of revolutionary battle cries, their combustibles of students' rallies and workers' committees. Rifles were passed to civilians and armies mobilized their tanks and artillery. Lieutenants on the march demanded to know the loyalties of their colonels and ministers in the capital tested the sympathies of their colleagues. Around them a whole country quite literally rose as one man, prepared to barter its life for its dignity.

And not a shot was fired. A few offices and jail cells exchanged occupants, but there was no rioting in the streets, no bloody flags waving over the broken windows of authority. The foreign divisions went out of their barracks and returned to them. The angry lieutenants saw some of their superiors leave, and re-pledged their own loyalty. The anti-peoples' administration became the peoples' administration—so far as the eye could see, with a minimum of significant changes. The revolution won, far more than the world at the time realized. It also lost.

The events could only have happened at the time they did, in the context of a Communist society which had been shaken to its center by the death of a dictator and the consequent stirring of life among the 310,000,000 people who had lived under him. Any Communist could have predicted the exact boiling point of the October Revolution, given the signs leading to it; although to people outside the System it would not appear so simple. For a Communist it would be enough to know that the disturbance was occasioned by the approaching meeting, on October 19, of the Eighth Plenum of the Polish United Workers Party (the organizational euphemism for Communism in that country), just eight months after the 20th Plenum of the Communist Party of the USSR.

A Party plenum in any Communist country is a serious thing. In its tensions of its build-up and climaxes it resembles the time of elections in a democracy. (An *election* in Communist politics has a totally different function, resembling that of a mass-meeting or the applause and demonstration part of a U.S. national political convention.) It is at the plenum, and only then, that the various forces struggling constantly within any Communist leadership must come at least briefly to the surface, before going out to receive the compulsory approval of the multitude.

The counterplay of factions or of personality within the ruling oligarchy is difficult to disguise at such an event, particularly in the absence of an utter police dictatorship. Even the tightest censorship of the press cannot prevent some sounds of these struggles from escaping to the outside. The Plenum's announcements are masked always with the dramatic clichés of "friendly debate," "Party spirit" and "fraternal criticism." But, whether in Bulgaria or North Korea, they have their own decisive and quite opposite meaning to the initiate. The position of a man's name in a Politburo announcement, a significant phrase added to a closing speech, the reapportionment of Party tasks, the weight however slight of the intra-Party criticism—all these can be matters of life or death to a man, a faction or a country. On the occasion of the Eighth Plenum in Warsaw, the Polish United Workers Party showed far more than the normal tensions visible to the trained Party eye. The Party as it was constituted literally broke apart. A new and for a long time undefined organism took its place.

The underlying cause of this fissioning process was the death of Josef Stalin in 1953. The consequent wave of reaction to "Stalinism" spread through the most tightly regimented Communist countries. Over a three year period, it grew to dangerous proportions, with the downfall of Beria and the succession of dog-fights among the leadership. On February 16, 1956 Nikita Khrushchev found it necessary to exorcise Stalin's ghost in his famous secret speech to the Twentieth Party Congress, one of the really extraordinary addresses of our time. Khrushchev attached "Stalin's despotism" as having disfigured Communism in every respect, from mass executions ("let my cry of horror reach your ears") to the adulteration of school textbooks. With this speech crashed the colossal Father Image which had, unfortunately for Khrushchev's purpose, been all too inextricably fitted into the masonry of Communist belief and practice.

In Poland, the largest of the Russian satellite countries, the ultimate effect of death and denunciation was impossible to control: the more so since President Boleslaw Bierut, the efficient Stalinist dictator of Poland, died in March, 1956, in the course of a visit to the Soviet Union. With Bierut out of the way, there was no one even remotely capable of stemming the tide of anti-Stalinist resentment that was sweeping his country. The resentment was shared by the young Communists, who had become disgusted with the corrupt administration. To their way of thinking, the Stalinist apparatus had brutally violated the tenets of true Marxism. It was shared even more vehemently by the mass of the Polish people, exploited and collectivized by the Russians, who by 1956 hated the Russians with a violence exceeding even the wartime hatred of the Germans.

At Poznan, on June 28, workers of the Cegielski factory rioted, after a prolonged dispute with regime representatives over their declining wages. They were joined by other elements of the population. The rioting became a bloody demonstration against the government, which only Army reinforcements were able to quell. The Poznan disturbance lasted two days, and it took on the dimensions of a full-scale revolt. Poznan, admittedly, was not a very "progressive" region by Communist standards. In the prewar Polish republic, popular sentiment in Poznan regarded Poland's old dictator, Josef Pilsudski, as a dangerous socialist. But this time rebellion was led by legitimately Socialist workers, who marched against the security police barracks singing the old battle songs of the Second International. That the rebellion was quelled quickly was due only to the accident of its spontaneity. It had neither plan nor leadership behind it. For the first Army troops called in to assist the police behaved very much like the Hungarian troops who marched into Budapest a few months later. They either made common cause with the workers, or took the vaguest of half-measures against them.

In its first post-mortems the regime pretended that Poznan was a demonstration of "provocateurs," "imperialist agents," "the reactionary underground" and other elements in Communist demonology. But this was not enough to bottle the immediate popular pressure building up inside Poland, the combination of an observed dislocation in the Communist high command and the poverty of both farmers and factory workers through a decade of Russification. After some scared consultation, the Party leadership acknowledged that "serious grievances" existed, and promised to correct them. In July, at the Seventh Plenum, it significantly accepted the resignation of Jacob Berman, Communism's *éminence grise* in Poland, who had dominated politics throughout the Stalinist period.

Between July and October the mutters of popular discontent rose to an audible roar, magnified to the last decibel by the exposés of the youthful party press, which had grown bolder in denouncing the hierarchy. The pro-Russian faction in charge of the Party grew desperate. Unable to rely any longer on local Party committees, it tried the expedient of rehabilitating former Party leaders who had been deposed and imprisoned, because of their nationalist activities, on Soviet orders. In August Wladyslaw Gomulka was restored to full Party membership from the limbo of obscurity in which he had been living, supported by a government sinecure, since his release from prison in December, 1954.

Gomulka had been deposed as First Secretary of the Party in 1949 for following the heresy of "national Communism," which is to say that he objected to Poland's becoming a Russian colony— although he remained in principle a dedicated grass-roots Communist. The fact of his later imprisonment, and the grounds, were well-known. As a result, he was the only Communist in Poland with any chance of commanding some popular support. He was also a Communist whose doctrinaire idea of "end-justifies-whatever-means" had been considerably humanized by his long confinement.

On October 15, just before the Eighth Plenum, the Polish Politburo held a meeting at which, in the bare announcement of the Party paper, "Comrade Wladyslaw Gomulka took part." This served to announce the fact that the pro-Soviet faction in Poland had thrown in the sponge, for the meeting secretly decided on Gomulka's elevation as Party Secretary. Their hand had been forced principally by two of the insiders. Premier Joseph Cyrankiewicz, a former Social Democrat, was not the most powerful man in the Communist councils. But his influence was considerable, because of his control of the official government administration. Since before Poznan he had used his authority to maneuver non-Stalinists into positions of power. Edward Ochab, the First Secretary of the Party itself, had been accounted a Stalinist. But the gross pressure which Moscow exerted on him, during a six month tenure, made him a better Polish nationalist than anyone had the right to expect. "We have had too many programs written in imported ink," he once snapped during a Party debate. It was this feeling which prompted Ochab to invite Gomulka into private discussions as early as September. In October, he turned his authority over to the other man.

The desperate reshuffling of the Party deck only made more intense the feeling for revolution, which was sweeping Poland as fully as it spread over Hungary. The non-Communist mass of the people took its cue from the bewildered, self-reproaching gestures of the Communists. The resentments of ten years crystallized. By mid-October the entire Polish nation was on the march against its governors. In Cracow, patriotic Army officers made common cause with the angry intellectuals in the universities and on the Party newspapers. A student delegation drove out to Nowa Huta, the huge steel mill complex outside Cracow, and joined forces with the workers. At Gdansk, Lodz, Katowice—everywhere in Poland, the same thing happened. In Warsaw angry students climbed the statue of Feliks Dzierzynski, the Communist Polish nobleman nicknamed "the Hangman," who had organized the Cheka, the first Soviet security police, for Lenin. The next morning, passersby cheered when they saw the statue's hands dripping with red paint. For people who had lived for ten years under a security system closely modelled on Dzierzynski's, this was no idle gesture.

The security system itself, normally the ultimate prop of a Communist regime, was too extensively shot with discontent to be effective. It had never recovered from the damaging revelations of Joseph Swiatlo, a lieutenant-colonel in its Tenth Department (charged with the care of high political prisoners) who had escaped to the West in December 1953, as an aftermath of the Beria execution in Moscow. In 1954 Swiatlo broadcast his story of inner corruption and cruelty back to Poland, over Radio Free Europe.

Even the best-organized secret police cannot stand public exposure, and the regime found it impossible to throw off the Swiatlo charges. Some leaders of the U.B. (*Urzad Bezpiéczenstwa*), or the Bezpieka, as the state security ministry was commonly called, had already been removed on popular demand. When the pro-Soviet group in the Politburo gave the U.B. a long list of names for arrest and proscription, just before the Plenum, the police not only admitted their inability to make the desired arrests, they gave a direct refusal.

The names included those of Gomulka and the anti-Soviet members of the Politburo, to say nothing of the intellectuals who had been writing all the inflammatory articles in the press. Organized by the pro-Gomulka Warsaw Party committee, groups of armed workers came to guard them all. But the guard was not necessary. Even the most faithful Soviet agents inside Poland had to concede the truth of Premier Cyrankiewicz' remark, made at a Party meeting: "If the secret police terror is to be reestablished, the community is resolved to settle its accounts with the System, even to the shedding of blood."

The last card the Russians had to play was the Polish Army, and their own. The Polish troops were under the command of Marshal Konstanty Rokossowski, a Pole who had gone to Russia at the age of 17 and joined the Soviet Army. He led Soviet troops in fact to the "liberation" of Poland, after conveniently waiting for the Polish resistance forces to destroy themselves in the 1944 Warsaw Uprising against the Germans, before completing his advance. The Russian distrust of the Poles was evident in the large number of Russian officers seconded to the Polish Army. With few exceptions, the important officers in the staff and higher field commands were Soviet citizens.

Rokossowski was a member of the Politburo in Warsaw and as such the permanent representative of the Soviet mailed fist. His own personal feelings in the crisis are a matter of speculation. Some Poles feel that he was secretly in sympathy with them, mindful of the fact that he had himself been imprisoned by Stalin's old M.V.D. for three years, up to his recall to the Army in 1941 (a fact that accounted at least for the absence of all his natural teeth). The evidence suggests he set out to do his job first and foremost as a Soviet officer, although he was close enough to the Poles to appreciate what his action could lead to. "If you want to step in and start a massacre, go ahead," Gomulka said to him, "but you can be sure no one will support you in this."

With this warning in his ears, Rokossowski had started his mobilization. Its backbone was of course the Soviet troops. Two

weeks before the Politburo began its Eighth Plenum deliberations, the Soviet garrisons based on Legnica in the west began
preparations for a march on the capital. At least one Soviet
division crept into Poland from the east, making its way across
the country to join the concentrations in the forests around Legnica. This brought the total available inside Poland to seven, with
many times that number ready to move in, not only from the Soviet
Union, but from the heavy garrison establishment in East Germany. By the time the crisis came, warships had been sighted
in the Gulf of Gdansk, keeping watch outside the Polish Navy
headquarters at Gdynia. The Soviet air strength was of course
overwhelming.

Against this formidable potential military intervention the
Poles had only the 50,000 members of the Internal Security
Corps, the K.B.W., as they were popularly (or rather unpopularly)
known, military formations attached to the secret police.* The
irony of freedom being defended by the formal representatives of
coercion had a logical explanation. In the maneuverings that led
to October, Cyrankiewicz had used his authority as Prime Minister
to appoint General Waclaw Komar to command this corps. Komar,
only released from prison a few months before, was an old supporter of Gomulka's. His appointment came on August 24, which
gave him just enough time to consolidate his hold on the K.B.W.
By October his troops were at the disposal of the Gomulka factions,
well-armed and rather grateful for being on a popular side, for a
change.

These were the opposing constants. Between them was the big
x factor in the October calculations, the 350,000 Russian-led
troops of the Polish Army. No Army units had as yet shown any
reaction to the chaos that threatened the country. But the soldiers
and officers were obviously interested in what was going on.
When a growing number of officers, field and company grade,
were being seen in the company of local pro-Gomulka commit-

---

* The K.B.W. was organized as a compact little army of its own, for imple-
menting the purposes of the Ministry of State Security. Patterned after the
uniformed forces of the Soviet K.G.B., it was equally comparable to the
Waffen-SS formations of Nazi Germany. Formerly, the K.B.W. worked
directly under the Ministry's orders. U.B. officers held reserve commissions
in the K.B.W., as well.

tee men, it was not hard to guess what their orders to the troops
would be, in case of any violence. For the Russians, the inactiv-
ity of the troops ordered out at Poznan was an uncomfortable
portent of what might happen now, given Warsaw's leadership.

Travel has a broadening influence. With the Polish crisis about
to break, this thought, if nothing else, might have comforted the
leaders of the Soviet Politburo, as they flew in for a landing at
Warsaw airport early in the damp morning of October 19. Without either an invitation or much advance billing, Khrushchev,
Mikoyan, Molotov and Kaganovitch walked onto the field to meet
the quickly marshalled Polish reception committee. They were
in a collective rage, which was not mitigated by the half-hour's
delay in landing that was forced on them by the Warsaw control
tower. Khrushchev himself was screaming about "traitors." "We
shed our blood for this country," he yelled at Ochab and Cyrankiewicz, "and now you want to sell out to the Americans and the
Zionists."* The threat behind his words was visible. A dozen
Russian generals, including the commander of the Warsaw Pact
armies, Marshal Ivan Konev, were on hand to accompany the
politicians.

It was afternoon before the Russians sat down to talk, in the
porticoed Belvedere Palace, an early nineteenth century landmark
originally built for a Russian grand duke. There was no time
wasted on preliminaries. Khrushchev and the others made it clear
that they wanted the lid put back on Poland before popular pressures blew it off, or forced the Russians to reimpose it themselves.
Politeness was not the strong point of the Russian argument;
Khrushchev started the discussions in the Belvedere with some
typically pungent comments about the Polish leadership's behavior. When one man answered him in Polish, Khrushchev
asked him sharply in Russian who he was. "I am Gomulka," he
replied, "whom you put in prison for three years."

The conversations continued on this undiplomatic level. They
were a strange mixture of toughness and conciliation, for neither
side had the comfort of precedent or habit to support such a peculiar situation. The military threat behind the Soviet delegation

---

* A not unusual example of Khrushchev's anti-Semitism breaking into the
open.

was speedily brought into the open. At the start of the talks Ochab told Khrushchev that the Poles would not negotiate if the Soviet forces now approaching Lodz continued their march on Warsaw. The Russians explained the march as a misunderstanding, and Konev promised to order the troops halted. (Rokossowski later gave similar reassurances inside the Polish Politburo.)

Such molifying gestures aside, the meeting resounded to Russian table-thumping. The Poles were surprised not so much by Khrushchev's bluster, as by the universal threatening attitude, even that of Mikoyan, whom they had always considered something of a moderate. What the Russians wanted was an immediate stabilization of the Polish Politburo, substantially as it then was. Gomulka could join, they conceded, as long as the basic balance of the membership remained the same, i.e., pro-Soviet. There would be no concessions to popular opinion, of the sort they had been hearing about. All of this Khrushchev restated in his own speech, which lasted an hour and a half, until well after midnight. Nor did he leave any doubts about his alternative. If opposed, the Russians would use all the force they had.

When Khrushchev had finished, Gomulka made the Polish reply. "Now I shall speak," he said, "not here, but over the radio to the Polish nation, and I shall tell them the whole truth about what has been happening here."

At this Khrushchev retreated. In a transformation which the world has since seen re-enacted, the leopard changed his spots and retracted his claws. His roars gave way to a conciliatory chewing-over the bones of the agenda. Although Mikoyan later gave the Poles a parting barrage of threats and exclamations in *his* speech, it was not substantive. The Russians gave ground on every position they had sought to deny: independence of the USSR in internal Polish affairs; the end of the secret police and Church persecution; the end of forced collective farming; and what for the Soviet Union became a truly agonizing reappraisal of Russian-Polish trade relations. Marshal Rokossowski, also, and most of his Russian army advisers were to go.

In his leave-taking at the airport, Khrushchev proved himself a trouper to the last. The first challenge now was succeeded by a long and friendly hand-shake with Gomulka, who the next day was proclaimed *de facto* ruler of Poland as First Secretary of the Party's Central Committee. Marshal Rokossowski, Marshal Konev and the other Russian generals also took their leave. Most of them returned to the Red Army headquarters at Legnica, to make some important adjustments in their tactical planning.

There was no doubt in the minds of the Poles that the Russians had come to put down the "revolution" without anything more than a token compromise, on the kind of impromptu trip that professional diplomats have so much difficulty in understanding. They yielded to the facts, when it was evident that all the facts were against them. For, despite the assurances of outright Russian agents like Franciszek Mazur, the pro-Soviet wing of the Polish Party was demoralized and hopelessly discredited. By contrast Gomulka and Cyrankiewicz showed a surprising firmness and had the evident support of the Polish people behind them.

On this score Soviet Ambassador Panteleimon Ponomarenko's intelligence was sure. The calm of the evening streets in Warsaw's center, he had warned his superiors, was deceptive. In the suburbs and factory districts around the city, workers' committees were organized and ready to be armed. In each of the 16 big factory complexes around Warsaw, duty shifts of this improvised militia remained at their posts night and day through the weekend, ready to alert their units for an instant march on the city. The workers' groups acted with rare coolness. It was one of their leaders at the Zeran factory who prevented angry crowds from going off forthwith to attack the Russians.

The foot patrols of General Komar's K.B.W. militia, whom the Russian delegates had observed walking the tree-shaded streets of Aleje Ujazdowskie, were only token detachments. The main strength of Komar's troops was deployed around the city of Warsaw, in the way of any action from the Soviet garrisons. Early on Saturday morning, one of Komar's detachments had in fact stopped a tank column of the Soviet Army at Sochaczew, some 25 miles west of Warsaw. No one fired, but the Army column turned back.

The students in Warsaw were in ferment, led on by the editorial heresy which militant Party intellectuals were getting into virtually all of the Party papers. Throughout the meetings of the Plenum, they kept up a sequence of rallies and cheering demonstrations, in the old Polish university tradition. But this time they had the advantage of a firm alliance with the workers and the pro-Gomulka Communist Party functionaries.

The Polish October, in sum, was about as close as any country ever came in real life to experiencing the spontaneous "rally" of workers, peasants and the intelligentsia which is such a staple of Communist folklore. Imprisoned as they were by the ring of armed Polish troops and militia, Khrushchev and his friends were in something of the same helpless position as the Socialist Revolutionary deputies in the Petrograd Duma on the busy day in January, 1918 when Lenin and his Soviet troops marched in to end their deliberations. For once the boot was on the other foot.

The final military element in Khrushchev's calculations, which he had hoped would be decisive, was no more dependable than the pro-Soviet politicians. Marshal Rokossowski was forced to admit that the Polish Army he commanded was no longer, in the Communist sense of the word, "reliable." Military action now would be Poznan writ large, or perhaps worse. Almost all the Polish Army units were now controlled root and branch by their Polish officers and increasingly committed to support of the government. At least one air unit, reporting to Warsaw on the appearance of an unreported Soviet tank column, suffixed the information with the question: "Shall we bomb them?"

There was nonetheless an anxious wait in Polish Party headquarters after the Russians had gone home. It needed only one order to advance, signed by either Rokossowski or his Polish subordinate General "Gas-pipe" Witaszewski,* to pull the trigger. But Khrushchev remained true to his word, although there was little doubt that he took what, from the Russians' point of view, was a huge calculated risk. He took the risk, also, against the advice of other members of the Politburo. On Monday night he had a long talk with Gomulka on the telephone, just a few hours after the Poles had announced the wildly acclaimed bit of negative information that Rokossowski had not been re-elected

---

* General Kazimierz Witaszewski, Deputy Defense Minister, was a veteran Communist supporter in Poland. He got his nickname because of his fondness for certain forms of direct physical persuasion as an interrogation method.

to the Politburo. The conversation was cordial, ending with an invitation to Gomulka to visit Moscow on Friday.

Gomulka accepted, thereby giving his close supporters a collective attack of jitters. At the earnest request of Cyrankiewicz and others he began to reconsider. The outbreak of trouble in Budapest confirmed his hesitation and he begged off. But the bargain with Khrushchev stuck. Konev, and later Rokossowski, returned to the Soviet Union. The Soviet troops returned to their barracks.

Barely three weeks afterward the Russian tanks were mopping up in the streets of Budapest. No one took the Hungarian disaster harder than the Poles themselves. It was Polish correspondents like Wiktor Woroszylski, later the editor of *Nowa Kultura,* who told the story of the Hungarian fight the more poignantly for their own deep commitment to its aims. Through the whole period youth rallies were held almost everywhere in Poland, to get money, clothes and medicine for the Hungarians. Some guns and ammunition were smuggled into Hungary beneath the straw at the bottom of Polish relief shipments, although as often as not these were detected by the vigilance of the Czech frontier guards, who remained obediently Communist throughout. The suppression in Hungary seemed to signal a general failure of the whole movement for freedom behind the Iron Curtain. No one was more sensible of this than the new Polish leadership, which had counted on the Hungarians as valuable allies for Gomulka's new drive towards a nationalist version of Communism.

That the Poles survived the Hungarian debacle with their new concessions intact was a victory of circumstance and leadership. It was a victory of circumstance because Poland happened to be bigger. The unity of the Polish Army with the people made the Russians aware that a Polish suppression would be far longer and more dangerous than their action against the disorganized 10,000,000 Hungarians. The nearness of Poland to East Germany, whose population was hardly regarded as "dependable" by the Communists, made the risk of intervention a double one. Particularly in the confused state of Russian leadership—for Khrushchev had by no means finalized his seizure to power—it was a risk which the Russians would do anything in their power to avoid.

Beyond the fortune of their size and location, however, the

Poles had the advantage of another priceless national commodity: able, courageous and intuitive leadership. The Hungarian revolt failed precisely for the lack of leadership. Imre Nagy was an indecisive man who could represent, but could not impose. There was no one on the scene in Hungary who could brake and channel the spontaneous outbreak of hatred against the Russians into a stable government which would nonetheless recognize the fact of Russian power. And the fact of Russian power, given the ostrich-like attitude of American power in this crisis, was the big, inescapable consideration. The men who directed the Polish revolution were highly practical patriots, the sort of people who can keep one eye on the stars above and the other on the shoals in front. As his past record and his imprisonment indicated, Gomulka was made of far more independent stuff than the average Party boss. This reputation earned him immediate popular support. Yet in marshalling the indignation at the Russian spoliation of Poland, he never forgot that the Russian power must somehow be placated.

Cyrankiewicz, who played a key role in assisting Gomulka, was unpopular with the country for having betrayed his own Socialist Party to the Communists in 1948. Yet he was a good enough Pole to want the country's independence. He had elements of courage in his make-up (he had never attacked Gomulka, for one thing, in the period of his "disgrace"). He was smart enough to realize long before October, 1956 that independence of the Russians could only be achieved and maintained by keeping up the orderly appearance of the government machinery. This he did, the while pointing the machinery steadily away from Moscow, through a long and deliberate shifting of important office-holders.

The third central figure in the Polish leadership, although he held no government position, was possibly even more important than the two others in realizing the October Revolution. He was the Primate of the Roman Catholic Church in Poland, Stefan Cardinal Wyszynski. Released from imprisonment when Gomulka took power, Wyszynski used the overwhelming moral weight of a patriotic church in a Catholic country to stabilize popular support behind Gomulka. It was due to him that the crisis did not turn into an anti-Russian crusade, which would have brought on Soviet Army intervention. For unlike Cardinal Mindszenty in Hungary, the

Polish primate conceded the fact that the church would have to live for a long time behind the Iron Curtain, with little hope of physical liberation. To regain the church's freedom in worship and doctrine, he was willing to make common political cause with men whose ideology he detested. It was a strange and unique bargain that he struck with Gomulka, but it was maintained.

Between them these leaders channeled the bursting indignation that made possible the Polish October. They made of *their* October a half-permanent historical phenomenon of greater significance to the world's future, possibly, than either Hungary or Yugoslavia. Hungary, for all its courage, was snuffed out. Yugoslavia had its revolt against the Russians adroitly controlled by a national dictator. The principal comfort for the modern Yugoslav, outside of certain limited economic and political ameliorations, is that the dictator is a local product.

Poland remains at least partially free, its government a constant compromise between the orders of the ruling oligarchy, the wishes of the governed and pressures from Moscow. However dedicated it is to Communism by its leaders, the Polish nation has at least regained some of the checks and balances that premise a free society. If it is not wholly free, neither is it slave. And if the contradiction between the leadership and the people remains great, its example continues nonetheless to work powerfully on the other Communist countries. It is, half-consciously at least, the agent of democracy east of the Elbe.

A one-time political satellite thus whirling half out of its orbit is a strange phenomenon. Given life in this peculiar form only by the tensions of the world around it, Poland in the Gomulka period has impressed even the casual tourist as a peculiarly eccentric country. It is a place where Marxist theoreticians argue with Americans in night clubs, without any worry at being seen there. It is a place where a military officer, pledged to defend the ideals of international Communism, will walk into High Mass on Sunday without thinking to hide his presence. It is a place where conversation is free, although the attempt to translate free conversation into print can have swift and embarrassing consequences. TV commercials can be permitted on the same channels that pledge the "workers' society" to a world free from private enterprise.

Under a Communist government, the most disillusioned Polish citizens are a group of believing Marxists who cut their teeth on the collected works of Lenin. The most contented citizens are violently anti-Communist farmers, whose political and social views would seem reactionary to a right-wing Republican in the United States. Such contradictions are of course not lost on the Poles themselves, still less their strange position in international affairs. "How do you run an army," a Polish battalion commander once asked in bewilderment, "when you tell the troops that we must swear to the eternal 'anti-imperialist' aims of our Warsaw Pact, but if the Americans don't give us more money, we'll starve?"

Such topsy-turviness does not make Poland an easy place to live in. Nothing is so frustrating to the human soul as a revolution that is frozen at its half-way point—not repressed, nor failed of its momentum, but simply frozen by the necessity of spraying some kind of political ether over all of its members. Even Polish press circles are accustomed to describe their October aftermath as one long "Thermidor." Crane Brinton, in his book "The Anatomy of Revolution," characterized the original Thermidor period* as "a convalescence from the fever of revolution." In Poland the description would be somewhat different. The very factor that made for the Polish revolution's initial success was the disciplined leadership of Gomulka and his Party faction. Yet this made it inevitable that the revolution would not even *reach* a dangerous fever point.

Everyone in the Warsaw Government was well acquainted with the revolutionary fury that showed itself at Poznan, where the mood of the rioting crowds speedily changed from being anti-secret police to being anti-Communist. However nationalist he is, Gomulka himself remains a Communist, whose practical inclination to offer the incentives of freedom is always tempered by the old Communist's distrust of the uncontrolled processes of democracy. Very early in the game, the angry young intellectuals found this out. At their first big meeting with Gomulka, they were chagrined to find that he by no means shared their love of free

---

* In France, Thermidor began with the fall of Robespierre on July 27, 1794 —the 9th of Thermidor in the Revolutionary calendar. Brinton sets the beginning of the English Thermidor as Cromwell's stabilizing seizure of power, of the Russian—conceivably—as the enactment of the New Economic Policy in 1921.

speech and political experiment. Speaking privately to a small group later, he said only half-jokingly, "If you do not stop all this talk, I shall have to put you in jail next year." He nearly did.

Gomulka must of course reckon with Khrushchev and Co., looking constantly over his shoulder. Their pressure need not be direct to be effective. Each orbiting *sputnik,* for example, made it harder for him to keep away from Moscow's political gravitational field; there is no clearer symptom of the Soviet strength in missilery than the rising pitch of Gomulka's anti-American foreign policy statements through 1958. Yet, even granting Poland's extreme international sensitivity, Gomulka's domestic political course, veering back and forth between a return to absolutism and the preservation of democratic freedom, has on occasion looked as bewildering as Dr. Dolittle's legendary childhood toy, the Push-me Pull-you.

His ambivalence extends to every feature of Polish life. The Church has its ancient treasures returned to it and priests are allowed to study in Rome; at the same time the government institutes an increasingly vigorous anti-religious organization and continues its support of the Soviet agent Boleslaw Piasecki, who presides over the Party's front organization of "Catholic" fellow travelers. Gomulka's strongest statement at the Ninth Plenum of May, 1957, in public, was the denunciation of Leszek Kolakowski, a young Marxist philosophy professor who has searchingly asked for more democracy in Poland's government. His most scathing attack, in private, was made on one Kazimierz Mijal, a spokesman for the pro-Soviet Communist group, as a Russian "agent." At the Twelfth Plenum, a year and a half later, he continued to defend his "centrist" policy against both pro-democrats and pro-Russians. Few areas of the national life have escaped the strange contradictions of a revolution which has shown a startling facility for shifting its feet between the brake and the accelerator.

A condition of progress frozen in mid-passage would be hard on any people. It is especially hard on the Poles, whose long record of suppression, revolt and, when the occasion offered, conquest, includes countless examples of suicidal bravery, but very few examples of calculated prudence. "Impatience," as Gomulka's Education Minister and house theoretician, Wladyslaw Bienkowski, expressed it, "is a Polish political characteristic. They all talk of getting the fruits of October. What they must realize is that fruits ripen slowly." In the course of a more hortatory, and a deeply moving statement, Cardinal Wyszynski urged the people of Poland to take hold of the peculiar challenge that October had brought them. "You have proved that you can die for your country," he said, "what you must do now is something that may be harder—to live for your country."

*   *   *

The historical view of Poland from the United States has done more to compound the confusion than to help the understanding of Poland's Frozen Revolution. To the normal well-read American, not of Polish extraction himself, this is the country which produced (a) Paderewski and Chopin and (b) Kosciuszko, who served in Washington's Army; and (c) Pulaski, who also served in Washington's Army and had several towns and a peculiarly traffic-bound viaduct on the approaches to New York named after him. Over (c) there is some dispute and confusion, except among veteran movie-goers who recall that a Polish girl named Marie Walewska (played by Garbo) enticed Charles Boyer (as Napoleon) briefly on the road to Moscow in 1812. We recall Pilsudski, as a dictator with a moustache, who died. There is the memory of the heroic Warsaw resistance of 1944 and the brave stand of the city against the Germans in 1939; the recollection of concentration camps and a loose guiltiness about the American desertion of the legitimate London Polish government, and its adherents inside Poland, at both Yalta and Potsdam. As for the country itself, it is remote, if not primitive—something traditionally "eastern." Nothing could be more indicative of the Western European fixation that has encumbered the American mentality for the nearly two centuries since this country ceased to be a Western European colony.

It is a pleasing shock, therefore, to find that Poles are a sophisticated people—often, indeed, to the over-ripeness of cynicism.*

---

* In an article in the banned liberal weekly *Po Prostu,* in May, 1957, the *avant-garde* young Marxist critic Roman Zimand developed the idea of cynicism in its political application. "The modern awareness of the Polish nation," he wrote, "has been shaped in such a manner that it has been systematically deceived by its rulers. Hence the universal skepticism

With similar surprise, a tourist in Poland discovers very speedily that the Polish national culture is extraordinarily richer than the half-remembered history of eighteenth century partitions suggested. The honestly patrician eminence of Wawel, the old castle in Cracow, looking over the upper reaches of the Vistula; the bulky serenity of the mediaeval city walls of Lublin, majestic at moonrise over the cobbled streets; the charm of the seventeenth century Old Town of Warsaw, painfully reconstructed though it be—these recall a powerful and a supple tradition.

The people are worthy of their heritage. There is a genuine flair to the Poles, which few other peoples in or out of Europe can equal, an innate sense of taste which makes a simple poster advertising a movie into a work of art, or turns a student cellar playhouse into a candle-lit theatre. Charm and grace are hard to kill, even in a country so long blighted by the mediocrity of the Communist dispensation. Nowhere else do so many Communists kiss so many ladies' hands.

When there is gaiety, it is the world's most pervasive. Bows are exchanged, toasts are expended, in such a prodigious knocking-back of vodka, the national jet propellant, that "Warsaw morning after," like Parisian liver, has become the great occupational hazard of the traveler in this country. Conversation spreads without constraint. The Poles are among the world's talkiest peoples. Their talk covers an infinity of subjects (and sins) and flavors itself with a kind of carroway-seed humor, made tarter and drier than most by an inherited national tradition of disappointment. The jokes about the Russians are not so prevalent in Gomulka's Poland as they were before the October, when a quick joke told behind a cupped hand was almost the only form of national protest; but they do occur, and the points are sharp and sure. At the height of the

---

towards all official theses. This attitude was strengthened by the fact that this skepticism was frequently an integral part of the demonstration of national dignity. This trait of the national character would not be so bad if it were not combined with another trait which contradicts the former, namely a childish confidence in all opinions contrary to the official thesis. It is needless to speak about the consequence of this mixture. But the most peculiar thing is the fact that in the last fifty years there has not been a single government in Poland which has taken account of these glaring national traits."

Russian intervention in Budapest, Poles would indicate the pictures of tanks firing at scattered students in the streets of Budapest, and repeat with bitterness what was once a popular Communist slogan: "The target of Socialism is the individual." When a Soviet aid program was announced, the café wits announced that the Russians had just come through with a huge new gift for the Poles: "500,000 pairs of shoes—to be repaired." At news of the first *sputnik* the inevitable comment in Poland was: "The only satellite that ever got away from Russia."

Most of the humor, in the central European tradition, has this sort of political note in it. When Gomulka was allegedly depending on the support of Mao Tse Tung, for fending off the Russians, a student cabaret skit had one newscaster asking another: "And how are things in Poland?" "Excellent," was the reply (echoing a once meaningless tag line from an old Polish play) "the Chinese are holding fast."

For all the political jokes, there is not much vocal interest in current politics among the bulk of the population. The Frozen Revolution has brought with it an almost studied political apathy, especially among the youth. The mass desertion of the Communist youth organization, once membership was no longer compulsory, was signal and extraordinary. Nor was it accompanied by any urge to join other youth organizations, either public or unofficial. Only the Catholic groups can command any loyalty, and their spread is heavily restricted by terms of the unofficial truce between the Cardinal and the First Secretary of the Party. The brightest student I met in Warsaw was studying Oriental Art. The most attractive of the students I saw in Cracow were studying dramatics or ancient literature.

There *would* be a surge of interest in English and American studies, given the equipment for more of them. The national distaste for learning Russian is accompanied by a corresponding desire to speak English. But here, as in so many other things, the dead hand of the Communist decade has left its touch. Two years after the 1956 October, thousands of interested English students in Polish schools were left with no better reading material than a few ancient volumes of Dickens, or English-language Communist propaganda literature.

The apathy in politics comes of course from the disappointment that October could not go further. It is prevented from becoming direct, angry discontent by the shared knowledge of almost all the Polish people that international facts are against them. The phrase "our geographical position" is heard over and over in Polish discussions. It has become the limiting convention of the national life.

The popular shunning of politics is nowhere better dramatized than among the deputies of the Polish Parliament, the 450-year-old Sejm. Almost half of the 459 deputies are not official Communist representatives. Although only the Roman Catholic Znak group of members, ten strong, is organized as anything like an independent voting group, many of the independents have strong ideas of their own (which they are, however, increasingly cautious in exhibiting). The reconstructed white building of the Sejm on Wiejska Street,* just by the river, is one of the handsomer examples of contemporary Parliamentary. Its interior, like the cleanliness of the outside, is spacious and rather grand—a complex of stairways in marble, long, well-furnished galleries, an impressive library and a commodious chamber. There, through the long debates on new economic programs, conducted on scrupulously parliamentary rules of order, Wladyslaw Gomulka sits inconspicuously among the other tenants of the government bench, his finely sculptured head resting on one hand, half-drowsing in appearance, sensitively alert in the fact. His constant presence epitomizes both the Sejm's possibilities and its frustration. His impatience in the "excessive" debate explains why the independent members are chary of being seen talking to Western newspapermen or visitors in the outside halls.

At the beginning of the October Revolution, Gomulka pledged himself to a return to parliamentary government. This being done, he has shown a consistent reluctance to abandon any facet of his government to the free play of Parliamentary processes. The Party, it was decided, must still make the decisions. It was too risky to

---

* First used by the pre-war Sejm immediately after Poland gained its independence in 1918, the building originally housed a girls' school. This structural ancestry long offered opportunity for Warsaw's wits to comment on the gossipy nature of the Sejm proceedings.

initiate really free debate—and voting power. This might return the actual ruling privileges of the Party to representatives who do in many cases honestly express the hopes of the people behind them, even if they were elected on a single slate.

But now again comes a contradiction of the tendencies towards heavy-handed Party rule that developed since 1957. Gomulka has not, for all his Communist conservatism, reduced the Sejm to the rubbery existence of the Supreme Soviet, or its carbon copies elsewhere in the "socialist camp." Debate of a sort does go on. Sometimes it has an effect. Opinions contrary to government policy are heard—even if they are largely restricted to the private proceedings of the Sejm committees. A man can be expelled from the Communist Party and still retain his parliamentary seat. The white halls of the Sejm look down on the nearest thing to a free representative assembly which the Communist world has ever permitted. It is a matter which may hold great meaning for the world, and certainly for the historian; but it is a nail-biting experience for an independent delegate.

For all that they shun audience participation in this curiously frustrating kind of government, the Poles support Gomulka because he is by any standards a Polish patriot. Patriotism in Poland is more obvious than anywhere in Europe. Through so many Polish generations, the feeling of patriotism has had to substitute for all the tangible trappings and processes of independent government, so that it has become almost a tangible thing in itself. The Polish eagle is a supremely unnatural looking bird, even as national eagles go, with the stiff stylized wings and the ancient crown on its skull. (The crown, of course, is not present in the current official depiction.) Its feathers are beaten and torn. But its head is unbowed, and it has, as history witnesses, never stopped squawking.

The nearest thing to a Polish patriot is an Irish patriot, and in many ways national feeling in these two frontier posts of Catholic Europe is the same. It would occur to writers of few other nations to call Poland, as its great poet Adam Mickiewicz apostrophized, "the Christ among nations"; but probably only a Puritan fear of blasphemy in print has stopped Irish poets from saying the same. Writing on modern Polish literature, the Times Literary Supplement found its only comparisons in Ireland and the literature of the Irish Revival—the world of Yeats, Synge, O'Casey and the Black and Tans. Noting the fact that years of foreign rule had conditioned the minds of Polish poets to associate certain poetic images with certain national feelings, the Times quoted the recently deceased poet, Jan Lechon, who once said that he would like "to see Spring as a Spring and not as Poland" for a change. Witness, for example, the constant use, following the 1956 Revolution, of the term "Springtime in October."

The poets of Poland—and in Poland a poet is a man of stature—have never tired, either, of dwelling on the challenging westernness of their country. On the map Warsaw and Belgrade are virtually in line with each other, on a north-south axis. But Belgrade is unmistakably an Eastern city; it is Balkan, Orthodox and pan-Slavic. The modern buildings all look as if they have been copied from somewhere else. Warsaw, visitors are chronically surprised to find, is a thoroughly Western city. It lies, as Poles say in their atlases, in *central,* not in Eastern Europe. It is Catholic, more so than any European capital except Rome and more sincerely so than Rome, one suspects, as far as the spiritual feeling of the population is concerned.

Foreign travelers are at first appalled by the labored reconstruction of the Renaissance houses in Warsaw's Old Town, down to the last reframed Latin motto on the walls and the archaic gilt arms and paintings. The Poles spent ten years in a painstaking rebuilding of their old stones, and spent so heavily that by 1955, when Communist Warsaw opened its doors to the noisy delegates of the World Youth Congress, the country's entire financial structure was breathing hard from the effort. Probably no other country in the world, given a capital city that was literally 85% destroyed, would so literally have restored it. But, even during the blackest Communist period, although few Communists would admit it, the rebuilding went on precisely to show the world that Warsaw was not Belgrade, or Moscow, or for that matter, Prague.

The city that the Old Town recreates is only part of the bursting capital which the Venetian Bernard Belotto (called Caneletto) painted in the late eighteenth century, a graceful amalgam of Baroque churches, high-crowned houses and high-stepping carriage horses. It is in fact a far older place, with its foundations in the northern Gothic of the High Middle Ages and the Renaissance. But even the oldest reconstructed remains show the hand of Italian and French artists, who came to Poland through the centuries in successive waves, as invited arbiters of the national taste. The surviving Gothic churches and the bravely decorated old town houses are visible proof, flaunted in the face of an Eastern occupation force, that Poland holds dear its links with the West. To an American, these whole reconstructed blocks of Warsaw seem like a metropolitan version of Colonial Williamsburg, done for far more pressing reasons. They give the same sense of national solidity, several times magnified.

One of the most heroic aspects of Poland's western connection, at least to the foreign traveler, is the Polish language. It is mute testimony (or at least the traveler is mute in trying to cope with it) of the fact that the original Slavic tribes of Poland first met and adopted the civilizing influences of Rome, rather than Byzantium. Russian or Serbian can at least be transliterated by a foreigner, with confidence that the Cyrillic letters will sound just the way they spell. But in Polish, the Latin alphabet has been twisted like the upper bends of the Vistula to accommodate contortionate Slavic sounds that Cicero never dreamed of. The pronunciation of a word like Rzeszow (pronounced jyé-zhov) or Walbrzych (pronounced vowb-jikh) requires an apprenticeship in a strange linguistic discipline. Only the patience of the Poles with foreigners makes this bearable, plus the fact that they themselves are apt to be impressive linguists.

All this is not to say that Poland is a transplanted outpost of Western Europe. A country which history long ago doomed to fight a two-front cultural war, Poland also faces east, and is influenced by the East. Warsaw and Cracow are among the few great Polish cities which are indisputably Polish. If Poznan is by ancient right and inheritance Polish, its other identity of Posen is also by ancient right and inheritance German, to say nothing of Wroclaw (Breslau). If Wilno is an ancient Polish stronghold in the northeast (despite its current occupation by the Russians) in its other incarnation Vilnius is the ancient Lithuanian capital.

Lwow may be a great outpost of Polish culture, but it has its own meaning to the Ukrainians.

This mixture of creeds and cultures has been made easy by Poland's geography. From the tree-shaded banks of the western Oder to the sluggishly flowing Bug in the east, Poland is a plain. In its pre-war boundaries, when both current borders were sited farther east, it was virtually the same thing. Vast and unbroken the Polish plain stretches, wrinkled only by its rivers and the low-lying hills. In the far south its flatness gives way to the rising heights of the Carpathian foothills. To the northeast some natural border territory is afforded by the lakes and the evergreen forests of the Masurian hills. But these are only exceptions to the rule in this one-storey country. Few areas on the world's surface would make a Swiss Army man more uncomfortable.

If Belgium could once have been called the 'cockpit of Europe,' Poland would correspondingly qualify for the title of Europe's arena. Since the Tatar archers galloped in view of Cracow in the thirteenth century, foreign armies have raced across its borders, killed its people and burned its towns. The Germans and the Russians, through history, have been the principal offenders, their excesses in modern times dwarfing in horror anything ever attempted by the ancients. The Poles, to give them their due, have been seldom backward in reciprocating on their neighbors' land whenever they got the chance, generally with more success on the Russian side than on the German. Nations that are glorious in defeat generally have the habit of squandering their blue chips, whenever they get ahead.

The marks of all this war still rest heavily on Poland's cities. Even Warsaw, the object of this unprecedented national effort in rebuilding, retains traces of the war and successive occupations on almost every block, from the patched bullet holes in spruced-up apartment buildings to the small plaques that dot the city. They tell us, for example, that on a certain spot near the river four students were killed in the Warsaw Uprising, or in a certain block on Aleje Ujazdowskie, not very far from the new American embassy, a group of patriots in the anti-Communist Home Army assassinated General Kutschera, head of the Gestapo forces in Warsaw, in 1944.

The farm country, as almost everywhere in the world, shows less stain. Barring the exceptional cases of China and parts of Russia, the scorched-earth policy is a relic of ancient war-making; modern war, an urban invention, fittingly works its worst on the world's cities. The fields in Poland are hence much the same as they always were, especially since the government began its policy of returning the compulsorily joined collectives back to private ownership. They are rich with wheat, rye and potatoes, especially in the south, although not very heavily populated. The enforced drive to industrialize in the first ten years of Communism turned thousands of potentially useful farm laborers into economically unprofitable factory hands. In the process they made the old agricultural surpluses nothing more than a statistical memory.

The people who live on the farms are considerably more changed than their land. This is not to say that many of them are Marxist converts. That Communism has had little success among the Polish peasants is Central Europe's understatement of the decade. Not so with Gomulka's impact on them. "He gave us back our land. He is a good man" could sum up the rural reaction to him. But the villagers do not like his friends, or what he says he stands for. Their lives, increasingly prosperous these days, center as always on the church, the land and the strictly run family. When they support the Communist Gomulka, it is to the degree that he has safeguarded this ancient trinity.

The youth of the farms, while holding on to this substance of tradition, have scarcely been as insulated as their parents from the changes of the last decade. Among other things, the old Communist systems of forced collectivization and forced industrialization shook up the population by putting villagers in factories and townsmen on the farms indiscriminately. In one sense this worked against the Communists; local feuds and old provincial differences grew dimmer, only to be lost in the general indignation of the Polish people. It also worked for them. The youth in the provinces, thanks to Communist missionary work, have a better chance for an education than their fathers did; most of them view the move to the cities as an improvement in their social status. But, like the students from the cities, they show few signs of any active Communist belief and many signs of their positive antipathy.

They all share the national craze for jazz, which for years was one of the few outlets for their anti-Communist sympathies. At dance halls or Houses of Culture all over the country, serious young workers, farmers and students are studying Louie Armstrong—not quite the way Lenin planned it. In Poland, an affection for jazz has its political overtones. When a few Americans visited a jam session in the provinces in 1957, the leader, a young engineering student, managed to pour out a definitive introduction in English, while he was shaking hands: "I like jazz. We all like America. We hate the Russians."

But beyond this obvious identification, jazz has a deep satisfaction to these children of the Communist decade. The eccentricity and the honest exuberance of a jazz combination are effective, if peculiar antidotes to a world which pledges itself to reduce every individual soul to the dimensions of a replaceable bolt on an assembly line. This is true throughout the European Communist countries, in Russia not the least. But with the Poles, as in other matters, jazz suffers less from "Marxist-Leninist" disapproval.

The walled mediocrity of Communism, although now breached, still causes violent reaction among Poland's youth. The smartest of them have developed an apolitical cynicism to life that would make Jean Paul Sartre look like Little Orphan Annie. It is a tragic experience for youngsters in their late teens or early twenties to be twice disillusioned. Those of them who were equipped for life by the disciplinary processes of Party schools, the youth organization, or Marxist university courses, had their Red coloration largely washed off in the months around October, 1956. But, barring some who have again become good Catholics, they have replaced it with no other.

Their political neutrality has the aggressiveness of disappointment about it. They do not attack Gomulka—although occasionally, as on the suppression of the famous youth magazine *Po Prostu* in September, 1957, student riots do break out. But they will not defend his government, or make much effort to participate in it. They congratulate themselves on their cynicism, the more so as they fear to hope. And in some of the human husks who form the Party cadres on whom Gomulka has chosen to rely, they find ample documentation for the most cynical of political theories. As the heroine of Marek Hlasko's bitter young story *The Eighth Day of the Week* expressed it: "Little dirty deals are mentioned in a loud voice; big ones are whispered about. No one ever tells the truth. And, who knows, every truth is perhaps the biggest dirty deal."

The protest is valid. For the Frozen Revolution has kept Poland confined in the stained overalls of a Communist society, however many reforms have been made. This society *has* a seedy kind of internationalism about it that early strikes the eye. Plac Konstytucji in Warsaw is a square lined by new gray official buildings with the huge cornices and squat pillars favored by architects of the Stalin Period. Immense stone lanterns, actually street lights, stand at strategic points on the square's perimeter, looking like fugitives from an Dionysiac procession. It is almost an exact replica of *Strassbergerplatz* in East Berlin, where the grossness of the architecture is just as thoroughly detested by the population.

There are other externals of the Communist Society—the seedy book-stores packed with badly illustrated propaganda, the ever-present "fraternal delegations" from elsewhere in the "people's camp," the tattered signboards with their promise of a bargain-basement brotherhood of man. In Poland, the degree of freedom already introduced has made the retention of these things doubly frustrating to the nation. The frustration is imposed in great part by a government that, through choice and through necessity, must keep up the cast-iron structure of a Communism which the entire people has quite vociferously abandoned. When freedom is the commodity involved, half a loaf often seems worse than none. Of course this is not so, and the Poles recognize it. What they must also recognize is that only by an unprecedented national productive effort can they earn themselves a little elbow room, both in freedom and in purchasing power.

However widely they differ in their philosophies, both the Cardinal and the First Secretary of the Party know that an unprecedented work drive is Poland's only hope for remaining free of complete Soviet domination, or the anarchy that would invite Soviet attack. Such a drive is a hard thing to ask of simple people, who have seen their world shattered three times around them in the course of two decades, and who hoped too much in their "October." But they also achieved more than they or anyone else had a right to expect, more success and more complications.

"In October," wrote the Polish Catholic member of the Sejm, Stanislaw Stomma, "we thought that a solution had been found, that we had caught Ariadne's thread which would lead us out of the labyrinth. It was discovered that matters were much more difficult than had been expected."

2

The Contrary Communist
and How He Grew

> "Dictatorship is the rule of one part of society over the whole of society and, moreover, rule basing itself directly on force . . ."

> —*Lenin*

W LADYSLAW GOMULKA was released from confinement on Christmas Eve, 1954 and driven back to Warsaw. He had been in his private jail, at Miedzeszyn, near Warsaw, for almost three years. In that time he had rarely been disturbed. The U.B. had given him only about 15 solid days' worth of its time, if all the interrogations had been counted. His stubbornness and his wealth of knowledge about intimate Party affairs made further interrogation unprofitable. But his isolation had been complete. His only contacts with the country were through a few jailors and U.B. officials. He had a small library provided for his use, but he was never much of a reader. He is presumed to have done some thinking.

While he was thus isolated, his reputation grew without him. In the years when he was in power, most Poles had either disliked or actively hated him. He was identified with the messily successful effort of the Communists to crush all semblance of political opposition, while they laid the foundations for their post-war Soviet satrapy. All Communists, in that period, seemed indistinguishably evil. But a man in a dark cell comes to perceive a wide spectrum of shadow, and the grayer form of darkness can look quite bright. So the Polish people, when the extent of their confinement was realized, gradually came to understand certain differences between a nationalist Communist like Gomulka and the foreign Communist organization that was crushing their lives.

Gomulka, it was argued, was not exactly a Soviet satrap. It was widely known that he went to jail for resisting the Russians. People forgot his earlier brutal suppression of the Peasant Party and the legitimate Social Democrats. They remembered only that he had tried to stop the Soviet Union's colonization of Poland. He became a passively popular figure. After such long imprisonment, he may have been, as the Stalinist Communists said, a "myth." But he was the only conceivably popular myth that any Communist government could hope to conjure into existence.

Long before the climactic October Revolution the Communist leadership in Warsaw was demoralized. Given the bankruptcy of force rule and the unstable conditions in Moscow, the Moscow Poles realized that they must come to terms with the population; And the population's mood was ugly. For months before the October Revolution several factions in the Central Committee had been trying to draft Gomulka and his myth for their own purposes. The Russian agents of the Natolin group,* hardly classed as friends of his, wanted to use him as a decoy, so they could continue the old system under apparently new auspices. The other more nationalist faction, as yet not very well formed, needed both his popularity and his immediate leadership. In the view of the people like the one-time Socialist, Premier Cyrankiewicz, Gomulka was the one man capable of turning the indignation against Communism into domestic concessions instead of open war.

---

* This segment of the Party which was frankly pro-Soviet in all its activities. It was so called because its members used to caucus in the Rococco palace of Natolin, near Warsaw.

With this struggle over his "myth's" possession still unresolved, Gomulka was released to assume the country's leadership. There is no doubt but that all factions which planned to use him counted on this leadership as being more or less titular. There is no doubt, either, that Gomulka almost immediately exceeded the scope of their plans for him. He became not an agent, but a principal, using the same people who had hoped to use him. He showed a political intuition and a firmness of governance which proved that the months of lonely reflection in imprisonment had not been wasted. He also put the stamp of his own personality on a brief, but significant period in his country's history.

Of all the ironies in the Communist scriptures, one of the greatest is the statement of Frederick Engels, made in the course of a discussion about the ideal state: "The government of persons is replaced by the administration of things." As it turned out, the behaviour of persons became the decisive element in all the real-life attempts at enacting the Marxist fable. The blind force of history triumphing over the inconsequentials of individual human characters has regularly dissolved into a chain of rivalries between very sharply marked personalities. In the U.S.S.R. it was Lenin vs. Trotsky vs. Kamenev vs. Bukharin vs. Stalin; or it was Beria vs. Malenkov vs. Khrushchev. Similarly in the satellites. Down through the years the administration of things has been thus replaced by the working-out of Lenin's more realistic question *"Kto kovo?"*— freely translated as "Who is doing what with what to whom?" The justifying theories came later.

There is no mystery in this evolution. The weakness of the cast-iron Marxist-Leninist theories in actual practice is by now intimately sensed by most of the Party rulers. For time has shown Marx to have been a hopeless prisoner of the ideas and circumstances of his era. Because of this inherent weakness—the contradictions in history, natural law and economic practice stated baldly as truths—any popular groupings on theoretical lines or political issues are potentially very dangerous to the System.

All members of the post-war oligarchies have instinctively realized the danger to the whole System of organizing any movement under the banner of a special idea (although it is of course standard operating procedure with the Communists to identify purged members of the oligarchy with all sorts of proscribed theories, as justification of their downfall). Except for the odd maverick like Bukharin or Milovan Djilas, the idea content in modern Communism is low. There are almost no real "issue" politics left. Even the serious talk about "dogmatism" vs. "revisionism," for all its theoretical window-dressing, reflects only opposing tactics of rulership.*

All this made the personalization of Gomulka's policy almost inevitable, given his strong will and definite ideas. It was compounding the irony that this happened. Among the world's Communist leaders Gomulka is almost the only one who is honestly not interested in cultivating his private power. He is a modest man, and a simple one, who genuinely believes something of what the book said about the ideal selflessness of Communism. He dislikes having his picture hung in public places. The absence of the hero-on-the-wall is one of the most refreshing things about modern Communist Poland, when contrasted either with the ever-changing czar-worship in Russia or the Tito-Hero signs and slogans in Yugoslavia. Yet this opponent of the "cult of personality" was fated to have his country known as Gomulka's Poland, his supporters called Gomulkists, his "Polish road to Socialism" called Gomulkism. In addition, he found himself half-blessed, half-cursed with a personal popularity that no Communist leader has known before— and probably since.

"The Polish road to Socialism," the history of the next two years showed, proved to be a curious, winding thoroughfare, a labyrinthine with political tunnels, underpasses and traffic intersections— all demonstrably two-way. Yet, given Gomulka's background and premises, it was the most honest, possibly the only honest attempt in modern times to construct a Communist society gradually, the way the books said it should work, without resorting to the terror and falsity that had by now been built into the Russian road to socialism. Its most important ideological basis is the mind and will of Wladyslaw Gomulka.

The two things that most distinguish this man are honesty and

---

* That is, as long as the disputants remain adherents of the System. It is true, as we shall note later, that many of the people denounced as revisionist have actually broken with the System completely.

patriotism. They are now rare virtues in a Communist, although before the 1938 purges there were quite a few others in Europe and Asia who possessed them. They make him intrinsically an object of Russian suspicion. "They hate Gomulka because he has gone too far away from their idea of Communism," a Polish writer told me, in the course of a Warsaw discussion. A lady companion corrected him. "The Russians hate him," she said, "because he exists."

The Communist experience in Poland is by no means unique. Wherever this system has spread itself, it has attempted roughly the same goals, made similar mistakes, perpetrated similar crimes, and provoked similar factions. The peculiar interest of Poland to the historian is that there, uniquely, the innermost strugglings of a Communist society were laid bare and shown up as evil and unworkable, like a slimy moss world suddenly brought into the open by the removal of its sheltering flat rock.

To the end, Gomulka has refused to believe this society unworkable. He was brought up in it. To a great extent he lives in a cage made of its premises. Paradoxically, nothing so demonstrates the wrongs and imperfections of this system than his life and struggles with it. He is not only the leader of the Communist Party in Poland. His life explains its history and inevitable rotting process, in Poland or anywhere else.

A more subtle man, given Gomulka's honesty, would recognize the absurdities. Perhaps Gomulka does. (Although, with 25 Russian divisions hemming the country inside the Iron Curtain, one wonders whether this recognition would have practical value.) But this is doubtful. He is a narrow-minded man. The same stubbornness which frustrated his prison interrogators has kept intact within him the hard prejudices of a grass-roots Communist organizer of the pre-war era. It is almost impossible to reason with him, as both political opponents and friends have discovered.

A more austere character could scarcely be invented. In his habits as well as his appearance, Gomulka is a secularist monk. Not overmuch concerned with the Marxist form of theology, he is obsessed with the Marxist version of holiness—the single-minded devotion of the individual to the cause of Communism. His life is uncomplicated by hobbies, athletics, the arts, intellectual pastimes or mistresses. About his only relaxation, acquaintances used to observe, was walking his dog around the block near the small apartment in the Praga district of Warsaw where he lived. His wife Zofia, herself the daughter of a Communist, has been with him through all the troubles; and they understand each other well. But he has never given much time to his only son. Due to the father's consistently strong feelings on the cult of personality, the son, now an electrical engineer, has had to go by another name than his real one, to avoid any possibility of favoritism.

Gomulka needs little sleep. Five hours a night will do him. Almost his entire waking life is given over to state business, and he lets his characteristic impatience loose on people who do not share his seriousness. There is no doubt that his Communism is disfigured, from the Leninist point of view, by his strong feelings of fairness and human justice. His loyalty to friends is tremendous, as is his capacity to remember injuries and nurse grudges. Sincere compromise is not part of his make-up. When he was coming up for trial in 1951, Stalin himself tried to save him for the Politburo, doubtless realizing the value of having at least one legitimate representative of the Polish working class in the mass of police informers, turn-coat journalists, Moscow-bred theoreticians and ambitious university Marxists that composed the Polish Central Committee. But Gomulka refused to remain in the Politburo unless his enemies, Hilary Minc and Jakob Berman, were removed. Since both of them, like Boleslaw Bierut, were Soviet agents, Stalin felt the price too high.

The grudges, impatiences and friendships are almost unfailingly hidden from the world by a moat of mannered aloofness. Gomulka is one of those people who keeps the world at arm's length, so he may concentrate on saving it in his peculiar fashion. Among Communist leaders, he has some kinship to the austerity of Lenin. As for contemporaries of other persuasions, he shows some notable similarities to General Charles de Gaulle. His version of legitimacy may be far different, but he shares de Gaulle's inflexible concept of patriotism. His sense of personal commitment to the country is virtually religious.

Like most of the world's Communist leaders outside Russia, Gomulka's life story is as much a hare-and-hounds proposition for the historian as it was for the pre-war police. Until the end of World War II, his whole existence was spent in a shadow world of illegal meetings, police raids and clandestine pamphleteering, against a background of bitter internal struggles within the Comintern and the Party. The closest parallel to his career is that of Tito's. But Gomulka, even more than Tito, played his game within his own country, more insulated than most Communists from the pulls of rival factions in Moscow.

He was born in 1905, in the mining town of Krosno, in southeastern Poland. His father, a worker in the oil fields, had spent some time working as a miner in Pennsylvania, although he had returned to Poland well before his son was born. Gomulka started working early. He became a blacksmith's apprentice at the age of 14. Scarcely two years later, he was working at organizing a union. He became a Communist at 20, when he was already an official in the chemical industry trade union. In 1932, he was arrested for the first time by police of Marshal Pilsudski's semi-dictatorial state after a labor riot in Lodz. He was also wounded there. A police bullet smashed the nerves in one leg and he has limped ever since.

Four years later he was jailed again as the result of his underground Party organizing work. Given a seven-year sentence, he remained in prison until the German invasion of September, 1939. As it happened, the second jail sentence probably saved his life, for it kept him away from Moscow.

*   *   *

Lenin planned the Bolshevik revolution from Cracow, a city of which he always remained fond. Russian-speaking Poles, like the secret policeman Feliks Dzierzynski and Joseph Unszlicht, once head of the Soviet Air Force, held some of the key positions in the early days of Communist rule in Russia. Rosa Luxemburg, the Polish female revolutionary who almost Communized Berlin, was one of the early apostles of Marxism. Yet the Polish Communist Party, from its birth on December 16, 1918, perennially managed to assert itself as a group of extraordinary heterodoxy, constantly suspected of deviationism by the high command in Moscow. The suspicion was just. Polish patriotism is inherently hostile to Russia; the Polish imagination is inherently hostile to Bolshevism.

The Party was outlawed in Poland the year after its founding, and it remained illegal until the Russian army reestablished it in 1944. Beyond this fact, it labored under some significant handicaps. In 1920, the Soviet Army invaded Poland, to be checked only by the hasty efforts of Marshal Pilsudski and the French General Maxime Weygand* at the approaches to Warsaw. The "miracle of Warsaw" had in fact been stimulated by Pilsudski's preceding invasion of the Ukraine in alliance with Petlura's Ukrainian nationalist forces. Nonetheless, the spectacle of Marshal Budenny's Red cavalry swarming over the Polish countryside was not much of an ad for "Leninist internationalism." At least one prominent member of the Polish Party's central committee, Domsky by name, denounced the Soviet invasion in a German Communist paper. (In those early days Communists were allowed to exhibit differences in public.) But most of the others welcomed the Red troops. At Bialystok Polish Communists set up their own puppet state, under the guns of the Soviet Army. It ominously prefigured the Lublin government of 1944.

None of this early activity was calculated to reassure the Poles about their new Communist Party's patriotism. On the other hand, the Party's support of Marshal Pilsudski in his 1926 nationalist *coup d'etat* was more than enough to dampen its claim to be a proletarian revolutionary movement. Even judged by the tortuous historical standards of the world's Communist parties, there are few such recorded cases of a political organization being hoisted on two of its own petards at the same time.

The Polish Party was far smaller, partly as a result, than the well-organized Communist parties of Germany, France or Czechoslovakia. In 1931, the year of its highest pre-war strength, the Party claimed barely 14,000 regular members, with less than 10,000 additional candidates in the youth movements. The Socialists were infinitely more popular among the workers. Little was even attempted, in the European Communist tradition, in the vil-

---

* As may be imagined, controversy has sprung up over the exact degree of Weygand's participation. It was, in any case, Pilsudski's army; and in view of Weygand's World War II record, we might conclude that Polish strategy predominated in this success.

lages—although the Polish Socialists had considerable rural strength.

The Polish Communists did have their moments. They played a big part in provoking the general strike of 1923, which one-time Polish Communists like Isaac Deutscher still wistfully call the "revolution *manqué*." They sowed many a seed among the poor and restless university youth of the period between the wars. A small but meaningful number of frustrated law or philosophy graduates found its way into Communist underground work in Poland, or across the border. There were moments when its leadership was able to break surface into the national life of the country. In the election of 1928, for example, Communist candidates, many of them running under the banner of legal "front" organizations, received 829,416 votes out of some 11,750,000 votes cast. But the Party's gains from general economic discontent were always scratched out either by its own bitter domestic feuds, or the suspicion of its bosses in Moscow.

The prominence of the personality factor in Communist leadership makes for a cave-world of splinter factions and counter-factions. There is a race of historians, principally former Marxists, who joyfully record these matters, although they are not very widely read. But to most bystanders such a play of faction and counter-faction has relevance to history only as an index of growth and decay, as historically significant as the exact details of the heresies which flourished in mediaeval Byzantium.* So, without going into the intriguing discussion of how Barski broke with Vera Kostrzewa, or how Lenski's "Left-Wing ascendancy" gave way to the "Old-Guard split," it is sufficient to note that the Polish Party was excessively given to internal quarrels which hinged on various Communist heresies. The heresies were never allowed to work their way out of the Party bloodstream (as happened elsewhere in Europe), which might have led to a united national party effort. For the factional battleground was too close to the Soviet Union. Whenever the factional fighting grew audible, the Russians blew

---

* It is not without relevance that the hair-splitting ideological controversies of modern Communism find their closest parallel in the fine-grained, but athletically prosecuted disputes over Christology which were so prevalent in the Orthodoxy of the Eastern Roman Empire.

their whistle, and the teams either changed sides or marched off the field.

Stalin in particular distrusted Polish Communism as a hotbed of disobedience, tainted by Socialist infiltration. In 1923, the Communist Internationale accused the Polish Party of "opportunism, rightist-deviationism and failure to exploit a revolutionary situation"—i.e., the general strike. The next year Stalin again castigated the Polish leaders for their tendency towards Trotskyism. In 1926, Stalin began attacking the Polish Communists for their "May error" of that year in supporting the Pilsudski *coup*. He continued to press the charge. At succeeding Polish Party congresses, he packed its Politburo with Russians, or at the least Moscow Poles. By 1930, to an even greater degree than anywhere else in Europe, the ruling circles of the Party were completely dominated either by Moscow Poles, or outright Soviet agents. This was still not enough. With the Nazi-Soviet pact already in the diplomatic prospect, an active Communist Party in Poland could be of considerable embarrassment. The heresy of "nationalism," also, was perennially latent in the make-up of the Polish Communists. Stalin was no man to take chances with its untimely recurrence.

In 1937, Stalin began the large-scale liquidation of the entire Polish Party leadership. He continued it through 1938, when the Comintern formally announced the dissolution of the Polish Communists as a party of "spies and traitors." Shattered by the influence of "Trotskyists and Pilsudskiites," the announcement read, the party had become merely "an agent of fascism and the Polish political police." Those of the Polish leaders who were not already in the Soviet Union, as refugees, were enticed there and killed. Their names today are pronounced like a hollow litany in Polish Communist circles: "Warski, Lenski, Walecki, Kostrzewa. . . ." They are Polish names, and their memory served to do exactly the opposite of what Stalin did in his liquidation. They kept alive in even the most orthodox Party member a nationalist resentment against the Russians.

The 1938 liquidations almost completely cut off the Polish Communists from their significant past. (The hundred-odd Polish purge survivors released from Vorkuta and similar establishments in the 'fifties were mostly minor officials.) It left the Communists inside Poland without any leadership, except for a few second-rank organizers. Among these was Wladyslaw Gomulka, who happened to be safe in Pilsudski's jail from Stalin's vengeance. The liquidations started a process of chemical change in the outlook of Wladyslaw Gomulka, which culminated when he came to power 18 years later.

In the post-October period, someone asked Gomulka whether he had believed the Comintern charges leveled against the Party leadership. He said he had not. "Why then," came the question, "did he not protest?" The answer was made with typical lack of gloss: "I didn't have the courage, or I didn't have enough confidence in myself. But if Lenin had lived in Poland, he would certainly have protested in such circumstances."

The 1939 invasion of Poland caught Gomulka with a minimum of tangible inspiration or directives from Lenin or anyone else in the Party. He reacted in the manner of a good corporal suddenly left in charge of a platoon. He fought. No small part of his postwar popularity was due to the gradual realization that he was almost the only high-ranking Communist with a consistent record of fighting the Germans. He took part in the 1939 defense of Warsaw, although the records are pretty reticent in describing his exact role, and made his escape through the Russian-occupied part of Poland to the Ukraine. Through 1941 he had his headquarters in Lwow, staying there after the Germans overran eastern Poland, on their way to Russia. He did some organizing work among the workers in his old home town of Krosno, then beat a path back to Warsaw, in obedience to the immediate Party orders he was by then receiving. In 1942, he directed what by Communist reckoning was "the first armed terrorism" of the war, in bombings at the Central Station, and the Cafe Club in Warsaw. In December of that year he was made Secretary of the Warsaw Party organization.

The bombing of the Cafe Club in Warsaw was hardly an impressive achievement, compared to the activities of the Home Army, the tactical arm of the London-directed underground, which by that time had organized an entire network of underground sabotage and reprisal activity, including a regular system of judicial sentences passed and "executed" against collaborators with the Germans and notorious Gestapo agents. The "act of terrorism," as the non-Communist Polish underground realistically appraised it, consisted of throwing a single hand-grenade into a cafe where German soldiers were drinking beer. But at least it was a fair index of Gomulka's sentiments. With his assistant Marian Spychalski, he had asked the Cominform long before for permission to organize a massive anti-German underground. The request had, naturally enough, been ignored. The Polish Party itself, as a result of the Nazi-Soviet joint aggression, had been discredited to the point of evaporation. In his resistance policy, Corporal Gomulka had a pretty thin platoon to operate with.

In December, 1941, one Marceli Nowotko, a loyal Moscow Pole, had been parachuted into his original homeland with a new set of Communist orders. Through Nowotko Gomulka's policy of resistance was finally sanctioned. The Party was reorganized under the new name of Polish Workers Party. Efforts were made to build up something like a Communist resistance network, although one operating independently of the Home Army.

But there were some interesting premises to this Communist underground, about which Gomulka apparently knew little or nothing. The Russians had no wish to help the functioning underground of the London government in exile. On the contrary, they wanted to destroy it, as they ultimately did during the Warsaw Uprising of 1944. If the Communist underground was too weak to get any big results fighting the Nazis, it was strong and flexible enough, ran Moscow's reasoning processes, to sabotage the Home Army. So while Gomulka went ahead with his projects for striking at the Nazis, Nowotko and his two assistants, Pawel Finder and Boleslaw Bierut, were playing the game with a different set of ground rules. They opened a series of arms'-length contacts with the Gestapo, among others, in the process of working out the Russian orders. A "cell of disinformation" was founded for the purpose of tracing the leaders of the Home Army and others in the patriotic underground, so that they could be denounced by the Gestapo.*

* Much of this information, as well as other details of the Soviet secret police activity in Poland, is based on the revelations of Joseph Swiatlo, the U.B. lieutenant-colonel who escaped to West Berlin and later to the U. S. It checks out with the testimony of others concerned in the doings of those days.

From September 30, 1939, when the fleeing President of Poland transferred his powers to a former Cabinet minister, the government of Poland carried on the fight against Germany in every possible way. Its new Premier, General Wladyslaw Sikorski, not only raised Polish armies to fight in France, Italy and the Middle East; he presided over the most effective Underground movement in Europe, because the most comprehensive. The Home Army, backed by the passive resistance of the entire country, had a total strength well over 300,000. It worked quietly and effectively against the German occupation until its back was broken in the tragic Warsaw Uprising of 1944. The negative role of the Communist underground, such as it was, is all the more shocking, since its principal aim was the sabotage of the national resistance.

Attempting to trace the exact course of the movements and counter-movements in this underground battle is a little like getting lost in the subway. But whatever the exact amount of damage done, there is no doubt but that the disinformation cell of the Communists furnished information about the Home Army that was of great value to the Gestapo. There were cases of the London underground's activities actually being raided by Communist or Soviet personnel disguised as Gestapo agents. Most damaging of all, the Moscow Poles developed a swollen file of names connected with the Home Army, which was tragically activated the moment the Russians marched into Poland.

In 1943 Gomulka became First Secretary of the Party. It was not by any design of the Russians. Nowotko had been killed by a fellow Communist, who thought, logically enough, that his dealings with the Germans established his identity as a member of the Gestapo. Finder, who then succeeded to the Secretaryship, was killed in 1943 by the Gestapo. Their deaths weakened the Moscow faction of the Party. In November, 1943, the "native Polish" element was easily able to elect Gomulka. Fortuitously, communications with Moscow had gone out at the time, and they remained broken for six months. When the Russians reestablished their direct control, there was not much they could do about Gomulka's *fait accompli*.

It was a shock to the new Party Secretary to find out the existence of the disinformation cell. His discovery came about by pure chance. The disinformation cell sent the wrong address to the Gestapo one day. Trying to liquidate the Home Army printing shop in Grzybowska Street, they gave by mistake the address of the People's Army. The Gestapo, happy enough to liquidate a few Communists, for want of nationalist victims, made the People's Army printing shop a thing of the definite past. In the course of investigating this occurrence, Gomulka ran down at least some of the threads of intrigue that had all begun with Marceli Nowotko's parachute jump.

The active nationalist Communists, now that they were in charge, made several honest attempts to cooperate with the established Resistance, or elements of it. But the inheritance of suspicion was too hard to overcome, in most cases. With the Socialists Gomulka made a little headway. He also showed very early in the game his tendency, later pronounced, to base the hopes of the future workers' paradise on a firm alliance of Communist and Socialist elements.

If Gomulka did anything but wait during the 1944 Warsaw Uprising, history does not show it. By that time the Communists were being actively directed by the Russians, through parachuted agents and so-called "partisan bands" which rolled westward in the comity of the Red Army. When the Red Army finally arrived in Warsaw, in January, 1945, it was accompanied by several divisions of Polish troops, who had been recruited behind the lines in Russia. (Only a small part of the Poles held in the U.S.S.R. were permitted to join the Polish Army in the West.) The entire strength of the Party and its sympathizers at this time, including those in uniform, was at its most optimistic 20,000. The Polish troops under Soviet command were by no means all Communists. They included non-Communists who had been forcibly impressed or who had volunteered, either deprived by circumstances from joining the London Polish armies or anxious to return to Poland with the military formations who were, so to speak, on the ground, not waiting fruitlessly on the Italian front or at RAF airdromes, wondering when their time would come.

On July 22, 1944, just 10 days before the start of the Warsaw Uprising, the Moscow Poles announced their "Committee of National Liberation" first formed at Chelm and later transferred to

Lublin. On August 5, 1944, after the Uprising had begun its fateful course, the representatives of the Lublin Poles arrived in Moscow to "negotiate" with Stalin and Premier Stanislaw Mikolajczyk of the London government. The course of the long negotiations that followed only postponed decision on the fate that was by now apparent. Using the bare minimum of props to cover up their aggrandizement, the Russians had taken over the country which fought hardest of any European nation for its liberation. Throughout Poland Soviet M.V.D. officers were busy, arresting, deporting, or assassinating, acting on the files which their loyal disinformation cell had accumulated. For all of Gomulka's honest efforts at some kind of honest nationalist Polish resistance, his Polish Workers' Party was universally known by the derisive nickname given by the legitimate Underground to the initials P.P.R. (for *Polska Partia Rabotnicza*). The words in Polish were *Platne Pacholki Rosji:* Paid Lackeys of Russia.

But it had the power. In 1945, thanks to a peculiar combination of luck and circumstance that included everything from big power relationships to the failure of a single wireless machine, Wladyslaw Gomulka found himself almost the most powerful citizen of a new "People's" Poland. Only the Moscow Pole, Boleslaw Bierut, ranked him. In the government administration Gomulka was Vice-Premier and Minister of the Recovered Territories, the immense western areas taken from Germany. In the party apparatus he retained his commanding situation of First Secretary. That he got to this eminence at all was a matter of some concern to his Russian comrades. In their milieu, this uncorrupted survival of the pre-war Communist Party looked rather like the honest church-going alderman who blunders into the councils of a corrupt political machine and is chosen mayor because he happens to have the only key to the Boss' cigar box.

Gomulka used his power for all it was worth. In the Western Territories he fought a losing but hard battle to deter the Russians from totally looting both cities and countryside. In 1945 he ordered Polish troops to shoot, if the Russians attempted any further looting from factories under his charge in the newly recovered Western Territories. He successfully protested the projected Russian arrest of Wincenty Witos, the old Peasant Party leader, which would have violated a safe conduct that he himself had issued. His vehicle of protest was a phone call directly to Stalin. For once, it achieved its object.

Within the Party, he continued the wartime sort of loose-construction Communism that led to his arrest. With the other "native" Communists in Poland—notably his friends Zenon Kliszko, Wladyslaw Bienkowski and Marian Spychalski—he sought to widen the membership structure of the Communists by mergers with Socialists, in particular. He openly preferred the pre-war nationalist tradition of the Socialists to the Moscow dependence of the Communists, and hoped to strengthen his own Party with transfusions from the Socialist party platforms. ("We are not a Communist party. We are a workers' party and a party of the nation.") He warned the Party to go slow on collectivising the farms, or interfering with other props of the established national order. In the Western Territories, he did not hesitate to use non-Communist technicians or administrators. His wartime experience had if anything made his convictions about this policy all the stronger. "Poland is not yet ripe for Communist rule," he had told the Peasant Party leader, Stanislaw Banczyk, in 1943, "We need 20, or maybe 30 or 40 years."

This devotion to gradualism did not make him a humanist before his time. He connived, cheated, threatened and bludgeoned as much as the other Communist leaders in their efforts to eliminate the legal and, judged by any fair standards, the majority opposition of the Peasants' Party and the Socialists from the scene. Although he warned against purges of "rightists" from the merging Socialists Party, he was ruthless in dragooning the Socialists into their reluctant baptism by subversion into the Polish United Workers Party. This ceremony took place in December 1948, after Gomulka had devoted much time to threatening the Socialists with the reprisals visited on any opponents of "workers unity." Reading the few books that were written about pre-October Communism in Poland, like Stanislaw Mikolajczyk's *The Rape of Poland* or the late Arthur Bliss Lane's *I Saw Poland Betrayed,* one can find no suggestion of the part Gomulka later played. To the non-Communist observer of the period, he was a dangerous and dedicated Party man, a little louder and more honest in his beliefs, but no different essentially from Moscow Poles like Bierut, Berman or Minc.

If the difference was undetected, it was nonetheless very real. The Russians realized that a nationalist like Gomulka was potentially dangerous to them, long before Tito appeared to dot the "i's" on their lesson. Within the Polish Party, Bierut, Berman and Minc, all of them obedient Russian agents, had resumed the direction of the Warsaw Poles, busy consolidating their Party strength, the while paying some lip service to Gomulka's ideas of a popular front.

Aside from these native Polish efforts, the Russians had several control devices of their own. The first one was the reorganized Polish Army. By mid-1944, five years before Marshal Rokossowski took formal command of the Poles, Soviet officers were "allowed" to take Polish citizenship, in order to fill out the gaps in officer material among the Poles. (Most of the surviving officer material was regarded by the Communists as politically "unreliable."

The next control agency, as with the other satellites, was the Soviet embassy. As the Russian control tightened, the position of the ambassador as an arbiter in Polish affairs grew more and more noticeable. The first post-war ambassador, Lebedev, was referred to with acerbity as the second Repnin, in memory of Catherine the Great's unsavory plenipotentiary.* But he was a relatively minor functionary. His replacement, Ponomarenko, was a member of the Central Committee of the Soviet Communist Party, besides being a diplomat. His crudeness became proverbial. In October, 1956, Ponomarenko's removal was one of the Poles' demands.

The final control agency was the ultimate instrument of the Russian state power, the secret police. Compared to the Communists' U.B., the pre-war Pilsudski police, who could be nasty on occasion, had the punitive power of a Keep-Off-The-Grass sign. The blue collar tips and hat bands of the U.B. and its military arm,

---

* Actually Prince Repnin did the Poles a service, by telling Catherine that her plan for forming a "Russian" party, composed of the Orthodox believers, was faulty. For this he was transferred.

the K.B.W. were borrowed directly from the M.V.D.* and in almost every other respect, except for foreign control, they were faithful copies of the Russian prototypes. A Russian officer (generally a meaningfully modest-ranking colonel) was installed as a "deputy" to the Polish U.B. functionary commanding each department. A Russian, however, directly commanded the important personnel department. In most cases the Russians faithfully kept up the forms of Polish independence, with that curious desperate regard the Soviet mind displays for at least the symbols of legitimate government relationships. But not for an instant was there any doubt about where authority dwelt. Occasionally, an especially bad-tempered Russian would break through the conventions. On his 50th birthday, Colonel Nikolai Orechwo, the Russian head of the personnel department, was handed a Polish medal by his superiors at headquarters. "I serve the Soviet Union" was his taut reply, a little too taut even for the Bezpieka Poles present at the ceremony.

Humankind has an interesting way of adjusting to its environment, then turning the very adjustment into a significant, though often unconscious trait of character. The poverty of lavish building material in Japan produced a national architectural cult of spareness and tasteful austerity. The lack of theoretical talents, and the leisure for using them, in the frontier days of the United States produced a practicality of outlook that influenced the whole new world of technology. The Russian lack of housing space, still a constant of Soviet living, has made a deep, but less appreciated contribution there to the normal human concept of privacy. Where everyone lives jumbled together, no one can have secrets—hence, no one should have secrets, and it is easy to learn whatever some one tries to keep hidden.

These feelings about privacy, intertwined with the original conspiratorial base of Soviet society, have been important bulwarks of the Soviet security system. Everything interlocks; everyone is

---

* This security organization, in its frequent changes of nomenclature, demonstrates the truth of the old adage "A rose by any other name. . . ." It set up shop as the Cheka in 1919, then evolved as the O.G.P.U., the N.K.V.D., the M.V.D., the M.G.B., and the K.G.B., successively. Through all these paper reorganizations, there were no fundamental changes in its mission, only improved efficiency.

useful; spying is a 24 hour-a-day job. This concept had doubtless been known in Poland, but the Russians demonstrated it to the ultimate degree, in their interlocking control of the secret police, and through them, of every corner of Polish society.

There were in effect a dozen key-holes in every Warsaw office, with as many different agencies or individuals looking through them. The wife of the offensive Colonel Orechwo, for example, was also a secretary of Boleslaw Bierut, assuring an optimum security watch on the leading Moscow Pole. Bierut had his own file in Moscow. But the dossiers on every other member of the Politburo were neatly recorded in the Tenth Department of the U.B., the special branch charged with the surveillance of Party members themselves. Each man had his flaws and past indiscretions carefully recorded here. Since a great number of the Party faithful had been involved in dubious dealings with either the Gestapo or the pre-war Polish police, there was ample ground for almost any kind of treason proceedings, if occasion suggested. Even the all-powerful Bierut had his tragic flaw. Jakob Berman, one of his most faithful assistants, kept up a lively file and surveillance system on the politically significant figure of Wanda Gorska, Bierut's mistress.

The old U.B. was swept away even before the October Revolution, largely as a result of the Swiatlo defection and subsequent broadcasts over Radio Free Europe. But before its suspension, it had been able to institute and maintain a police state in the classic manner. It did not operate on the basis of wholesale arrests, except for the mass liquidations and deportations of the legitimate underground immediately following the war. In line with standard Communist police procedure, it established a myth of omniscience, and some set boundaries of conduct. These boundaries placed crippling restrictions on what people in a normal society would consider freedom of movement, not to say thought. In Russian society they have become a commonplace. In Poland, both because of the nature of the people and the relative shortness of police rule, they never reached this point of inevitability; but the margin was close.

The Bezpieka was commanded by the Minister of State Security, one Stanislaw Radkiewicz, who was later arrested, tried and jailed by the Gomulka government. Like his department heads, Radkiewicz had a Soviet officer, in this case a general, at his elbow. Under them were eleven numbered departments and several special agencies. The first department concerned itself with counter-intelligence, mainly directed against foreign espionage activities, real or fancied. The second department was in charge of archives and censorship. The third department controlled the fight against "underground" movements, i.e. any organized guerilla fighters or remnants of the London government's network. The fourth department was in charge of "espionage" in industry and agriculture, which is to say it spied, or had the capacity for spying on every factory or collective in the country. The fifth department kept watch on youth organizations, trade unions and the puppet non-Communist political parties.

The sixth dealth with espionage outside the country, and for a time was extremely active. For some years after World War II Polish U.B. spy rings extracted a great deal of information about Western and specifically U.S. troop movements and political activities in Germany. The eighth department controlled transport; the ninth heavy industry and the mining and chemical industries. The tenth, as mentioned, saw to intra-Party relationships among the Communists. The eleventh manipulated the Communist attack on the Roman Catholic Church. Besides these numbered divisions, the U.B. contained an investigation bureau, which handled trials and "confessions" in all except official Party matters; a personnel department; an office in charge of safeguarding members of the government, and another in charge of radio monitoring, jamming, etc.

The principal unifying force through all the U.B. departments was the unsavory character of their members. In the police state tradition, the Communists swept up all the worst elements in Polish society, including every variety of informer, stool pigeon and police spy used by the Nazis and the Pilsudski police before them. Their privileges were great, including a system of special stores, commissaries and expensive residences, set in their own fenced-off compounds. As later revelations, and in some cases, trials brought out, they used their privileged position to commit every variety of crime and torture. U.B. leaders like Roman Romkowski, Anatol Fejgin, and Josef Rozansky were later proven guilty of extremes in sadism, made in the course of getting "confessions" from people who fell into their net. In their prison at Mokotow they conducted the kind of hearings that have since become well-known to the world outside—a process of constant interrogations, carried on day and night, blinding lights flashed in sleepless prisoners' eyes, beatings, forced marches, and sometimes murder.

The author of this grisly efficient police structure is said to be a man who later became something of a world personality. When Stefan Korbonski, the last Director of the wartime London Underground, was being interrogated at U.B. headquarters in 1945, he noticed a Russian in civilian clothes, wearing some sort of Soviet decoration in his buttonhole, walk unobtrusively into the room to listen in. After listening to the proceedings for an hour, he got up and left, the while all the U.B. personnel scrambled to attention. Guards identified him as "the real top-dog in the Ministry," a general in the M.V.D. He was called Malinov.

Just eleven years later, witnesses to the debacle in Budapest said that the turning point in the negotiations between the Hungarian and Soviet military delegations was reached when a person, "wearing no insignia of rank" walked into the room at Soviet Headquarters on Csepel Island, and announced the arrest of the Hungarian delegation. This was Colonel General Ivan A. Serov, head of the Soviet State Security after the fall of Beria, and Khrushchev's chief policeman until his replacement in December, 1958. Serov and Malinov, it has been reasonably suggested, were the same man.*

Through the last 20 years Serov was involved in the affairs of Poland in several unpleasant ways. At the beginning of World War II he superintended the deportation and arrest of Poles in the eastern provinces annexed by the Russians. He came back to Poland in 1944, and directed the mass arrests, deportations and murders of Home Army personnel, as well as certain important members of the legitimate Polish government. His techniques were subtle, at first, rather than blustering, and he preferred to work quietly and persuasively. "You need to find in every man's soul a

---

* Although reliable Russian sources have denied this identification, I have noted what seems to be a general conviction among Poles that it is so.

hearth," he said once, describing his interrogation technique, "and then start to dance from this place."

If Gomulka had any doubts about Russian interests in Poland, Serov and his men must have settled them. After the Communists were reestablished in Warsaw, he would appear every Thursday in Gomulka's old apartment on Szucha Avenue, for the secret weekly meetings of the Polish Communist hierarchy. There, quietly and simply, he would tell the Poles what to do. Whereupon they danced.

*   *   *

Since his return to power Wladyslaw Gomulka has danced to the Russian tune only fitfully, and with some pronounced variations of his own. In Stalin's day this eccentricity was not permitted. His collision with the Russian dancing masters made inevitable his departure from the Politburo; but to arrange this matter took the Moscow Poles some time. By 1948 they were ready to move. With the opposition groups eliminated, Mikolajczyk in exile, the influence of the "London" underground nullified, Boleslaw Bierut could act on his orders to make a Russian rubber stamp out of the Polish Party. The impending troubles with Tito made it all the more necessary to erase the "national Communist" opposition in a hurry.

The Cominform denounced Tito in June, 1948. Barely three months later the Central Committee opened an attack on Gomulka's stewardship as Secretary General. On September 6 he was voted out of this office, after a carefully prepared campaign of several months, waged against him by Bierut. He was accused specifically of "nationalist deviation," which included everything from a tendency to go soft on Tito's defection to his insistence that forced collectivization was premature, inefficient and ill-suited to the character of the Polish people.

Shortly afterward Gomulka was removed from the Politburo and his two ministerial posts in the government. He had only a small, if devoted following within the Party at that time and the majority of his non-Communist countrymen had not yet reached the point where they established degrees of coloration when assessing the Redness of their Communist rulers. So the Moscow Poles were able to set about their tasks without much interruption. Bierut told the U.B. to start making out a case, in preparation for the inevitable trial. The investigative branch began to comb the convictions and past histories of Gomulka's best friends, beginning with General Marian Spychalski.

By this time Gomulka's fate was evident; and Party friends started peeling away from his presence like sensitive artichoke leaves. Bierut and his two henchmen Minc and Berman set forth their new collectivization schemes without fear of interruption, pledging Poland lock stock and barrel to the interests of the Soviet Union. In November, 1949 the Central Committee opened its own kind of impeachment proceedings in earnest, for Gomulka still remained a member. Instead of simple nationalism, the new charges hinted at faulty appointments, toleration of spying and anti-Party elements, down to "permeation with the Pilsudski spirit." Calling him by his old Party code name Wieslaw, Edward Ochab, the same man who later turned into a Gomulka supporter, made the classic accusation against Gomulka: "In your present position, Comrade Wieslaw, you will become the symbol for the bourgeouisie, for the rich peasants, for reaction." At the same meeting Hilary Minc, the regime's economic czar, was more frank. Gomulka, he said, had a "complete lack of faith in the Soviet Union."

Along with his friends Spychalski and Kliszko, Gomulka was thrown out of the Central Committee. He responded, during the expulsion proceedings, with the usual phrases of Communist self-criticism. He conceded that he had perpetrated "a mountain of mistakes. . . . It never entered my head that Poland could progress along the way to Socialism without being supported by the Soviet Union but . . . it was difficult for me to shift my attitude as regards the Soviet Union to the ideological party plane." But there the self-criticism stopped. He still defended his own ideas about the "Polish road to socialism."

For about a year Gomulka survived in a curious kind of enforced limbo, stripped of his offices and influence, while the Moscow Poles set about a vacuum-cleaning of the entire Party. On August 2, 1951, Joseph Swiatlo, the same U.B. official who later escaped to the West, drove down from Warsaw with a few henchmen to the resort town of Krynica. At a few minutes past seven a.m. he knocked on the door of Gomulka's room at the New Resort Hotel and asked him to come up to Warsaw. Gomulka had a pistol under his pillow, but he was dissuaded from using it. After several hours of argument, he agreed to come with them. He and his wife Zofia drove back through Warsaw to their well-guarded jail at Miedzeszyn, a country house operated by the Tenth Department of the U.B.

The Russians kept pressing for an immediate show trial, like the public trial of Laszlo Rajk in Budapest in October 1949, or the later Prague proceedings against the Czech nationalist Communist suspect, Rudolph Slansky, in 1952. But the Poles, for all the ministrations of the U.B., were having difficulties. Gomulka was a tough man to break under questioning and too unreliable to risk being exhibited at a public hearing. He insisted on his innocence. When faced with wholly fictitious charges of collaboration against the Germans during World War II, he rejoined by threatening to tell the entire story of the collaboration of the Moscow Poles with the Gestapo, of which he had very sure knowledge.

The U.B. kept its distance, finally—although some of Gomulka's most trusted friends, notably Spychalski, had confessed to falsified "charges" against him. So did the Politburo. Of all the Communist parties in Eastern Europe, the Polish was the weakest. To damage the slight popular hold it enjoyed by a show trial and a killing was too risky. Of all the Communist parties in eastern Europe, also, the Polish had suffered the most bloodily from the Stalin purges of 1938. Bierut and Co. may have been Soviet agents; but they were keen enough to realize that a cycle of purges, once begun, may easily culminate in the elimination of the original executioners. The litany "Warski, Lenski, Walecki, Kostrzewa . . ." still echoed down the corridors of the new block-square Party building in Warsaw. In the end, it was probably their uneasy memory that saved Gomulka's life.

3

The Party on the Operating Table

> "Freedom only for the supporters of government, only for the members of one party—however numerous they may be—is no freedom at all. Freedom is always and exclusively freedom for the one who thinks differently."

> —*Rosa Luxemburg*

ONE OF THE most decisive speeches of our time was the Secret Report to the Twentieth Congress of the Communist Party of the Soviet Union, made by Nikita Khrushchev on the night of February 24, 1956. It was barroom oratory. For all the planning behind them, the wild-swinging denunciations of Stalin had the abrupt violence of a glass knocked off a table. This made it all the more effective, tactically speaking, for Khrushchev's purpose. Through his very violence, Khrushchev was able to secure the prestige of the ruling committee in Moscow and the Communist Party itself, by sharply focusing the rising national uncertainty and distrust on the monster crimes of Stalin and the "cult of personality."

On Saturday morning, October 20, 1956, Gomulka made a speech of his own to the Central Committee of the Polish Party, which will probably go down in history as the inescapably related step-child of Khrushchev's. He lacked the drama of Khrushchev's revelations. The crimes discussed were less enormous, his sense of political theatre less acute. Where Khrushchev spoke as a *post mortem* prosecuting attorney, Gomulka addressed his audience as a planner interrupted in his work, considering the obstacles criminally placed in his path. He was not attempting to persuade his audience, as the Russian was. When Gomulka spoke, his victory in the October Revolution had already been won. Where Khrushchev's speech was a tactical expedient, Gomulka's was more like a declaration of long-term strategy. Where Khrushchev attacked one personality, Gomulka denounced an entire era.

Both speeches, judged on the basis of what they proclaimed, were current successes and historical failures. Khrushchev succeeded in diverting the Soviet people from an increasingly dangerous subterranean fault-finding, by channeling their worry and indignation into a public phase of Stalinist witch-hunting. Gomulka succeeded in gathering popular enthusiasm for his program of "national Communism," probably the first time since the early days of Communism that any such enthusiasm had been raised, without heavy artificial stimulation. But in each one the seeds of ultimate failure were clearly visible.

In castigating the dead dictator, Khrushchev was unable in the long run to disengage the entire Communist Party leadership from the dictator's crimes. On the contrary he set off a chain reaction of criticism and enquiry that hurt the Party far beyond anything he had imagined would happen. The result proved to people who had never believed this before that enquiry is potentially fatal to a Communist system. For the new enquiry was followed by waves of counter-criticism and revived repression, as the Politburo finally realized they had opened a Pandora's box. In external affairs, like the executions of the Hungarian leaders, and inside the U.S.S.R., with the stifling of expression that culminated in the vilification of Boris Pasternak, the leaders resumed the tight exercise of power almost frankly as a power oligarchy. They continued, necessarily, to strip themselves of the decaying layers of ideology and "fraternal spirit" that had once been such a valuable window-dressing.*

---

* They felt the lack of windowdressing keenly—and their craving for *some* kind of Communist "legitimist" sanction in no small way explained the growing prestige power of Mao Tse Tung, the last first-generation Communist leader in the international movement.

In *his* speech, Gomulka opened the crack of Communist infalli-
bility even farther. He was fully as concerned as Khrushchev with
maintaining the power of the Party state. But in denouncing the
excesses of a whole system of government, his indignation and his
basic honesty carried him into much deeper water than he intended. The words he used were more general than Khrushchev's,
the implications drawn from them by a non-Communist population more general still. His speech had attacked specific abuses of
Communist rule. In the end, he found it cited as a text proving
that any system of Communist rule is unworkable and impossible
outside of the Utopian Communist scriptures. As Gomulka's rule
continued, the definitions he first gave of the rights of man and the
abuses of power posed a dilemma for their author that grew constantly more difficult.

Gomulka's speech started with a bitter recollection of things
past, the progress of the Moscow Poles' dictatorship since his own
arrest. ". . . Although only seven years have gone by since that
time," he began, ". . . these years constitute a closed historic
period. I am deeply convinced that that period has gone into the
irrevocable past. There has been much evil in those years. The
legacy which that period left the Party, the working class and the
nation is more than alarming in certain spheres of life. . . .

"After the conclusion of the Six Year Plan, which according to
its premises was meant to raise high the standard of living of the
working class and the entire nation, we are faced today . . . with
immense economic difficulties which grow from day to day. We
contracted important investment credits for expansion of industry,
and when the time came for payment of the first installments we
found ourselves in the situation of an insolvent bankrupt.

". . . the economic picture of cooperative farms . . . is a sad
picture. Despite great outlays, they had smaller results and greater
production costs. I do not mention the political aspect of the
problem. . . ."

He followed with his plans and warnings for the present. This
included a recognition, among other things, that the Poznan rioters
were right. "The working class recently gave a painful lesson to
the Party leadership and the government. In seizing the strike
weapon and in demonstrating in the streets on the black Thursday

last June, the Poznan workers shouted in a powerful voice: Enough! This cannot go on any longer! Turn back from the false road! The working class has never resorted to the strike, as a weapon of struggle for its rights, in a thoughtless manner. . . . The clumsy attempt at the presentation of the painful Poznan tragedy as the work of imperialist agents and provocateurs was very naive politically. . . .

"The Twentieth Congress of the Communist Party of the Soviet Union stimulated a turn in the political life of the country. An animating sound current went through the Party masses, the working classes, the entire community. People began to straighten their backs. The silent, enslaved minds began to shake off the poison of mendacity, falsehood and hypocrisy. The stiff clichés, previously predominant on Party platforms and at public meetings, as well as in the press, began to give place to living, creative words. . . .

"Governing the country requires that the working class and the working masses should give the credit of confidence to their representatives who hold the reins of government in the State. This is the moral basis of exercising power in the name of the working masses. The credit of confidence can be continuously renewed only on the condition that obligations towards those giving the credit are fulfilled. The loss of the credit of confidence of the working class means the loss of the moral basis of power. . . ."

In his long and moving statement, Gomulka went on to describe and denounce "the cult of the individual," as practiced in Russia and the satellites, the deterioration of the Communist Party, even the inequalities in "the relations between us and our great and friendly neighbor the Soviet Union." Always he specified ways of correcting the mess left by the Stalinist Poles: the unreal price structure, wasteful industrial management, destructive forced collectivization of agriculture. Most prominently, he discussed his plans to rehabilitate the Communist Party on a basis of "democracy."

Of all these things, nothing was stranger to hear from the head of a Communist Party than his insistence on "the moral basis of power." Lenin, to be sure, had talked about morality with great fluency, and Communists have "moralized" ever since. But the

Leninist version of morality is, as Lenin artfully put it, "entirely subordinated to the interests of the class struggle of the proletariet," (i.e. to what Lenin says these interests are). It posits its own peculiar penalties for critics.* Gomulka's definition was more like the ancient rational recognition of a basic contract between rulers and people, rooted in the natural law.

In the next three months this concept of morality had its first test. The energies released by the Polish October were far from sated by assurances that the Party would pull up its boots and start some honest work. The non-Communist majority in the country was anxious to see the whole structure of Communism swept out along with its abuses. The young Party intellectuals, finally giving free rein to their suppressed logic, were riding high, past intra-party democracy, in the direction of a modified parliamentary government. "Socialist Parliamentarianism" became a popular slogan among the eggheadery. The evils of legislatures, one of the perennial exhibits in the Communist chamber of horrors, were discovered to inhere instead, as Professor Julian Hochfeld suggested, only "in the political and economic contents of their systems." Gomulka's own convictions were cited about the Party being the "leading" not the "ruling" Party, in sharp contradistinction to the usage among Khrushchev and the Russians.

The only two "other" political parties permitted in Poland were the Peasant Party and the Democratic Party, both orderlies of the Communists, but at least potential sources for a political opposition. People recalled Gomulka's early convictions about building something new in Poland, rather than performing a pullmotor revival of standard Communism. In November 1956 during the course of a speech to Party workers, he restated this: "The building of socialism provides for the cooperation of other, non-Marxist political parties, which, however, support socialism. There are also possibilities for the progressive Catholic movement to participate in building a system of social justice. . . ." But at the same time, he gave the delegates a tough reminder that the future of Poland

---

* "And the Menshiviks and Socialist-Revolutionaries, all of whom preach this sort of thing, are astonished when we say that we shall shoot those people who say such things. They are amazed; but surely it is clear . . ."
—Lenin's speech at the 11th Congress of the CPSU in 1922.

could be reconstituted in no other formal image but that of the present "People's Republic."

An election had been promised for January 20, 1957. With the entire country aroused and angry, as well as relieved, Gomulka faced the unique dilemma of a Communist leader who had the courage to let some air into his closed society. If he went ahead with a free election, as promised, the fresh draughts might well blow down all retaining walls; the people would very possibly elect every non- or anti-Communist who showed his name on the ballot. The result would be temporary chaos and a sure return of Russian troops. If on the other hand he ran through a typical faked election, with the usual forced Communist majority, the result would be revolution—and a sure return of Russian troops.

He was saved from the dilemma by a combination of honesty and shrewdness. In 1947 he had helped rig as crooked an election as ever disgraced the map of Europe. Although he would still justify the ends for which he had then crushed the "counter-revolutionary" parties, his own sufferings under Communism had made the means now repugnant to him. He decided to honor his October pledges to the Polish people. At the same time he set out to show them, by a combination of explanation, appeal and vicarious threat, that the Russians would not permit a repudiation of any Communist government at the polls.

Rarely in modern history has a government sent out a more candid appeal to its citizens. "Listen to this summons," he said to the country on the day before the elections, "It is one of deep political wisdom. Listen to the voice of reason. Let us be wise on Election day." There followed his famous predictions: "To cross out the candidates of our Party means to cross out the independence of our country, to cross out Poland from the map of European states."

His appeal got heavy support from the Roman Catholic hierarchy. Cardinal Wyszynski was faithful to the terms of the new truce between church and state. After a conference with Premier Cyrankiewicz, whose billiard ball head was beginning to show some worried furrows, the Primate presided over a letter of the Polish hierarchy to the Roman Catholic parishes of Poland. Its injunction was very clear. "The Sunday of January 20," the bishops wrote, "is a day of general elections to the Sejm. Catholic citizens have their obligation to discharge their duties in this election. The Catholic clergy will hold divine services in such a way that all the faithful can discharge their religious duties and their voting duties without impediment."

The Cardinal's letter, Gomulka's own honesty and the national instinct for self-preservation did the trick. The voters gave 98.1% of their votes to the official candidates of the Front of National Unity. An amazing 94% of those eligible went to the polls. That they were voting for Gomulka, not for the Communist Party was very clear from any analysis of the balloting. In all, 722 candidates were nominated by the Front for the 459 seats in the Sejm, which gave at least some latitude of choice in a single-ticket election. Many of the obvious "Stalinists" were not returned. The highest individual totals outside of Gomulka's went to Eligiusz Lassota, the editor of the violently anti-Stalinist *Po Prostu*, and two non-Party candidates, one of them a Catholic writer. In numerous cases, preferred Party candidates were returned at the bottom of the lists and non-Party people moved up to the top. Officially, the Polish United Workers Party received only 237 of the seats (although naturally fellow-travelers or others of the obedient occupied much of the balance). If the populace had to accept a single-slate election, Gomulka's new government had been forced to make the officially picked candidates as palatable and as non-Party as possible.

The election was a great victory for Gomulka's national Communism and a signal defeat for the Soviet Union's international variety. The most accurate expression of its international implications was a cartoon in the Swiss weekly *Die Weltwoche,* showing the same headline "Communist Victory in the Polish elections" being received with wild acclaim in the White House and with gnashing of teeth in the Kremlin. In this description, no reportorial exaggeration was involved.

Gomulka had little doubt about the nature of the verdict. It was dictated by confidence in him, as a leader, and by expediency— "in the land of the blind," the Poles might have phrased it, "vote the straight one-eyed ticket." In the circumstances he had a clear choice of vehicles for traveling down the Polish road to Socialism:

the Party or the State. With the new Sejm in session and a governmental mechanism which for the first time in a decade had been brought to some independence of the ruling Party, he had every encouragement for choosing the State, i.e. for activating the formal government organism which orthodox Communist Party rule prefers to have atrophy. The Communist Party was demoralized by the events since 1953. It was out of touch with the Polish people and, considering their mood, glad of it. Even a semi-parliamentary government, under the aegis of the United Workers Party, would have been applauded by most of the population. It would also have given a broad channel to the anti-Party energies coursing through the country.

At the same time it would have rung the alarm bell in Moscow. For all of Khrushchev's ad lib liberalism, his principal aim since coming to power was to restore the Communist Party in the Soviet Union and elsewhere to a position of unquestioned rule. Many of his political and industrial reforms, from the 1956 abolition of the Moscow industrial ministries to the 1958 laws requiring factory work of students, make sense chiefly in the larger context of restoring the Communist Party to power as the only arbiter of national policy against the rising influence of the technicians, the managers, and the increasingly skeptical intellectuals. The revelations of the Twentieth Party Congress, to say nothing of the cumulative effect of Stalinism, led to a pronounced loosening of "discipline" among the Russians, a less reverent view towards the ruling Party. Khrushchev's response was to strengthen the Party to the utmost, in an effort to shore up the foundations of the Soviet state. And, broadly speaking, he succeeded in doing so. Like Lenin and Stalin before him, if far more desperately, Khrushchev realized that the Communist ruling class cannot permit any rival body of control, or it will ultimately lose to it—in any country.

Gomulka decided on Party rule for Poland not alone because he appreciated the effect of his actions on the Russians. ("Do you want the tanks to come in here?" was a question he more than once asked during Party arguments.) But also, as an old Communist, his world was bounded by the Party. If the Party had erred, his reasoning ran, the errors could be corrected by new ideas and new men. All of this correction should be done within the Party framework. He never tired of citing the metaphor of a spent car that needed only some spare parts to make it go like new.

Without being philosophers, even "humanitarian" Communists share the ancient distrust of thinkers in the Hobbes tradition for the good sense of their fellow-men. Gomulka could not face the "anarchy" that would come with a government divorced from Party rule. He is no world traveler, and he can honestly be believed to base his knowledge of the outside world and parliamentary government solely on his own limited experience with them. "Would you rather have 75 political parties?" he asked groups of Polish workers during the question-and-answer sessions he held in those months. Always he justified the Party choice by at least the expressed conviction that the only alternative was the corrupt "anarchy" of pre-war Poland.*

Having decided on rule by the Party, Gomulka's job was cut out for him. He had to make the Party into at least a fighting echo of the Utopian organization which stood behind all of his speeches like an out-of-date Platonic universal: a "socialism" humane yet severe when faced with crisis; broad enough to admit disagreement and confess failures, yet narrow enough to ensure doctrinal loyalty; patriotic yet loyal to the ideals of international Communism and committed to the withering away of the nationalist state.

He conceded that the Polish Party's past sins were against it (to say nothing of the failings of the Soviet comrades) but he implored the people to distinguish the ideal from the blemished malfunction. "In this often ruthless struggle," he once told the weakened "Socialist" Youth Organization, "the pure idea of socialism comes into contact with the dirt of the past and may sometimes be soiled with this dirt. When this happens, some people seeing the stain on socialism focus all their attention on it, losing

---

* The Polish attempt at recovery after World War I was hampered by a basic imbalance of economic resources, made more serious by crop failures and poor markets for Poland's staple crops. From the birth of the republic there was also the destructive rivalry between Roman Dmowski's National Party and the Pilsudski forces. Without going into this complicated history, it is enough to say that the Communists' neat explanation for the Republic's failings was specious and self-serving.

socialism from their sight. . . . But just as the dirt which collects on the human body is not the natural characteristic of the body . . . a stain on socialism is never socialism itself."

*   *   *

Even reckoned by Communist standards, the stains on the body of Polish "socialism" needed the services of a powerful detergent. It was not that the Poles were less susceptible to Communism than others in Eastern Europe, or the Russians themselves. They had simply been circumstantially put in the position where Communism lost its police power, and where a Communist leader was generally humane about the use of political coercion. The result showed only how pathetically dependent is the Marxist-Leninist state on coercion and police power. They are the indispensable elements that give it shape and direction. There is not even much content without them.

As a simple study in numbers and edifices, the Polish United Workers Party looked impressive even at the point of collapse in 1956. When Gomulka set out to reform it, he found that the membership rolls had swelled since the 1948 days when he last had access to them. The organization was a far cry from the small group of activists who had brought their carpet bags back into Poland in 1944 and 1945. Party strength stood at, roughly, 1,300,000. The membership was organized in the approved Soviet pattern. The Central Committee exerted its decisions down through its nerve centers in the provincial committees and secretaryships, enforcing its guidance—and, in theory at least, drawing its basic strength—at the primary level of the small local party cells.

At the top power was concentrated in the Central Committee's Politburo and the Party Secretaryship. They controlled between them the other normal devices of a Communist power state newspapers, lectures, schools and "spontaneous" organizations, along with the Secret police. *Trybuna Ludu,* the official Party newspaper, was charged, along with several theoretical journals, with chalking the Party line with the utmost legibility (consonant with saving the skins of its editors). There was a Moscow teletype in the *Trybuna's* offices, and each night the Poles received a daily ration of mandatory announcements and news releases from Headquarters.

The same people who controlled *Trybuna* presided over the small but important group of Party schools. They were of varying complexity. The shortest and simplest, the "Senatorska Street" School, gave a three or four months course to party activists from the provinces. The highest, the Institute of Social Sciences, amounted to a concentrated four year course in modern Marxist manipulation. Only carefully selected Party workers could matriculate, and then after a period of three years' detailed (and secret) observation of their every movement. In their four year span, they studied every particle of the Communist *Weltanschauung*—in law, agriculture, pedagogy, history and religion, literary criticism and architecture. Graduates might be expected to go far.

The *Lektorat* was an official lecture agency, centrally directed, specializing in exhortation and excuses. Its speakers were sent out regularly from Warsaw to assist local Party bosses in making the current line believable, as well as to keep up some form of enthusiasm in the Party trade unions, youth groups and the like. For months after October 1956 the *Lektorat* was demoralized and virtually defunct. Its framework remained, but it was a long time before Party zealots could begin to build on it again.

With all this organization the Polish Communist Party was a barely walking corpse. The summons of Gomulka to power was index enough of the old leadership's inability to cope with the situation. The party following was in an even worse condition. It had virtually ceased to exist below the level of the district committee. The young intellectuals on whom the party counted for tactical leadership were busily involved in thinking their way out of Marxism all together, or finding their Utopian ideas about the new Marxism crushed by political realities (see Chapter 4). Most of the rank-and-file activists were distressingly passive. If originally honest Communists, they were demoralized by the successive exposures of the Party—it is a commentary on the Soviet system that many of the highest Polish leaders were genuinely surprised at learning of the Stalinist excesses—and its obvious lack of the slightest appeal or even contact with "the working masses" of Poland. But great numbers of the card-carriers were literally just that, people who had taken out Party membership as a means of

getting better jobs or of sheer survival. These "rice-Communists,"*
by no means disturbed at the break-up of Party discipline, went
about their daily round with composure. They didn't throw their
Party cards away; but they were hardly waving them around.

The few Party members who retained their zealotry were forced
to artifice even to get much of a crowd at local meetings of the
aktiv. Others made concessions to the individual views of their
members, especially on religion, that would have had Lenin flop-
ping over in his stone-cold mausoleum. In August 1957 a veteran
Silesian Communist named Eryk Opiela wrote a letter to the editor
of the ideological magazine *Nowe Drogi,* describing his own plight,
which was very typical.

"Our primary Party organization with 15 members," he wrote,
"has no more than three or four members with Marxist viewpoints.
At the time of the last meeting devoted to the resolutions of the
Plenum of the Central Committee of the Polish United Workers
Party, I said among other things that personally I saw no possibility of reconciling our viewpoints with those of the Catholics. Immediately I met strong opposition from those present. The majority
of those at the meeting ostentatiously declared that they were
practicing Catholics, that in 1946–1947 the Party had not ex-
cluded Catholics, that nobody was being reproached for his philosophy, that the Party was not a Communist one but a workers'
Party and that, therefore, full tolerance should be applied. . . .
In my opinion the Party cannot be the meeting ground for two
different philosophies."

This was a slippery ball for the editors to field. But they succeeded, summoning all the double-talk at their disposal, in this
sort of reply: "Your conviction is right that it is impossible to
reconcile the Marxist philosophy with religion. One should not
forget that in spite of this the materialistic philosophy is not an
indispensable condition for Party membership. Our Party is not
just an association of the adherents of Marxist philosophy but first
and foremost an organization of political struggle for the building

---

* In the days when Christian missionaries preached the faith freely in China,
a distressingly numerous by-product of their labors was the so-called "rice-
Christian," a Chinese who espoused Christianity solely to get food, shelter
or a good job with a European firm. In our contemporary world, "rice-
Communists" are more usual.

of a socialist society which will become communist in the future. The conclusion is that a believer can belong to the Party and that it should not be said that comrades who recognize the principles of our program and carry out, in their sector, the Party's policy, but maintain their religious views, should be removed from the Party in the interests of its Marxist character. This does not mean, of course, that we should tolerate the behaviour of the members who would undertake religious propaganda or play the role of the representatives of the clerical, Christian Democratic social program. . . . In order, however, to avoid mistakes, one should be able to differentiate religious views from religious and clerical propaganda. . . ."

The converse of this "Separation of Church and State" theory was dramatized by a cartoon in an issue of the Polish satirical weekly *Szpilki*. It showed a penitent kneeling in a church confessional. From inside the priest's box came the question: "And are you a believing Communist, my son, or just a practicing one?"

When they took power, Gomulka and his aides had no illusions about the strength of the Party organization through which they willed to work. In a speech at Katowice in December, 1956, Gomulka acknowledged that the Party had cut itself off from the workers. "One must state with regret," he said, "that we comrades have seen how many of our activists were afraid to go to the working class; this is a sad phenomenon. When we have not gone to the working class, direct to the factory, there has arisen a vacuum, and there is no vacuum in nature. We have not gone, somebody else has come. . . ."

Gomulka hoped to put new life in the Party structure by introducing that kind of intra-Party debate which the history of Marxism has consistently honored by the breach, rather than the observance. In the same speech at Katowice, he said: "Our democratization is compassed by some definite limits. It all comes down within the Party—first and foremost—to giving Party members, the Party masses, a chance to elect those authorities to the Party whom they trust most. And that is broadly conceived democracy . . . this democracy would sometimes submit the wrong people for the Party leadership and reject valuable people, but this will only be momentary, provisional, temporary. A worthless man will sooner or later be removed by these same Party members, and a better man will be chosen in his place. . . ." Or, as Gomulka's chief theoretician Wladyslaw Bienkowski explained it, absentmindedly folding paper airplanes during an interview with foreign journalists in his Ministry of Education, "The October period weakened the rule of the Party apparatus, but it will be strengthened by democratization. Members of the apparatus should now be elected in free elections. We don't want *apparatchiks.*"

These happy hopes, as they gradually found out, were as unreal as the broad smiles on the faces of Stalinist era youth posters. Where democratization inside the Party was permitted, the organizations speedily fell apart, as party members took their differing viewpoints to their logical conclusions, whether about religion, collectivization of agriculture, or freedom of the press. Such democratization was speedily recognized in Warsaw as dangerous. Where organizations held together, it was exactly by virtue of the *apparatchik* in control. Like democratic political parties, Communism has its ward-heelers. But a ward-heeler in the Communist Party anywhere, by virtue of participation in crimes against the people and his enjoyment of luxuries denied them, gradually becomes not so much a political functionary, as a member of a distinct ruling class. This class is set apart from the rest of its country by privilege and hatred. It hangs together for the mutual protection of its members. It supports the government, at any cost, to preserve its life.

This group exists in Poland as in every Communist country, and it was well categorized in Milovan Djilas' book *The New Class.* This new class, as Djilas points out, is essentially an ownership class, for all its proclaimed fictions of acting as the mere agent of "the people," "socialism" or "the workers." "The new class," Djilas wrote, "instinctively feels that national goods are, in fact, its property, and that even the terms social and state property denote a general legal fiction. The new class also thinks that any breach of its totalitarian authority might imperil its ownership. Consequently, the new class opposes any type of freedom, ostensibly for the purpose of preserving "socialist ownership."

The New Class reproduces with extraordinary speed in a bureaucratic (if not a biological) context. The ratio of size to efficiency, also, is as inverse as any capitalist Parkinson's Law could imagine. On his arrival from prison, the story goes, Gomulka looked in disbelief at the huge new party headquarters on Nowy Swiat in Warsaw. "What is that," he asked the people with him, "a hotel?" He was told the building's identity. "What," he asked again, "do they do with all those people?"

Each new group of recruits to the proliferating New Class defends its privileges with the greed of the capitalists in Communist folklore. Its members grow accustomed to live in special houses, to obtain their goods and luxuries (virtually without cost) at special stores, to enjoy the services of private tailors, hair-dressers and importers. In the Bierut era the Second Department of the U.B. used to send agents to Western Europe to select special wines and southern fruits for use at Bierut's quarters in the Belvedere Palace, and at several hunting lodges he maintained in other parts of the country.

The virus of privileges, the more infectious according to rank, worth and the amount of incriminating evidence one Party member may have had on another, had long since entered the bloodstream of most Party officials. It became an article of faith to defend them. As the privileges attracted more recruits, the weakest and the most venal members of society flocked to have their loyalty proved and get their Party cards.

Gomulka had no sympathy for these *apparatchiks*. He is a hairshirt Communist, an idealist from an older primitive version of the cult. He denounced the mass of the Party. His reformer's attitude in this respect, was at one with the mood of the young October idealists. Nor was it unknown in the Soviet Union, where it was enunciated by young Russian writers like Vladimir Dudintsev, whose book, *Not By Bread Alone,* a moralizing Soviet "Executive Suite," made a temporary stir until the Party clapped a muzzle over its modest indignation. "I never did believe in vulgar Communism," says Dudintsev's hero Lopatkin, "Those who think that under Communism everyone will strut around in cloth-of-gold are mistaken. The petty bourgeois whose heart is in the good things of life expects from Communism merely the filling of his belly. But in true Communism, many objects of crazy luxury, born out of the idleness of the rich, will be abolished."

Even such oblique fictional calls to hair-shirt Communism are regarded by the New Class as serious threats.* In Poland Gomulka's hair-shirt Communism, in charge of an entire government, scared the New Class far more than he inspired it. His attack on the excesses of Communist administration threatened the very structure of their power. His ideas of thrift and "worker's morality" were unwelcome to a group that had grown wedded to its privileges. As a result the men of what Poles called the *Konserwa,* from high party officials to petty invoice-inkers, did their level best to sabotage every effort at reform. The only real goal of these Marxist "revolutionists" was to keep things as far as possible as they were. Like old-fashioned American ward-heelers, they were at root a vested interest, concerned primarily with keeping its vest on. "We try to activate the comrades," another article in *Nowe Drogi* confessed, "but unfortunately each prospect dies a natural death."

With the bureaucracy dragging its feet underneath him, and only barely loyal to the new administration, Gomulka had to begin his balancing act between the two opposed sets of higher-ups: the "revisionists" and the "dogmatists"—an emergent, impatient Left and a die-hard, irreconcilable Right. On the Left were most prominently the young intellectuals who had fired the October Revolution with their militant editorializing. There were in addition the former Social Democratic faction headed by Cyrankiewicz (if a group so sullied by Communist collaboration could still use this respectable name) and a few of the Communist Party theoreticians. The Right ranged from outright Soviet agents like Franciszek Mazur and his friends to orthodox old-line Stalinists whose definition of Communism stopped short of complete Russian appeasement, but who wanted in all other respects a strict adherence to the established Soviet Communist line.

The gradations inside both factions were vast (there is still argument over exactly how many sub-factions are included in each side); but there was no doubt of their mutual hostility. The Left revisionists wanted to take a rational broom to the whole system of present-day Communism and sweep it clear of "dogmatism."

* Dudintsev, for one, had to recant, in a preface to a "revised" edition of his book in 1957.

They claimed that the Stalinists had hopelessly twisted Communism into a frozen bureaucratic cult, where the letter withered all of Marx's and Lenin's original spirit. Most of them also protested the institutionalized cruelty of the police power. The dogmatists insisted that the iron rule of the Party, necessarily cruel on occasion, was the most important component of Communism. Too much discussion automatically leads to the heresy of deviation, they felt. So much for the "democratization" tendencies of the other side.

This division came as no surprise to Gomulka. The fight between the revisionists and the dogmatists is as old as Marxism itself. The use of right and left is confusing to an outsider, especially to an American accustomed to associate the term "left wing" with Communist world domination. In fact, it has shifted even inside the Communist movement.* But every Communist Party, like the Empire of Lilliput, has always been divided on these lines between its Imperialists and Big-Endians.

Originally, Gomulka's version of national Communism occupied a middle-ground between the two wings. It was not any elaborately worked-out theory. Gomulka is first and foremost a tactician, along with Khrushchev the leading current exponent of Lenin's adopted maxim, *"On s'engage, puis on voit."* But he had done some thinking in his prison days, and he set forth a few basic premises to go by when he came to power. The first was national independence. The second was gradualism. Even the Communist Rome, he reminded his followers, could not be built in a day. With this went realism— Gomulka had a grass-roots' organizer's feel of what could and what could not be accomplished. The last was his principle of "humane socialism," a wedding of modern Communist practice and machinery with an idea of the rule of law, half rediscovered.

* As Bertram Wolfe notes in his book, *Khrushchev and Stalin's Ghost,* Socialists in pre-revolutionary Russia used "Left" to designate the people who wanted to distribute more wealth to the masses; "Right" to indicate those who wanted emphasis on industrial development first. In later Soviet usage, the people who put the welfare of the masses first now comprise the "Right danger," while those who want an industrial build-up are classified "Left." In this, as in other aspects of modern Marxism, one is forcibly reminded of the old Abbott and Costello comedy baseball routine: "Who's on first?"

In practice Gomulka's national Communism had several concrete objectives. All of them, predictable on the basis of his past record in government, had been suggested by his October 21st speech. The first was to stop the forced collectivization of agriculture, as obviously destructive to the economy. The next was to alter the heedless pace of industrialization, slackening the pursuit of heavy industry for its own sake (and the Russians') and putting some emphasis on consumer goods production. Workers were to be given a voice in the management of their factories. Private initiative in certain fields e.g. handicrafts, retail trade, was to be encouraged.

All of these plans showed Gomulka's tendency to tailor the political garment up to a point according to the nature of the people and the circumstances of their time. "In the past period," Bienkowski had criticized, "we wanted to build Socialism in a desert. At first it was necessary to roll the terrain, to destroy the various form of social life, to eradicate the roots, because they could give rise to capitalist shoots. This idea is anti-Marxist, anti-rational and in fact purely idealistic."

Gomulka's view of "national Communism" was not Titoism. The Poles borrowed only one idea from the Yugoslavs, the system of workers' councils, i.e. groups of elected workers acting as an active board of directors for a factory's management. Even this, for various reasons, they ultimately turned against.* But it had old roots in the Communist movement. In Gomulka's national Communism almost every student of Marxism could see the active ghost of Nikolai Bukharin, the brilliant Soviet theoretician, once head of the Communist Internationale, whom Stalin destroyed in 1938.

Lenin called Bukharin "the most valuable and the most important theoretician in the Party." Although Bukharin was an internationalist at first, along with Trotsky, he later went over to Stalin's position and wrote the major thesis advocating "socialism in one country." But his idea of one-country socialism was far

* In Yugoslavia, which is to all intents and purposes a strict dictatorship the workers councils could be counted on for obedience to rigid party political orders, whatever their economic "independence." In Poland, organized more loosely, their political freedom posed too many problems for the Gomulka administration.

different from Stalin's. Bukharin wanted to 'balance' the elements
of the Soviet economy, working out its problems smoothly and
gradually, without undue hardship to the workers and peasants in
whose name the whole process was being done. Planning, in Bukharin's book, was not something that could be done with a slide-
rule or a few strokes of a typewriter. It was a complex operation,
which must be constantly adjusted to needs and changes of circumstances. He opposed forced collectivization. At one point he
frankly called on the peasants to enrich themselves. The village
peasants, he argued, could be the better absorbed into the general
Soviet economy if such absorption were smooth and natural. He
demanded an increase of consumer goods—what Khrushchev two
decades later caustically called "cotton-dress industrialization"—
step by step with the expansion of industry. "The acuteness of the
goods famine," he wrote in the 'twenties, "must be genuinely alle-
viated, and not in some remote future, but within the next few
years. A start must be made immediately . . . lest the queue and
the waiting list begin to look like our way of life."

The later proprietors of the queue and the waiting-list have
never ceased to attack Bukharin with a ritual fury, even when they
themselves made their consumer concessions, as with Malenkov
and Khrushchev. (Khrushchev disinterred his idea for a few comments in his February speech at the Twentieth Party Congress.)
But they have never been able to keep Bukharin's skeleton locked
in the closet. His ideas permeated international Communism very
early in the game, notably through his influence as head of the
Comintern in the 'twenties; and old Communists like Gomulka
and his friends were not likely to forget them. For the record they
deny it. Gomulka's national Communism, as its most persuasive
spokesman Bienkowski once explained, is nothing more than "a
return to Leninism." "Does it recall Bukharin?" "Not really. . . ."
For a modern Communist to admit a debt to Bukharin, in short,
is as embarrassing as it is for an American Eisenhower Republican
to concede that his party's social welfare ideas derive from Franklin D. Roosevelt and its foreign policy from Harry S. Truman.

Actually, Gomulka is Bukharin all over again. Nothing could
be more hostile to the aims of the property-holding New Class
than the ideas of this long-dead Marxist, who like Gomulka was

also an honest man, and rather humane. Besides being humane, he was the apostle of the practical and the reasonable, two virtues most incompatible with modern Marxism.

While the dogmatists thundered against his new program, Gomulka ran into heavy weather from the young revisionists who had first supported him. With them it was not a question of his going *too* far leftward, but of not going far enough. As the struggle and fate of the embattled intellectuals shows, they lacked the realism to match their zeal. Their continued criticism of Gomulka's caution showed little regard for the Russian divisions which made such caution inevitable. They also lacked the popular touch to transform their advanced ideas into any mass movement, or even into a large cadre.

*   *   *

In Gomulka's effort to remake Polish Communism into his own self-contradicting image, he had few trustworthy associates, or even competent untrustworthy ones. The lack of managerial talent became a perennial defect of his regime. It was honest enough to alienate the more talented members of the New Class bureaucracy, not honest or imaginative enough to use the considerable non-Communist talent available among Poles inside and outside the country.

In the Communist Party mechanism proper, Gomulka's search for a new cadre has not gone much beyond a few close advisors. The closest of the inner circle is Zenon Kliszko, an old-line Communist who worked with Gomulka in the underground of the thirties, and followed him down the apparently rosy path of national Communism in 1945. As Vice Minister of Justice, Kliszko was one of Gomulka's principal assistants, although he kept conspicuously out of the limelight. He was arrested in 1951, after the fall of Gomulka and tried on the usual charges of every thing from deviationism to intriguing with "western European" espionage circles. Like the others arrested with Gomulka he was sentenced to jail. He stayed there, like the others, until 1954. Unlike the others, however, he did not confess to any false accusations against the boss. He is probably the one man in Poland whom Gomulka completely trusts.

The other inner circle members are General Marian Spychalski, Minister of Defense, and the aforementioned Wladislaw Bienkowski, Minister of Education. Spychalski, an architect from Lodz, is a veteran egghead Communist of the thirties, who stayed with Gomulka during the early stages of the World War II resistance. He went to Russian-occupied Poland, finally, to join the Russian-equipped Kosciuszko division of General Zygmunt Berling, which the Russians sponsored. He became, first, the division's chief of staff, and finally, the virtual political commissar of the Communist Polish Army. In the immediate pre-war days, he was the effective force behind Marshal Rola-Zymierski, the cashiered pre-war General whom the Communists elevated temporarily to nominal command of their armed forces.*

Spychalski was arrested in 1951, after Gomulka's downfall, and put in prison, after a reasonably spectacular trial, complete with confessions. He implicated Gomulka in testimony to the U.B. agents who interrogated him, and his evidence was the principal prop in the jerry-built case against Gomulka that was never used. His sins in this regard were apparently forgiven him.

Bienkowski is Gomulka's theoretician, the dialectical mechanic of his "Polish road to socialism." Like Gomulka he is a pre-war Communist who used Warsaw, rather than Moscow, as the focus of his ideology. He became Vice Minister of Education in 1945 and for a few years followed Gomulka up the ladder. In 1949, apparently because true intellectuals have a reputation for being harmless, he escaped the severe penalties of the other Gomulka followers. He hibernated as director of the National Library until the October revolution. Since the October, he has become what amounts to Gomulka's private Harry Hopkins. He handles many of the tough negotiating jobs—with Zenon Kliszko he conducted

---

* Zymierski was a fairly typical study of the rise and fall of a Soviet agent in his own country. His pre-war service as Vice-Minister of National Defense was climaxed by a six year jail sentence for corruption in office. During World War II, he offered his services to the Home Army, but was rejected. He ultimately became a double agent, working for the Gestapo and Soviet intelligence, and performing good service for both. The Russians ordered his installation as Commander in Chief of the Polish Army, in which capacity he continued to report to Soviet intelligence. After the Soviet Marshal Rokossowski took over this job in November, 1949, Zymierski's presence was superfluous. He was arrested in 1951.

the Church-State negotiations with Cardinal Wyszynski. He also does the explaining, to foreigners, when the regime wants to put its best-shod foot forward. Bienkowski is the one high Warsaw official traditionally accessible to foreign correspondents.

There are several others now known as Gomulkists, or at least ipso facto Gomulkists, since they hold high office under the present government. Ignacy Loga-Sowinski, a member of the Central Committee's Politburo and head of the Trade Union Council, is an idealogue of sorts. Oscar Lange, the Chairman of the Economic Council, is a former University of Chicago professor, in his American residence a 1930 vintage 'parlor pink' who dislikes Communist excesses (especially when he has to participate) but who managed to serve through the Stalinist period. These and others of the inner circle have been used by previous "administrations" Stefan Jedrychowski, for example, became a minister and a leading economic planner early in the Bierut regime. Lange's Deputy, Czeslaw Bobrowski, has served in the Polish administration since the Pilsudski era, barring World War II. Before the October Revolution, he went into exile from his post as Ambassador to Sweden, in protest against the Stalinism of the Party. It may be a comforting thought to economic observers that, in whatever direction the Polish economy is steered, Bobrowski always manages to remain somewhere in the vicinity of the helm.

With all these bureaucratic weathervanes in operation, Gomulka's reliance on a very limited circle of advisors is understandable. It is here that all semblance to a Communist 'Eisenhower' program—otherwise rather a facile comparison—vanishes. Eisenhower has actually been surrounded by a great many capable men, unfortunately men of varying view. Gomulka works alone. He is the eastern European political version of that favorite American TV character, the frontier marshal who sleeps in his clothes in the local saloon, always ready to uproot evil the instant it appears, painfully conscious that the townspeople are not really on his side and that even "the boys" around his own poker table are most of them susceptible to the lure of a few more silver dollars from the opposing gang.

As his loyal second fiddle, Gomulka enjoys the talented obligato support of Joseph Cyrankiewicz. Since January 1947 (excepting the year beginning July 1952) he has been Premier of Poland. Cyrankiewicz reached this office when he was only 36, and he is a person of unquestioned talent. As Polish Communist administrators go, he is a good one. But as a personality he is one of the most debatable people in the country. Opinion varies as to whether he is a high-minded patriot, who suffered the Bierut regime along with those less prominent in its administration, or a combination of the Vicar of Bray and the acquisitive hero of Budd Schulberg's story "What Makes Sammy Run."

In 1947 Cyrankiewicz helped Gomulka take over the Socialist Party and merge it with the Communists in the United Workers group. He is not without courage. He lived through imprisonment at Oswiecim, in fact helped organize a considerable underground there. But his speedy liquidation of the independent Socialist Party (he was its last Secretary General) is hard to explain away. In the worst of the Stalinist days, he was a front man for the Bierut government, the parade liberal, the "Westerner" in a group of committed Soviet agents. As such, he was not much liked by the Poles.

After Poznan, the evidence shows that Cyrankiewicz got in some good blows against the rotting Party system. His capture of the administration machinery, as noted, was a big factor in Gomulka's return to power. But, although many credit his efforts for the success of the October, he has not shared much of Gomulka's popularity. He is not a popular figure, too remote, too intellectualized, too tarred with the smelly brush of the Bierut government. His wife, Nina Andrycz, is a well-known Warsaw actress. It is a standing local joke to speculate whether he is not an even better master of stagecraft himself.

Attacked (or prodded) by both "dogmatists" and "revisionists," Gomulka's established policy was to tread a cautious median measure down what was to be the world's waviest Party line. In actual fact, he is not this much of a middle man; in a strict ideological sense Gomulkism is far more like revisionism than dogmatism, however much its founder is forced to tighten the party reins. But a position ostensibly in the middle is a negotiable asset in a Communist country. Lenin used it to great advantage himself, always managing to make his position appear as the reasonable center view, his opponents' as unhealthy extremism. It has been very wearing on Gomulka. Each Party plenum has been a shifting battle-ground, that demands a political cats'-eyes vigilance. On the whole, Gomulka showed himself to have grasped Lenin's principles. Even by Soviet standards, he is one of the world's champion plenum-fighters.

Poland at plenum time resembles a crowd of sports writers watching a critical and complicated wrestling match from a distance of a mile, with foggy field-glasses. The Central Committee meetings usually last for three or four days. They are closed. Only the results are announced publicly, in a closing statement. The terseness of the announcements generally underlines the bitterness of the controversy that goes on inside the committee rooms. For the press, especially foreign wire service men, it is a highly uncomfortable period of spading up rumors—the chance remark by a friend of a Committee member's over 3 a.m. vodka, a few words dropped by a *Trybuna Ludu* editor at the Journalists' Club, a raised eyebrow at a question during an official interview. The loquacity of the Poles complicates matters. Almost everyone has a theory about the current aspects of the *Kto-Kovo* relationship. The truth of the theories only becomes evident after the meeting is over, and sometimes not for a long while.

The Ninth Plenum, in May 1957 was perhaps the most decisive of Gomulka's stewardship. It was the first to be held after the October Revolution had been stabilized. Taking advantage of the favorable temperature, the dogmatists were ready for an open attack on Gomulka's new liberal policies, specifically the concept of the "Polish road to socialism." The revisionists had for some months made their position known. Dissatisfied with Gomulka's apparent withdrawal of the October concessions (actually he had not promised so much as they had inferred), they preceded the Plenum with long demands to preserve the freedoms of October. Their articles showed all the anger of disillusionment. A great many Polish newspaper readers felt the same way.

Gomulka led off the Party sessions on May 15 with a cruel, heavy attack on the left wing. He reminded Leszek Kolakowski, the brilliant neo-Marxist philosopher (at least he still called himself a Marxist then), and the others like him that they were trying to push October too far, that he did not intend to give up the authority structure of a monolithic Communist party. He stated the issue as bluntly as he could: "No party member can accept only one part of democratic centralism, that is accept democracy and reject centralism." So there. While gloom started to fall over the advance spectators drinking *Exportova* at the Journalists' Club, Gomulka interrupted the proceedings to go to the attractive new sports stadium across the river, where the last lap of the Berlin-Prague-Warsaw bicycle race was being run.

The final portion of the People's Bicycle Race, much to the disgust of the Polish crowds, was won by a Russian. Possibly emboldened by this, the dogmatists began their expected attack with new spirit. Successive speeches ripped apart every plank of the Gomulka platform. They dealt with decentralization, the farm policy, industrial democracy, the alliance with the church. The most vicious attack was made by one Kazimierz Mijal, a middle-ranking member of the Natolin group, who called the whole Gomulka policy "a return to capitalism." He wanted, instead, a return to "internationalism," i.e. recognition of the leading role of the Soviet Union. The leaders like Mazur and Zenon Nowak were too cautious to come out with this denunciation themselves. But in the context of the other attacks, Mijal's charge represented a clear demand by the "right" that Gomulka come to heel, and restore the country to satellite status.

At this Gomulka fought back. "I thought," he began, "we would hear only one first Secretary's report at this meeting—mine. It seems we have heard two. I shall have an answer." In two and a half hours of invective, he told the 80 members of the Committee just what he thought of "dogmatism"—as great a danger as revisionism to true Communist thought. In fact, beneath this ideological bit of ruffles and flourishes, he was restating Poland's independence and his own absolute rule of the Party.

He had no hesitation in naming names. When some one referred to the "Hungarian incident," Gomulka replied, "It wasn't an incident. It was a tragedy. . . . What do you want? Russian tanks in the streets again?" As for "internationalism," he went on, was the liquidation of the Polish Communist leaders in 1938 internationalism? Was the devastation of the Western Territories by Soviet troops in 1945 internationalism? The Hungarian Stalinist

leaders Rakosi and Gero, he went on, had always told the Budapest crowds that the Soviet Union was at the head of the Socialist
camp. "In the end," he said, "Soviet tanks were in the first position."

Whether or not Gomulka had been forwarned of the Stalinist
attack (as is probable), his counter charge was most effective.
The actual members of the Natolin group in the Central Committee numbered only 23 at that time. There were only about
five real revisionists, fifteen "social democrats," about fifteen of
Gomulka's persuasion, under 20 "centrists," old-line Communists who had prospered under Stalin, but wanted Polish independence. Gomulka's speech mobilized all of these forces to give
the Natolin group a crushing defeat. Since he had already attacked
the revisionists, no centrist could accuse him of any dangerous
capitalist tendencies.

Lenin's tactics had won. For all the speechmaking, Gomulka's
policy of loose construction Communism remained the same as it
had been. Revisionists, too weak to hope for power themselves,
were relieved that an internal pro-Russian reaction had been fended
off. The others were more than ever assured of Gomulka's leadership.

Through later plenums a similar pattern has been repeated.
The naked assault on Gomulka's authority has not been repeated;
but the agents of the Soviet Union are always ready to exploit
any difficulty of the regime. By the ground rules under which he
operates, Gomulka cannot expel all of them. He can, however,
exploit their tactical mistakes, dismiss spokesmen and discipline
others. In March 1958, at the Eleventh Plenum, he threw Wiktor
Klosciewicz off the Central Committee for his attacks on economic
policy, backed always by the charge that relations had been allowed to deteriorate with the Soviet Union. He has disposed of
others differently. In 1958 Franciscek Mazur was sent off to the
more congenial atmosphere of Prague as Polish Ambassador. In
their places he has substituted his own men, gradually shaping the
Central Committee as the instrument of his peculiar program. His
much advertised personal acceptance by Khrushchev ("my closest
friend") in their 1958 meetings was of material assistance in
doing this. Thanks to Gomulka's support of Soviet aggressive

foreign policy, the Russians clipped the wings of their own agents.

By the 12th Plenum, in October, 1958, Gomulka enjoyed a working majority of 50 votes among the 75 Central Committee members. He was able to dismiss revisionists and dogmatists with equal contempt. It was fashionable to be a Gomulka "centrist."

The corollary to the inner-circle in-fighting was Gomulka's drive to capture the lower Party organization. After the October of 1956 the lack of central governance over the Communist Party was painfully obvious. As the non-Party journalist Edward Osmanczyk wrote the following year: "The authority of Gomulka does not have a sufficiently wide foundation in the personal authority of the Party active and this is, in my opinion, a serious liability in the national account."

Gomulka's first step was to cut the swollen Party membership down to size. Immediately after the revolution the Gomulka faction began to scan with clear disfavor the ranks of the New Class bureaucrats, in the spirit of Savonarola's Florentine followers, had they been suddenly allowed authority over the swollen court of Pope Alexander VI. But for a year after the October, Gomulka had to suffer the disapproving dead weight of a bureaucracy basically interested only in saving its own jobs.

In October, 1957 Gomulka felt strong enough to move. He made a speech at the Tenth Plenum of the Party announcing a purge of "notorious idlers, trouble-makers and demagogues" inside the Party. After taking his usual swipes at "dogmatism" and "revisionism" (principally the latter) he told the Central Committee that the Party Congress set for December would be postponed until the reconstruction of "a conscious, militant Party completely devoted to the cause of Socialism." It was finally scheduled for March, 1959. The Party, he said, has "lost many of the features of the working class . . . dissolved in the non-Party masses." Backing up his feelings about loss of contact with the workers, his statisticians reported that only 39.9% of the membership of the Polish United Workers Party were actually workers. Fully 38.8% were "mental workers," including bureaucrats. This would put the membership of the New Class in Poland at something under 520,000.

The Party "verification program" has since been a continuing process. By February 25, 1958 some 20,890 ostensibly true believers had been expelled outright, while 129,895 were stricken from the registers. Numbers of these were the "careerists, self-seekers, revisionists, liquidators and conservative elements"—the obstructive *Konserwa* that he had been denouncing. Others were thrown out for humbler reasons like drunkenness, scandalous behaviour, grafting, or taking advantage of their position. By the end of 1958, the number of Party members was down to less than 1,100,000.

No one in the Gomulka faction even pretended satisfaction with this achievement. As a steady running fire of Party press comment has confirmed, the program of verification foundered on the old problem of "quis custodiet ipsos custodes." What could be called orthodoxy in a Communist Party, when the national Party philosophy was identical with principles denounced elsewhere in the Communist bloc as evil heresy? What was a Party ward-heeler's loyalty worth to a government dedicated to removing his ilk for sheer inefficiency? What did the new-found freedom of discussion mean to a Communist, if it would likely as not lead to his expulsion from the Party? The Party, it was observed, was more influenced by the voluntary resignations of some of its leading young idealogues than by the attempted purging of the verification program. The latter, as practiced in the local Party *aktivs,* had all the vigor of hastily staged debates. Its failure only underlined the demoralization of Poland's rank-and-file Party members; it hardly corrected it.

Standing among the wreckage of verification and high-echelon Party bickering, Gomulka saw that even if he controlled the Party machinery completely, it was not equipped to accomplish the subtle balance between authoritarian leadership and intra-Party democracy for which he had once hoped. God may be able to "write straight with crooked lines," as Charles Peguy put it; but an institution so beset with human failings as the Polish United Workers' Party could only adapt its tactics to the instrument, and write crooked, too. By the middle of 1958 Gomulka had hardened a noticeable trend towards dictatorial rule. The shape of his acts and utterances had stayed far from the braver hopes of October 21, 1956.

At the Sixth Congress of the Polish Trades Unions, in April 1958, Gomulka denied the worker's right to strike, a right which had until then been virtually conceded. The same man who once justified the Poznan workers' rebellion now said, "Under our conditions strikes are to be considered as being directed against the socialist system. In our country the workers have enough legal ways of removing shortcomings. If they strike in spite of this they cannot count on sympathy either from the Party or the authorities." Although what he said was diluted by later concessive remarks from his assistants, the impact was too strong to ignore.

At the same meeting Gomulka clipped the wings of the emerging workers' council movement more sharply than before. There were practical reasons for this (see Chapter 8). The principle of running a factory by a committee of workers, although a laudable step towards democracy inside a Communist country, is demonstrably not the most efficient way to run a factory. No one would be quicker to admit this than prominent American free enterprisers like Walter Reuther and George Meany. Many Polish workers, left to themselves, would have sacrificed the urgent needs of the economy to demands for more wages. They were understandably slow to appreciate the fact that the faults of the Russian economic colonization would take a long and desperate effort to cure; any true prosperity for Poland could only be preceded by more austerity still.

Over and above such tactical objections, the regime had a fundamental political problem with strikes, potential strikes, or workers' councils: the Communist Party organizations were too weak and disorganized to control them. And without energetic control measures by the Party units, such economic movements, growing strong and clamorous, would certainly end by encroaching on the political power.

The need for a strong Party government, as it seemed to Gomulka, and the concurrent lack of one had its effect in other fields. Principally, it caused the growing tightening of censorship. The Party intellectuals found life under Gomulkism increasingly uncomfortable. As hopeful publications, like the ill-fated magazine *Europa,* died aborning on the censor's desk, the angry young novelists and the probing critics of Marxism headed for the bunkers. There was a sober reminder of past Stalinist days in statements like that of the Propaganda director Andrzej Werblan, who said at a Party cultural meeting that "in the future, neither time nor money will be wasted on the publication of demoralizing works which do not contribute to the Socialists reconstruction of the state." Whether in youth movements, the universities, or journalism, Gomulka's Party headquarters moved in to check the spread of the October freedom. Its weakness made inevitable the fact that there would be little "democratic centralism" involved in the process.

Yet it is unfair and inaccurate to present these developments as the inevitable erosion of the October reforms, a retreat whose lost ground would never be regained. Step by step with the persecution of the revisionists, Gomulka continued his infinitely more delicate job of prying the Moscow Poles out of the Party leadership. Poland remained the only place in the Communist world where a man could resign from the Party and still earn a living. If Gomulka was becoming more repressive by Polish norms, by outside Communist standards he remained a dangerous revisionist.

In this lies the heart of the matter. From the beginning of 1957 the leadership of the Soviet Union has been fighting tooth-and-nail to eliminate "revisionism" as a factor inside the bloc. Its dangers are written large and clear. Since the execution of Beria in 1953, the tempting idea of a loosened Communist society, always striving to be freer, has infected even the people of the Soviet Union. The damage done by revisionism to previously safe Russian satellites like Bulgaria and Romania—to say nothing of outposts like East Germany—has been immense. For when freedom is introduced into the life of a country, it spreads unless contained. Similarly with blocs and alliances. The slightest amount of free discussion, even within the framework of "Marxist" thinking, causes concern in Moscow for the safety of a world Party leadership that is now stripped of almost all its ideology, all its idealism, all its revolutionary enthusiasm.

In restricted fields, the modern Communist society can tolerate a certain amount of freedom, if it happens to be expedient. The case of the pampered and on the whole uncoerced Soviet scientists shows this. But any such zone of freedom must be hermetically sealed off from the rest of the society, to avoid the widespread political changes that they would bring. The Russian scientists in the Soviet Union, for example, safe behind the moat of their sub- sidies, honors, chauffered cars, expensive TV sets and satisfied professional interests, are effectively cut off from spreading their ideas and their ways of thinking to the country at large. As political facts, Gomulka and his system cannot be thus easily quarantined.

In the face of what has since amounted to "re-Stalinization," the iconoclasm of Khrushchev's Twentieth Congress speech was spe- cious. He realized that the time had passed when the old-fashioned dictatorship could perpetuate itself without concessions. Hence his politically violent reaction to Stalin's kind of iconolatry. He de- nounced it so that the leadership could survive, as first an oligarchy, next a dictatorship of a looser variety. Once the rule was solidly secured, he has inched his way back to a rigid pattern of authority, or as rigid a pattern as changed circumstances permit. The very existence of Gomulka's kind of country poses a recurring threat to this pattern. Freedom is contagious.

All of Gomulka's outward conformity to the reimposed Soviet order has not saved him from renewed Russian pressure—a de- velopment he doubtless anticipated. As late as August, 1958, when Poland's dyed-in-the-wool revisionist writers were feeling the sting of Gomulka's revived censorship, the Soviet monthly *Zvezda* threw out a chain-shot broadside against Polish literature in gen- eral as a dangerous fosterer of revisionism, and if not even more deadly heresies. On August 17, the reply came back, politely but firmly, from the literary department of the Party's *Trybuna Ludu* in Warsaw. Its author, Jan Szczepanski, now chief of the cultural department of the paper, was not a man associated in Polish minds with freedom of speech. And he paid a lip service to Khrushchev's revived idea of Socialist Realism in art, one of the things the October Revolution had fought against. But even Szczepanski, speaking for the Polish Party, could not let this Ice-Age criticism pass. "I cannot agree to the intolerance of other forms of art" he wrote, "and to the monopoly of Socialist Realism. From such a monopoly nothing good arises."

This may not have sounded courageous to a forthright Ameri- can, sitting comfortably in his living room. But to a Pole living behind a wall of Soviet divisions and long since disillusioned by any talk of American "liberation," it passed for courage.

Viewed even from a two-year perspective, Gomulka's speech in October 1956 could be denounced as specious, but it was sincere, for all the confusion that existed between his concept of liberties and those of his supporters. His later backtracking from its optimistic promise was inseparable from the immense pressure which the Russians have since applied, to force the deviator into as close as possible an approximation of the old satellite position. They realize that the roll-back cannot be complete, without risking another upheaval like the October. But they make it as complete as possible.

In the circumstances, effectively cut off from anything but token support from the outside world, Gomulka finds it hard to resist. *"Raison d'etat"* is a familiar word in Polish government circles. When a revisionist-minded official speaks of censorship, or the decline of workers' councils, or Gomulka's fraternal visits to Moscow or Kadar's Budapest, he starts by pointing to the map. *"Raison d'etat"* is another word for Europe's most unfortunate geography.

Against such pressures the man who talked so much about "the moral basis of power" has gradually found that a veiled force, or threats thereof, must do the job which Utopian Communism failed to do. Gomulka is no fool. He realizes how his hopes for a libertarian "national Communist" Party were dashed on reality. As the self-nominated rebuilder of Communism in Poland, he resembles a trusting surgeon who sets out to reconstruct a tired, sick old reprobate on the operating table, only to discover too late in the game that the organs are hopelessly diseased: the heart is weak, the stomach is ulcerous and the liver beyond makeshift surgery. In Gomulka's case, given the present international situation, he must nonetheless keep the patient on the table, trying to sound hopeful while examining his diseased condition. Or he may set him up, pretending that nothing really has happened.

4

The Intellectuals' Revolt

> "Rabbi," asked the young Communist member of the
> congregation, "can you build socialism in one country?"
> "Yes," said the rabbi, after a moment of thought, "you
> can build socialism in one country, but you have to live in
> another."
>
> —*as quoted by Czeslaw Milosz*

SOME 700 MILES southwest of the actual Lenin and Stalin
mausoleum in Moscow stands an expensive 34-story eyesore that
historians may some day nominate as its ideological headstone.
Architecturally speaking, the Palace of Culture in Warsaw is a
triumph of Ivan-the-Terrible Modern. An unmercifully permanent-
looking mass of huge square pillars and fluted cornices, lowering
over its own leveled square, its tower insultingly dominates Warsaw's European skyline. Coming back to Warsaw on the Lublin
road, one sees it long before reaching the street-car termini that
set off the city outskirts. It is the only really high structure after
the large radio towers outside the city, where centered, in the
days before October, the regime's jamming apparatus against
broadcasts from the West.

The Palace was Josef Stalin's personal gift to Poland's satellite government, built in 1953 by imported Russian labor. It was intended to act as a huge classroom in current Soviet Communism —housing the headquarters of Poland's press, propaganda and cultural activities, from which the nation could have its daily dialectic spooned to it. In official theory it remained so. In practice it became for Poland a monument to the withering away of Communism, as an active ideological commodity. The locked and unused offices in the upper stories, so noticeable in 1957, were testimonials of the Soviet System's failure to teach, convert or convince the youth of its occupied countries. Only the basement night club drew a really popular following. In the summer of 1957, to the accompaniment of great enthusiasm, Miss Warsaw was crowned there. She was delegated to participate in the international Miss Universe contest of that year, along with other national champions, wearing provocative capitalist attire.

Few symbols of any System have done their job so well in reverse. The prime users of the Palace were supposed to be the new generation of Poland, educated for Communism since 1945. But it was precisely this youth who led the revolt in October, 1956, against what they still half-euphemistically called "Stalinism." The editors of the revolutionary press were in their twenties. So were the leaders of the student demonstrations, many of the factory workers, the young officers, and the entrepreneurs of anti-Russian cabaret entertainment. Their revolt, and their subsequent apathy and discontent, make the sharpest comment on the failure of modern Marxism, as it is understood in the West, to win any more ideological converts.*

Polish youth is not a monolith. It hates the Soviet symbol in different ways, and for different reasons. For three representatives of the younger generation, the Palace can mean three widely separated, if commonly unpleasant things. K. is a lieutenant in the Polish Army, determinedly apolitical, certainly not pro-Communist, but neither is he anti-Communist in any positive way. He sees the Palace of Culture exactly the way his grandfathers saw the Russian garrison buildings, or the expensively-built nineteenth

---

* The successes of Communism in underdeveloped Asian countries are another story, and a more frightening one. They have had little to do, however, with the spread or perception of either Marxist or Leninist theory.

century Russian orthodox cathedral, as the symbol of Russian imperialism and Polish national humiliation. He tries to avoid walking by it, unless he has some business there or in the vicinity.

W. thinks of the Palace primarily as an alien aesthetic eyesore. He is an art student, which gives him legitimate cause for making this statement in the course of his daily round. But the feeling which stirs his judgment is too strong to be merely professional. It is the cheapness of this expensive Soviet structure that he hates. He hates it because the last ten years of Communism have put a standardizing cheapness on everything in his life. "It is not only," he says, "that they have driven my family into one packed room of a four-family apartment; it is not only that their combination of rationing and bureaucratic crookedness has made the Black Market a necessity in my life instead of an illegal device for profit." All this could happen under other circumstances, and he would understand them. But W. and tens of thousands like him have grasped very solidly the difference between privation and cheapness, between the admitted want that comes from being nationally poor and the want that is officially disguised by a conspiracy of brightly painted posters, massed parades and absurdly comforting slogans. He has abandoned politics, of almost any variety. His overriding emotion is a despairing contempt that dwarfs the vaguely comparable emotions of intellectual hot-rodders like the so-called "Beat Generation" in the U.S. or the "angry young men" of Britain.

G., a young journalist, represents only a small minority of Polish youth, yet he and his group have been far more central to the story of Gomulka's Poland than any of the others. It was his kind who made the real mockery out of Stalin's Palace of Culture; yet paradoxically they were also the ones who had believed everything in its original charter. He knows it as an intellectual battleground, still littered with the abandoned wreckage of retreated arguments, the unburied paragraphs of long-dead manifestos.

G. is "political" by training and inclination. He no longer has his Communist Party card, although he would still insist that he is a true "Marxist-Leninist." He grew up in the Communist Pioneers after the war, graduated to youth organizations organized on the model of the Russian Komsomols and, finally, entered the Party. In the months before October, 1956, he and some of his colleagues had been ever more loudly questioning the Communist faith they were supposed to uphold, indeed explain to those less ideologically fortunate. Until September, 1957, when the strongly critical weekly *Po Prostu* was suppressed, he looked on its offices in the Palace of Culture's tower as a field of intellectual struggle which might divert a corrupted Communist state from its stumbling downward path, back to the primitive innocence of a "purer" kind of Marxism. The content of this purity he and his friends had figured out on their intellectual drawing boards. Now the closed offices in the Palace mock him so, that he prefers not to stop by there, even for the worthwhile movies or concerts that are regularly put on. He still fights this old battle in his mind, but he fights as a man several times deceived.

None of these young men, neither among the frustrated Marxists nor the non-Communist majority, is unrelievedly outraged in his actions. The new Polish generation is in fact distinguished from its elders by an ingrained caution. It is the 50- or 60-year-olds who makes the more violent anti-regime statements to visitors. Most of those in the 20 to 40 bracket are visibly conscious of the Frozen Revolution's limitations.

The younger Poles are distinguished from their counterparts in other countries in that they have a slight sense of humor, or at least demonstrate a historic national capacity for taking repeated hard knocks with a wry smile. For a brief period, the humor and the indignation overcame the caution. On a visit to Warsaw or Cracow, before the 1958 tightening of regime censorship pressure, it was possible to see political cabaret satire as sharp as anything in non-Communist countries. A student theater in Cracow, for example, specialized in reading recent Russian pronouncements on Socialist Realism in the arts with appropriate gestures and comments, against the background of an incredibly awful piece of Communist poster-art—young pioneers stepping forward with gleaming picks and shovels and well-pressed smiles—which the students swore was an authentic survival. A helmeted woman with a heavy Russian accent produced some patter about local political conditions, and a stylized chorus interspersed its comments in language that was meaningless enough to pass as authentic 'existentialist.' The impressive and contagious aspect of the whole performance was its genuine humor, to say nothing of the considerable artistic talent of the performers.

In Warsaw the mood was similar. The same bulletin boards that had announced the rallying places at the time of the October Revolution were later covered with funny or half-funny political jokes, imitations of the hated Socialist Realist art (the emphasis on this phase is made advisedly—the Polish intelligentsia takes its art more seriously than most), or mock criticisms in Communese, e.g. "shows pronounced signs of deviationist enthusiasm," "revisionist wrecker," etc. The students, in private, were always ready with a quip or two about their political position, or lack of position. But few quips were without meaning. The students realized very well their importance, and the damage they had all done to world Communism. But they had also to live, sadly, with the concurrent realization that much of the damage had been conclusively fenced over at home.

When a Pole says he is an intellectual, he is in no mood for American-style "egghead" jokes. He is proclaiming a fixed social position, a way of life and a self-consciousness about both that would make Thomas Mann's Germanic self-probings on the subject seem casual. The universities are the *Inteligencja*'s compulsory spawning grounds. Poland's university tradition is one of the oldest and best-guarded in Europe. (The senior university, the Jagellonian at Cracow was founded in 1364.) The immediate historical antecedents of the Polish university intellectuals have been French, in the classic sense, and Russian and German, in the Romantic. Polish students have always had a hungry taste for the worlds of Fenelon and Montaigne. At the same time the Polish students of the Nineteenth Century were politically responsive to the continuing calls for revolution that came from the German Romantics, and the forerunners of Russia's own brief liberal and socialist tradition.

No student ethos in Europe was more politically conscious than the Polish. And in Poland's often unhappy circumstances, by 'politically conscious' is generally meant the ability and the courage to throw a paving block at an armed policeman. Through the years of foreign domination, after the dispersal of the Polish nobility as a cohesive political force, it was the *Inteligencja Polska* which shared with the clergy and the surviving noble families the leadership of the nation. In no other country has the egghead been so prominent, respected and institutionalized.

It was natural, therefore, that the Russians would pin great hopes in taking the new generation of the established Polish eggheadery, setting it atop the old tradition and making it the vehicle of Communist rule. (Like the Nazis, the Russians had done their wicked best to obliterate the intelligentsia of the generation preceding.) They had ten years to do the job, and they failed. For the October Revolution was touched off and kept burning by precisely the editors and writers who were expected to keep the population ideologically in step. In a series of exposes ranging from Lysenko-type biology to the excesses of the Polish foreign trade organization, they subjected the "excesses" of something called "Stalinism" to the critical eye of something which, almost to the end, they still call "Marxist-Leninism." The emergence of this partially free press made Poland each day less tenable for its Soviet governors.

Looking at Poland, or any Communist country, from the vantage point of an open society it is difficult to imagine the terrific impact of these published doubts in the System. They were written by a small and carefully selected minority of the Polish people, all of whom had long since had their reliability to Communism well proven, and sometimes in very nasty ways. When these tested reliables published their doubts, and in Party papers, it had the effect of an explosion. The great majority of the Polish population, hostile to Communism almost in its entirety, was quick to rally behind the only group in the country with permission and facilities to give this hostility voice. This eggheads' revolt offered the Poles the first real dose of hope they had had in years and incidentally restored the historical prestige of the Polish intelligentsia, which centuries of adversity had bound closer to the general population than anywhere else in Europe.

The most striking fact about the revolting eggheads was their youth. There were older writers who supported the movement. Many of them had long encouraged the growth of opposition to the regime's cast-iron Communism within their own circles—like the aging but intellectually spry poet Antoni Slonimski and the historian Jan Kott.

But it was the young who actually did the job. The 25-year-olds on the staffs of papers like *Po Prostu, Nowa Kultura, Sztandar Mlodych* and *Zycie Warszawy* were in contact with the organized workers and the Party groups as well, and they acted as catalyst for the others.

Foreign visitors to Poland never ceased to wonder at the almost universal youth of the *"enragés,"* as all participants in the Eggheads' Revolt came to be called. When they made their first contact with some hero of the neo-Communist intellectuals, either by accident over a bottle of Hungarian wine in the Warsaw Journalists' Club, or by appointment in his office (after often complicated negotiation) it was startling to find some bespectacled young man in a sweater, who looked less like a revolutionary leader than an articulate history graduate student, intent on talking out his Ph. D. thesis in political science.

The Intellectuals' Revolt in Poland was no upsurge of one nation's youth rebelling in isolation. It reflected in extreme the tensions that began with the death of Stalin throughout the Iron Curtain countries. If the extreme was due to the peculiar situation of the largest and most cohesively nationalist Eastern European satellite, it was very logical in its development. It can be said to Poland's credit that her youth followed the inconsistencies of Communism to their bitter conclusion long before anyone else in that grey world had either the intelligence, the courage or the intuition to do so.

The revolt of the *enragés* had its beginnings in 1945, when the Russians began their attempt at colonization. Facing the Europe it had so long coveted, Stalin's Russia stood at that moment like a barefoot caricature of the Third Rome for which the early Romanovs had striven.* It had welded to the Czars' broken ambitions all

---

* The idea of Moscow as the lawful orthodox successor of Rome and Constantinople had given a semi-annointed tone to Russian political expansion since the reign of Ivan the Terrible, and half consciously crept into the thinking even of his atheist Communist successors. ". . . All Christian Empires are fallen," wrote a Russian chronicler of the 16th Century, "and

the energy of a new and long frustrated Russian missionary zeal. To exploit this zeal, there was for the first time a clear military and political highway, heading west, between Brest-Litovsk and Berlin. But the problems in the involuntarily made mission lands were very different, transcending even the considerable physical contrasts between the forest people of Finland, the factory bourgeois of Czechoslovakia and the Slavic peasantry in Bulgaria.

Nowhere did the Russians have a tougher nut to crack than in Poland. Despite their war losses the Poles remained by far the largest and least digestible population in the future satellite bloc. They were traditionally the most anti-Russian, the most fervently religious, whose piety moreover had as often been directed against the Orthodox Russians as the atheist devil. The Polish resistance in World War II had amply demonstrated the national capacity for courage, fortitude and, on occasion, foolhardiness. The Polish Communist Party, as noted before, was also the smallest and least representative in the area.

It was essential, therefore, for the Russians to proselytize the youth as quickly as they could to make up for the resistance of the adults. They had a few advantages on their side. The Polish intelligentsia had been heart, soul and head of the resistance movement. By standing passively on the wrong bank of the Vistula, Marshal Rokossowski's temporarily non-fighting Soviet divisions had insured the destruction, in the 1944 Warsaw Uprising, of its most promising representatives. Poets had fallen in the streets trying to soak German tanks with home-made gasoline bottles. Literary critics and novelists had died behind their ammunitionless machine guns. Otherwise they suffered then or before the fate of Oswiecim (Auschwitz) or Majdanek, for the Germans were more or less determined to exterminate every Pole who could read.

The few intellectuals surviving the War and the Uprising had learned caution the hard way. They were disillusioned by the failure of the West to redeem its promises. They had no illusions about the Russians, but after years of hopelessly fighting against power, they had begun to respect power as an intellectual factor.

---

in their stead stands alone the Empire of our ruler in accord with the prophetic books. Two Romes have fallen, but the third stands and a fourth there will not be."

In the spring of 1945 an idiomatic translation of "If you can't lick 'em, join 'em" would have received implicit acquiescence among the Polish Intelligentsia's remnants. The minority of dissenters would have been either West in the emigration, wondering whether they should cast their lot with the people back home, whatever their oppressions; or leaving Poland en route to Vorkuta or worse places, picked up in the Russian round-up of the Polish patriotic resistance.

The next half-generation lacked even the mental reservations of its older brothers, for the teen-agers of 1945 had few undamaged memories of ancient faith, honor or traditions. What they saw principally was the futility of the present. If the only future was to be Communist, at least it promised "planification," after the demoralizing confusions of the German occupation. There was demonstrably neither freedom nor security to be felt standing in the moon-scape of the destroyed city of Warsaw, wondering where to find an older brother's grave inside the rubble of the Old Town.

*　　　　*　　　　*

The Russians brought with them from the East only a small group of Polish Communist or fellow-traveling intellectuals, but they were well house-broken. They had survived the deaths and deportations of families and friends, and the long-past purging of the Polish Party in Moscow. They had watched the mass deportation of roughly one and a half million Poles into the depths of Russia, for slave labor camps or worse. They had a clear idea of what had happened to the Polish officers in the shallow grave at Katyn.* They had a very good idea of what the Russians expected the new Poland to be—the leading buffer province of Communized eastern Europe, if not ultimately a Soviet Republic. Thus, as realists who learned the hard way, even the Lublin Government's group of trained posts, critics, novelists and Party line-layers appreciated the difficulties of colonizing their reluctant country.

---

* The existence of this massacre, which recurs in any discussion of Polish-Soviet relations, was first revealed, ironically, by the Germans in April, 1943. It is now well substantiated fact that between 5,000 and 10,000 Polish officers were massacred by the Soviet State Security forces in the forest of Katyn and elsewhere, in 1940.

Which made all the more urgent the job of attracting the younger generation.

One of the first acts of the new Lublin Polish government in 1944 was to set up a system of youth "pioneer" groups, modeled as exactly on the Russian prototype as the newly-created U.B. was patterned on the Russian secret police. To a youth that looked desperately for something solid, they offered ideals, advancement and membership in a club that did not set too exacting a standard for its recruits. The writer Wiktor Woroszylski, later the editor of the *enragé* standard-bearer, *Nowa Kultura,* described his reception into the Party in 1945: "I was received in an irregular way (to judge by the statutes). At the end of a brief examination ("Who were Marx and Lenin?"), the secretary of the district Committee, who was meeting me for the first time in his life, signed my application. Then, holding out a white cardboard, my Party card, he asked: "Where do you want to go? The Youth, the U.B., or Political Education?"

"I would surely have picked the U.B. [sic], if, a few days later, a fourth possibility had not presented itself. *Glos Ludu* [Voice of the People—then the Party paper] published my first rhymed bit of invective, pathetic and badly formed, titled *Before Berlin.* After which I was taken on as a reporter for the local edition."

"Thus began not so much my conscious life as my life of responsibility, a life where there was not on one side the Party, on another work, on another finally poetry, but where Communism was the supreme poetry and the daily effort, and poetry the road towards Communism. You smile wryly at this old-fashioned bombast. Too bad. That's what it was like."

There was no let-up in the drive to Communize Polish education. Where, for example, there had been throughout Poland only 27 institutions of higher education in 1939, with 49,000 students, by 1955 the total was raised to 84 schools, with 140,000 students.* Few of the students were even professed Communists, to say nothing of dedicated ones. But enough were attracted by the combination of lure and coercion to produce a hard core of young

---

* Admittedly, this figure was reached largely through educational gerrymandering, e.g. a single faculty would be divorced from its university and made into a separate institute of its own.

men, pledged to the Communist cause, and wholly convinced that everything wrong with Poland, or any place else, could be fixed up by a return to "orthodox Marxist-Leninism."

"Behind us," as Woroszylski continued, "stood the Party. The Party said the word—it must be done. We knew that victory depended on us, a victory which could not be reckoned beforehand. We knew no higher joy than that of sharing in the struggle for the Cause."

Young men like the future *enragé* editors worked, lied, cheated and persecuted for the sake of the Party, a fact that must be recalled in assessing the tragedy of their plight later. They participated at first without friction, as did their elders who had survived the German occupation. They enjoyed, like Eligiusz Lassota, the later editor of *Po Prostu,* "the joy of having a fine pistol," when mounting night guard over a Party installation. They gloried in the fact of their membership in the Polish New Class, as it was then emerging.

Their idealistic glory was short-lived, lasting about as long as the preliminary softening period in Poland's Russian colonization. Its crisis came in 1948, when Wladyslaw Gomulka was removed as Party Secretary, charged with the heresy of "national Communism." (Among his principal Cominform accusers the year before, had been a secretly aspiring Yugoslav national Communist named Tito.) Although Gomulka then, as now, did not much frequent intellectual circles, his downfall was the signal for the intellectual tightening process in Poland's Stalinization. The young eggheads who had been debating Marxist theory around their theoretical headquarters, the magazine *Kuznica* ("The Forge") found that any debate on the subject was becoming an increasingly dangerous luxury. The students who had enjoyed fighting the "reactionaries" of the non-Communist majority in Poland's 1946 "election" soon found out that their enthusiasm had really not been an important factor.

Probably the cruelest blow of all to the young Marxists (non-Communist Poles had more concrete worries) was the imposition of a rigid Soviet "Socialist realism" as the guidepost in the arts. The Poles are an artistic people, with a natural gift for design and expression that is shared by few other European races. Even during the first months of the Communist reign, the arts had begun to re-appear. Although making their formal bows to Marxism, critics still criticized a bit, novelists still wrote things which could be called novels, artists painted. By 1949 socialist realism was firmly imposed. The "beet and tractor literature," as the Poles called it, chugged on to the field. The graphic arts degenerated into a Soviet-style series of poster contests, with the orthodox pictures of smiling collective farmers that have rubbed the paint off museum walls from Riga to Shanghai.

The bulk of the population met Stalinization as something inevitable and expected. It was in fact only a change in degree from a system which already killed, robbed and deported with a thoroughness transcending even the German occupation. But the minority of pampered youth was frightened. The prospectus had sounded different, at the Party meetings in 1945 and 1946. Nothing had been said about classic Soviet furnishings like the distortions in history, the arbitrary silencing of orthodox Marxist articles, or the deliberate editing of works by long dead authors. "The fact was," wrote Woroszylski later, still wondering a bit, "that the revolution which we were defending had at the same time some counter-revolutionary habits and that our idea of the character of the Party was already an object of some mystery. . . ."

By 1952 the mold had set and so had the doubts. Again from Woroszylski: "The result of our sad evolution: who were we in 1952? The power of the people and the Party, as a few years before? No, we were no more than the official choristers of the Party and of the people's power. The Party—that was the directors; the power of the people—a pure abstraction. Every responsibility for shaping reality was slipping from our hands. All that was left was diligence in the 'creative cells' and paying the assessments when they came due. In our verse, all the while, we kept gargling our high-mindedness: 'We, the Party, the working class, People's Poland!' We did not understand how these tremendous words sounded suddenly so empty and false."

Such doubts had long been flickering in the general dark. Many of the brave manifestos of 1955 and 1956 had been written in 1953, but prudently kept in desk drawers through the years intervening. For ten years of Communism had taught even the most idealistic of young Marxists the necessity of the "double-think" process which Czeslaw Milosz in his *The Captive Mind* calls Ketman. It is best described as a kind of life-and-death gamesmanship designed to keep a modicum of utterly private (and useless) intellectual freedom, while vieing with one's desk neighbor in cries of approval for the slightest detail of the regime's program.

All over the Communist world the restrictions of Ketman were loosened by Stalin's death and its aftermath. Yet, paradoxically, it was only the death of Stalin that kept the little bands of true believers from losing their faith, at least for a couple of years. Along with like-minded people elsewhere in the Communist world, the Polish Intelligentsia watched with fascination the increasingly bold things that were said about the dead dictator in Russia. Long before Khrushchev's excited denunciation of Stalin leaked out of the Twentieth Party Congress in 1956, the Polish Communists and other national brothers under the skin were reconstructing their tattered Marxist belief through "de-Stalinization." If so much that was bad in the system could be traced to Stalin, their reasoning went, this means that mankind must be on the threshold of a restored, "pure" Marxist-Leninism.

In forging a new dictatorless Communism, the Poles felt that they would have a lot to teach the Russians. For the visits to Moscow made by members of the Communist Eggheadery left them far from comfortable. Woroszylski, whose experience was so typical of others in his generation, had the added blessing of a year in Moscow, in 1952. He wrote: "In spite of all my efforts, I did not feel at all like a Communist from the foreign country in the first country of workers and peasants, but like a suspect intruder into a secret fortress." Russian ignorance of the Marxism they had themselves so earnestly debated was profound. "What did the Russians think about Bukharin?" one of the Warsaw editors was asked, who had spent some time in Moscow. "Think of him?" he said, "The students whom I was with didn't even know who Bukharin was, or those who had heard his name knew that he was an enemy of the state and nothing more." Thus thoroughly had the Russians managed to eliminate all the anti-Stalinist opposition, through 30 years of history, or so it seemed to the Poles.

That the regime did not act quickly to stifle such recriminations, as they were voiced, was another index of how the uncertainty of Moscow had transmitted itself to the satellite capitals in the years between 1953 and 1956. The satellite leadership, if anything, was even more worried and confused than the members of the Soviet Central Committee playing musical chairs on the Kremlin steps. The rising doubts of the young Polish intellectuals accordingly found their way periodically into print. They began to criticize obliquely, in the debates about the country's educational and literary suffocation, which appeared in print as early as 1953. By late 1954, Polish writers found it safe to take public pot-shots at the whole theory of Socialist Realism in the arts and letters. But it was not until the next year that anyone felt bold enough to discuss Poland's political and social failures.

On August 21, 1955, a *Poem for Adults,* by the poet Adam Wazyk, was published in *Nowa Kultura.* Wazyk, then 50, was a reputable literary figure in the Communist world, who until that time had practiced Milosz' art of Ketman with great success. He had spent World War II in the Soviet Union, returning with the triumphant Lublin contingent at its close. He was one of the founders of the Marxist literary weekly, *Kuznica,* while still in the Communist Polish Army. He had remained a contributor after *Kuznica* was merged into *Nowa Kultura* in 1950 (for harboring potentially dangerous corporate thoughts). Through the first decade of Communist rule he continued to be for all intents and purposes a reliable supporter of the System.

The appearance of conformity was smashed with the *Poem for Adults,* immediately recognized as the most violent and radical criticism of a country under Communism ever to appear in a Communist-controlled press. Its pictures of life in Warsaw were like a series of George Grosz drawings, enough to destroy a decade of poster-mounting:

"In a freshly plastered street of new buildings, lime dust circles and a cloud rushes through the sky. Pulverizers, rolling in the street, press the surface. . . . Little and big children scatter under the chestnut trees, dragging wood for fuel from half-pulled-down scaffolds. . . . fifteen-year old whores walk

down the planks to the basement, their smiles seem made of
lime. . . ."

Wazyk's comments on the System were more fundamental:

> "They came and said:
> 'A Communist does not die.'
> No man has lived forever
> Only the memory of him is to remain.
> The more valuable the man,
> The greater the pain.
> They came and cried:
> under socialism
> a hurt finger does not hurt.
> They hurt their fingers.
> They felt the pain.
> They began to doubt. . . .
> On this earth we appeal on behalf of people
> Who are exhausted from work
> we appeal for locks that fit the door,
> for rooms with windows,
> for walls which do not rot,
> for contempt for papers,
> for a holy human time,
> for a safe return home,
> for a simple distinction between words and deeds. . . ."
>
> (translated by Paul Mayewski)

The poem's publication came only after a showdown fight between the "Stalinist" members of the *Nowa Kultura* editorial board
and the new *enragés* or "progressives." At that Wazyk and the
board turned out a quickly written final stanza, as a sop to authority, which vowed thinly that all these appeals and criticisms were
being made by good Communists. (. . . we appeal through our
Party.) But this gloss was very obvious to any reader and had no
braking effect whatever on the poem's impact. *Nowa Kultura* sold
like a confidential magazine in Hollywood. Copies were soon
getting heavy black-market prices, and hand-written versions were
circulated throughout the country, besides.

The regime acted quickly. The staff of *Nowa Kultura* was changed and Wazyk forced into temporary silence. He did not unship his pen again until April 1956. The official press cranked up a series of denunciations ("a bad and cruel half-truth"), but no one paid much attention to it. The cat was out of the bag. As further indication of the regime's predicament, Wazyk was not arrested.

The youth magazine *Po Prostu* had at first joined the conformist hue and cry at Wazyk's heresy, and its critic published an aggrieved denunciation. But very shortly afterwards, *Po Protsu* itself began a series of honest muck-raking exposés of the corruption inside Polish Communism, which widened the crack made by Nowa Kultura. *Po Prostu* ("Speaking Frankly" in English translation) then had a circulation of only 15,000 to go with its ambitious sub-title "The Voice of the Young Intelligentsia." But criticism proved a startling circulation-builder, and the specific exposé soon led to the general editorial indictment. Copies containing the critical articles sold out everywhere. Within a year circulation had risen to 150,000.

Other papers and magazines, including the organ of the Central Committee, *Trybuna Ludu,* jumped on the bandwagon. In March, 1956 the National Council of Culture and Art made a formal break with the whole program of socialist realism, and then some. "One of our most urgent tasks," said Antoni Slonimski at the Council's meeting, "should be to restore the Council to its true functions. This Red Salvation Army must finally leave off shaking the tambourine, leave off public confessions—I mean these self-criticisms made hastily and saying nothing. It must cease this pious ministry with regard to its flock. . . .

"Only a true democratisation of our public life, the reestablishment of public opinion, a return to our fidelity to rationalist thought, to a thought that is free and without fetters—only this can save us from Caesarism. . . .

"We are leaving the night of the middle ages. There are young forces in Poland, there are some healthy souls and characters who have awaited the moment of this transformation. We must today give them our pledge."

In a long and weighty speech Slonimski's colleague the literary critic Kott gave further public voice to all that the eggheads had been thinking. "Our Marxist analysis," he said, "serves through its researches into the past to discover objective truth. But it stops on the threshold of the contemporary era. With the aid, it seems, of the same scientific apparatus and the same concepts, we force ourselves not to learn the truth, but to explain reality. To explain and to justify it! At any price! It is this that before our eyes, from year to year, contemporary history becomes more and more a great mythology. If the facts present an obstacle, we modify the facts; if our real heroes pinch the truth, we pick some out of thin air."

These were strong words to say publicly in a Communist country. But by this time similar expressions could be read in almost any of the papers, *Po Prostu* and Woroszylski's *Nowa Kultura* still leading the pack. The Poznan riots came two months later. Then the criticism of Stalinism, Caesarism, statism, or the "cult of the individual" had become a full-dress symphony, with the brasses setting the beat.

When Gomulka defied the Russians in October, the Party intellectuals, now joined by a considerable number of non-Communists (who had previously prudently shut up) were his indispensable assistants. On October 20 when Gomulka stood up to take the cheers of the Warsaw crowds, Eligiusz Lassota, the 26-year-old editor of *Po Prostu* was at his side.

It was almost immediately thereafter that the trouble started. The *enragés* had provided priceless aid and leadership at the October revolution. They had for a few months actually led and channeled the mass discontent of the people against the regime's excesses, just the way the Marxist textbooks always said the intelligentsia should behave. Their tragedy was that they believed what they said, not knowing any better. The *enragés,* young or old, were no crypto-democrats, or pro-Americans. Most of them were on the contrary students who had learned their Marx too well for use anywhere outside the classroom. For each member of the *Po Prostu* editorial board, as they argued out their editorials in the Palace of Culture, believed that he was taking Poland into a purified new dimension of Marxism, which the whole world could not help but applaud.

The facts of international life and of Marxism were stacked

against them. Gomulka, for one thing, had never liked the intelligentsia. His seven years out of power, although they had given him considerable leisure time to ponder the Marxist classics, had, if anything, deepened his distrust of theoreticians. "Scribblers," he called them.

Once in power, he took the course of a veteran *Realpolitiker*. His objectives were to get Poland out from under Russian domination, put the country on its feet economically, and reestablish his own control over the Communist Party. In none of this program was there any place for a new purified Marxism. Since it was the party organization, not "pure Marxist-Leninism" which he considered the only suitable vehicle for governing Poland, the *enragé* journalists and writers speedidly got in his hair. "Do you want the *Moskals* (i.e. the Russians) to make a second Korea of us?" he snapped at a youth delegation after October, while listening to one of their appeals for a more democratic, "purer" Marxism. He realized more clearly than anyone that the Russian power had always to be reckoned with. He succeeded in facing down Khrushchev and Co. on October 19, 1956 and subsequently only because he made them realize that Poland would fight a second attempt at Russian colonization. This remained his big card. But to play it well, he needed the entire population, or at least large sections of it united behind him.

As a result Gomulka found himself constantly balancing two forces, neither of which counts idealistic Marxism as much of a virtue. A majority of the Poles hate it, lock, stock and barrel. The hatred is reinforced by the spiritual teachings of the Roman Catholic Church and intensified by the primitive and quite justified suspicions of Communism among the Polish peasantry. In gaining the support of the Church and the peasantry for the *status quo,* Gomulka had to soft-pedal several articles dear to the orthodox Marxist's heart, notably collectivization of agriculture, secret police authority and state control of the clergy.

As for the other end of the balancing act, Khrushchev and his divisions, Gomulka is well aware that the Russian leadership regards doctrinal Marxist purity as a middling incidental to the consolidation of a colonial empire, run by a tight managerial system. What the Russians really insist on, in Marxism's name, is what facilitates the Russification of a country, or at least, as in Poland's case, its firm alliance.

In his condition of constant political weighing and juggling, Gomulka welcomed the angry young intellectuals as cordially as a veteran tight-rope walker greets a couple of friendly helpers who insist on testing the strength of the wire, by jumping on it in the middle of his act. Poland could maintain its position only by loudly proclaiming the truth of two palpable and contradictory fictions: 1) that Poland is run by a tightly controlled Communist Party exactly like the Russian Party and owing loyalty to Moscow in every detail; and, 2) that Polish Communists are really "different" Communists, who will never hesitate to sacrifice Marxism and their power to the needs of the united Polish people.

Almost every day in every way, some egghead was throwing a verbal brick through one of these desperately proclaimed assertions of the "Polish road to socialism." Either they were shocking the Russians with their loud cries for freedom or they were disturbing the internal situation by reaffirming that no true freedom was possible without purifying what they came to call the "institutional Marxism" of the Party government.

Inside the party the Intellectuals' Revolt presented Gomulka with another dilemma. For it intensified the problem of the split between the "revisionists" and the "dogmatists." The intellectual revisionists constantly demanded "democracy," if only inside the Party Councils. Stalin and some of his successors, they charged, had betrayed the idea of "democratic centralism" by eliminating free discussion inside the party. Other excesses of Stalinism, notably its police activity, had driven a large and nasty gulf between the Party rulers and the people, which Marx or Lenin [sic] never envisioned. So ran their argument. The dogmatists responded with their customary vigorous vituperation.

Nikita Khrushchev owed his initial success in Russia to the ease with which he could leap from revisionism to dogmatism and back, like an equestrian acrobat with two performing horses. Gomulka is by Soviet standards a revisionist. But he is a revisionist of a very moderate order. He is in fact the one genuine moderate statesman whom the Communist system has produced. As events later showed, he was inevitably sensitive to Soviet pressure, which constantly made itself felt against the revisionists. For a long time after the October, 1956 stalemate with the Russians, this pressure eased, at least in the columns of the official Soviet mouthpieces like *Pravda* and *Izvestia;* but it continued in the form of sniping "literary" criticism in the Soviet weekly press. Finally, when the Russians came back to the open cultural offensive in 1958, Gomulka had more or less to agree with them.

It took the angry young intellectuals a long time to accept the fact that they had been abandoned by their leader. They never quite understood, to analogize from a more religious era, why Luther himself had deserted them and was apparently knuckling under to Pope and princes. So they became modern Anabaptists, ever more iconoclast, ever more critical of Marxism, until it became doubtful whether there was much Marxism left in them at all. "Our young journalism," wrote one of Gomulka's own entourage, Minister of Higher Education Stefan Zolkiewski in 1957, "abandons the grounds of Marxist philosophy in matters of morality. It abandons the concept of the morality of *results of actions* in favor of the ever more clearly existentialist morality of intention. Our journalism is creating an imaginary world for itself." Translated from Marxist double-think, this criticism stands as the most serious charge that one Communist can make against another: the *enragés* were abandoning the vital Marxist insistence that the end justifies the means.

For well over a year the young Marxist intelligentsia fought their many-sided battle in the open. Like the traditional Polish Army formation, they took on everybody at once. They attacked the new "clerical" influence in the school system. They attacked both the Party *apparatchiks* and anti-Marxists who were trying to take advantage of the Revolution. They particularly attacked the Communist Party governing body. "If the secretary of a local Party organization," wrote *Po Prostu* in 1957, "does something incorrect, he is brought to responsibility for it by the district committee. But to whom is the Central Committee of the Party legally responsible?" A sensitive point.

Partly to keep Moscow off his neck (for the Russians consistently demanded the *enragés'* suppression), Gomulka early began to criticize excess revisionism as equally dangerous with dogmatism.

To express his own middle-of-the-road policies, Gomulka took over the theoretical magazine *Polityka*. *Polityka* under its new management soon made enough angry disciplinary noises to please any old-line dogmatist—although it remained more liberal, slightly, than the official Party paper. For the criticism from the angry intellectuals was not doing the Party any good.

By the summer of 1957 Gomulka was snapping at the revisionists as much as he had snapped at the Stalinists, and less subtly. It was his own idea to single out Kolakowski, the young philosophy professor, as an example of the dangerous non-Marxist tendencies to which revisionism could lead. In Moscow for the Fortieth Anniversary of the Soviet Revolution, he denounced meddlesome "intellectuals" with a specially written piece for *Pravda*. There was little doubt, however unkind his criticism, that he had singled out the right people. For Kolakowski, after years of seeing through a glass darkly, was leading the parade of theoreticians who were rapidly reasoning themselves out of Marxism. "A mythology," he wrote, in an article which the regime tried to censor, "must be integral if it is to be effective. The death of gods is a chain reaction, one pulls the other along over the precipice, the abyss calls forth the abyss. . . . Hence the necessity, so well known to experienced priests, of maintaining the mythology as a system in which every detail is equally important and equally sacred . . . Stalinism therefore was a theology able to live thanks to its integral character . . . but its fall, too, must be as totalitarian as its rule. The gods are connected by chains of deception. They fall like houses made of cards. How imprudent it is to try to remove only one card . . ."

In September, 1957, *Po Prostu* was closed. Its editor, Lassota, was forced to resign from the Party. *Polityka* summed up its downfall in an editorial, with perhaps unconscious frankness: "Willingly or unwillingly *Po Prostu* was gradually joining the current of the total negation of the Party's policy. The critic of Stalinism became the critic of the political program. . . . The struggle against the wrong methods of building socialism during the previous period became transformed in the new conditions into the spreading of disbelief in the possibility of building socialism. . . .

". . . there are people who declare: the liquidation of *Po Prostu* means the suppression of freedom of speech, the stifling of criticism and a deviation from October. What can we say to this? Freedom of speech has defined boundaries in post-October Poland. These boundaries end where . . . propaganda, directed against the building of socialism in our country starts . . . they end where the vital interests of the State and nation starts. . . ."

The crackdown continued. An obedient Party hack named Leon Kruczkowski was made chairman of the Writers Union, in effect chief censor, and he began working with routine efficiency. The ambitious Western-connected literary magazine called *Europa* was suppressed before it started publishing. In protest ten of Poland's leading writers turned in their Party cards. They included, among others, Adam Wazyk, whose poem had sounded the alarms in October, and such distinguished fellow-*enragés* as Jan Kott and Pawel Hertz.

In the same month that *Po Prostu* was abolished, there appeared in *Nowa Kultura* a series of articles by Kolakowski, entitled "Responsibility and History," which powerfully heightened the urgency of Gomulka's repression. They were not overly noticed at the moment of their publication, partly because the complicated language Kolakowski uses was a little difficult for Gomulka's remaining house intellectuals to decipher. But they grew into a virtual *cause célèbre* after a few months' time. Kolakowski, a philosopher and scholar by both profession and instinct, presented in them a reasoned and fatal criticism of the Marxist state, which deserves to stand in a trinity with Djilas' *The New Class* and the incidental commentaries on Communism contained in the Russian Boris Pasternak's great novel *Doctor Zhivago*.

Pasternak saw the failings of the Communist system with the mystic eye of a poet, Djilas from the practical disillusionment of a prematurely aged revolutionary "political." Kolakowski concerned himself rather with the inner validity of the modern Marxist philosophy, through the basic metaphysical questioning of a Western man who is disturbed by the house in which he finds himself. Where Djilas and Pasternak asked respectively "How does it work?" and "What does it do to people?" Kolakowski concentrated on the moral question: "Can it be just?" In his essays he centered on the Marxist insistence, dusted off periodically by successively worse generations of Communists, that the inevitable force of history, moving in just the direction the System anticipated, is in itself philosophy, morality and social ethic, justifying any aberrations from previously established moral codes or generally conceded human feelings.

The shakiness of this history myth, as Kolakowski described it, is responsible for the "sectarianism" of the modern Communist government. This government he still politely described as the Polish "Stalinist" extreme, but the things he said about it offer a categorical description of the whole System's behavior, anywhere, especially the subject of its dealings with revisionists. "It has been known for centuries," he wrote, "that stakes are, first of all, for heretics and not for pagans. . . . The phenomenon with which we are dealing now cannot be simply explained by the natural self-defense of the political organisms against the invasion of foreign bodies which have penetrated them. This is not an immunization against disease-carrying elements, but an attempt to create an airtight, if possible, protective film against all stimuli able to bring revolutionary changes—a sign of a backward development in social processes.

"Sectarianism in political life—a sign of which is the extreme scrupulousness concerning the exact borders of the organization— is then a testimony to a double process occurring within it; it testifies to senile changes and the loss of procreative powers, and thus it testifies that the political organization has become a goal in itself, has isolated itself from the social tasks which have given rise to it, and has concentrated its own tasks on prolonging its own existence. Sectarianism is not a mistake of individuals; it is a social sign of approaching death . . . it is comparable with the sometimes brutal egotism of old age, which vaguely realizes that nature is turning against it. . . ."

But Kolakowski's purpose went far beyond simple description of the Communist state's political senility. The heart of his essays was the essentially "vague" character of Marx' historical determinism, the impossibility of formulating the Marxist dialectic into laws and, therefore, the utter need for the personal individual moral judgment—not the state's fake "determinism" as the fundamental factor in human decisions. "No one," he wrote, "is exempt from the moral responsibility for crime, merely because he is intellectually convinced of its inevitable victory. No one is exempt from the moral duty to fight against a system of government, a doctrine or social conditions which he considers to be vile and inhuman, by resorting to the argument that he finds them historically necessary. . . . The values of historical progress [after a quotation of Marx] are achieved through crime, and yet, these values do not cease to be values, and crimes do not cease to be crimes just as great works of art do not lose their greatness owing to the fact that the artist was prompted by the lowest motives . . . we see no reason for treating morality as a tool of great history."

"We are not Communists because we have considered Communism a historial necessity. We are Communists because we are on the side of the oppressed against their oppressors, on the side of the poor against their masters and on the side of the persecuted against their perscutors. . . ."

To oversimplify a tremendously complicated and often brilliant piece of philosophical argument: Kolakowski thus told his readers and himself that as the word is presently used, they could not be Communists at all. In his argument he had surgically separated every shred of moral justification from the historical base on which the modern Marxist system insists it stands. "The essential social commitment," he summarized, "is a moral one. Regardless of which historiography we should like to assume we shall be justly judged for everything we have done in its name." Therefore, he concluded, every repression of the System is immoral and individuals are bound to struggle against it.

Kolakowski was born in 1927. He has lived all his student and adult life under a Communist government. He was a member of the Communist youth organization and later of the Party and lectured at the Party schools. His early work in philosophy was directed against the usual "class enemies," citing the glories of "socialist liberation." It was no different from the early works of hundreds of bright young Marxists like him in Moscow, Bucharest, Prague or Peking. We must remember this to appreciate his achievement. For working with no more encouragement than his own reason, he stripped away the fallacies of his environment and argued his way back toward the essential body of rational truth that his ancestors had believed in through long centuries before him.

It was incidental that he still regarded himself as a "Marxist," for formal purposes, or that he insisted that the end could justify the means (but only inasmuch as it was a moral end). Essentially, he had broken not only with a formal Communist government process, but with the entire pattern of determinist thinking that had defaced Europe since people began misinterpreting Hegel in the last century. He rediscovered the natural law of Christianity as surely as Camus rediscovered it in his *L'Homme Revolté,* although the particular routes from Marxism and Existentialism had a markedly different set of landmarks. (Since Kolakowski's researches into mediaeval Christianity are so extensive that he often writes in the language of theology, the mention of "natural law" would not be very surprising to him.)

"Responsibility and History" had a tremendous effect on Polish intellectuals, and Kolakowski's rediscovery of moral truth turned the pace of inner moral defection from Communism into something like a toboggan slide. The precise enunciations of this disbelief among the young Marxist *enragés* varied, and were often confused. Given their heavy Communist upbringings, the rediscovery of morality almost recreated in them the old analogy of the prisoners, which Plato uses in the Republic. "Men dwelling in a kind of cave beneath the ground . . . with their legs and necks fettered since childhood,"* they were understandably confused by the light they saw at the end of their reasoning processes.

Few of his contemporaries, understandably, were able to reason their way out of Marxism with Kolakowski's clarity. Their conversations reflected the extreme tactical confusion of ideas in process of desperate remodeling. "One cannot come to socialism without revolution," a high-priced Party boss would explain, "yet revolution is a complicated thing . . . we in the underdeveloped countries had not the tradition of democracy you had in the United States. . . . It is the tragedy of Marxism that the U.S.S.R., the first country to establish it politically, was undeveloped. . . . Political democracy is not an idea in general but must be taken in its particu-

* The Republic. Book VII: 514.

lar cases. . . . We think that controlled democracy is one step towards true democracy. . . . We think that our processes will produce democracy. . . . It's the same point of view that Mr. Nehru had. . . . Naturally we reject the old Communist thesis that capitalism cannot produce. . . . Yes American capitalism seems to have much good in it—our local Party cell is organizing a discussion group about American capitalism. . . . No, I don't mind if you call me a Social Democrat. . . ."

*   *   *

In their poems and novels the intellectuals of Gomulka's Poland were able to express themselves more sharply, without the necessity of exploring philosophic premises. The end of enforced slogan-writing in 1956 released a long contained reservoir of literary talent, and some of its products were arresting. As would be expected, the mood and style of these writers is not calculated to please admirers of either Francoise Sagan or Elizabeth Bowen. Their themes are immediate: the crimes of youthful gangs in Warsaw, the wretchedness of living in overcrowded houses, the evils of the Stalinist period, with a heavy accent on police persecution, recreations of the war years. Out of the more serious books comes a fictional parallel to Kolakowski's re-tracing of Marxism. The Communist party characters, and what they stand for, come off very badly in a novel like Kazimierz Brandys' *The Mother of the Krols,* which the *Times Literary Supplement* called "the most successful attempt from inside the Communist camp at finding the truth about the degeneration of Communist ideology and practice." At its close, its hero, a veteran Communist leader from pre-war days, talks to another Communist, who had paid for his Spanish Civil War record with a long sentence in Soviet concentration camps. It is after the death of Stalin, and the hero suggests that "not all is lost," if the Stalin crimes can be recognized. "Not all is lost!" the other says, "What are you defending? What have you got left. . . . You fear infamy. But infamy has already taken place. The common man despises us. All, all is lost."

Even the best of these writers—young men like Leopold Tyrmand and Jerzy Andrzejewski or older names like Slonimski or Mieczyslaw Jastrun—are seldom heard of outside of Poland, although the part they played in speeding the general decline of Communist literary pretensions is considerable. But there has been one exception. Marek Hlasko, a 25 year old writer of great power, shot up to fame in the period immediately before and after the October Revolution with his angry, grim stories of life in the physical and moral debris of Polish cities. He has been compared to Faulkner, Erskine Caldwell or the early Steinbeck, with some justice. Both his themes and his indignation share something with many young American writers of the early 'thirties—although, having already experienced Communism in action, he lacks their type of left-wing social consciousness. The aim of his stories in general is to paint the hardships and crudities of life as they are, without the varnish that Social Realism used to cover them. But he focuses his photographic stories of misery with a rare understanding of their purpose not as a continuing art form, but a temporary literary reaction. "I personally do not believe in the future of this type of literature," he wrote in 1958, "but I am certain of its current necessity. I do not believe in cynicism. . . . But I do believe in mutiny; I believe in mutiny as the starting point for finding a place in life and society. I believe in mutiny as the highest value in youth. . . . And mutiny cannot be just; exactly as unjust is the world in which mutiny is born. . . ."

In the summer of 1958 a film version of Hlasko's story "The Eighth Day of the Week" won a prize at the Cannes festival. The story of a young architect and his student girl friend whose romance shatters because there is no place in Warsaw where they can be together, it is patently not a salute to the government housing industry. Gomulka personally ordered it withdrawn and refused permission to show it in Poland. While Hlasko was still in western Europe, on a visit, *Trybuna Ludu* cut loose on him with a violent anonymous attack as "a pupil of Orwell's, who denies the humanistic spirit of Socialism." "Hlaskoism," the article continued, was a widespread error among the young Polish writers, who refused to see anything but the dark side of their country's existence.

From Paris, Hlasko made a dignified reply to the charges. "It was from the papers," he wrote, "that I learned that Hlaskoism exists in literature. . . . It makes no difference about what they call disenchanted people, for it does not change the fact. . . . It was not I who made up Warsaw, that Warsaw which was for so many years a city without a smile; it was not I who made up the Warsaw in which people trembled with fear . . . it was not I who made up the Warsaw in which a girl was cheaper than a bottle of vodka—it was that Warsaw which made me."

The account of Hlasko's reception in official Warsaw is about as good a barometer obtainable of Gomulka's rising irritation with the intellectual revisionists. In 1957 he received the state publishing prize for his novel "The First Step in the Clouds." In 1958 he was able to get his two latest books published only outside of Poland, by the very excellent Polish magazine *Kultura* in Paris. In an open letter to *Kultura*'s editor, he added an interesting postscript to his own witness of the transition in official writing fads since the October. "Perhaps you will also be interested to know that this same narration of "Cemeteries" which earned me the tag of traitor and smuggler of anti-Communist weapons, was bought in December 1956 as a fragment by the editorial office of *Trybuna Ludu*. So, as you can see, the career of an author in totalitarianism is a dangerous thing. It is very easy to become, from a cooperator with the Party organ, a traitor and a good-for-nothing who is stamped by an anonymous informer."

Hlasko had repeatedly denied that he would leave Poland for good. Shortly after his last denial ("a writer is nothing without his homeland") he asked for and received asylum in Germany. His reasons for doing this were partly personal—and his action made things no easier for the writers who still tried to keep some free speech alive inside their country. But he had been heavily handled by the Gomulka government.

Hlasko later decided to return to Poland, but not before a tremendous furore had arisen over his departure. It only dramatized the fact that the cords of censorship, once reestablished, had been steadily tightened. On May 6, 1958, almost half a year before Hlasko's departure, a rising young Gomulka man named Andrzej Werblan had addressed the Press Commission of the Central Committee in Warsaw on the subject of the magazine *Nowa Kultura,* which had just had a forcible change of editors. Werblan, who had been Boleslaw Bierut's secretary before the October revolution, was demonstrably a man who was fast on his political feet, and pedalling smoothly. What he had to say about *Nowa Kultura* was virtually a general statement of the regime's attitude towards the writer.

The burden of Werblan's speech was the old Communist argument that freedom of expression is sharply conditioned by what is being expressed. He expressed the regime's disapproval at everything from efforts to publicize the men of the Home Army who died in the Warsaw Uprising (the regime's position was that they died bravely, but for a bad cause) to the publication in Polish of excerpts from James Joyce's Ulysses. He noted with dismay among the "negative phenomena" mentioned, the satire being produced in one of the small review cabarets in Cracow.* But in the course of these specific objections, he also enunciated some painful truths of the Gomulka position on domestic governance.

"The Communist Party," his lecture ran, "has the right and the duty to defend its superior position even with state force, as this is equivalent to the defense of the Socialist revolution. Without the leadership of the Communist Party there can be no socialism. . . .

"One cannot and one ought not to idealize the masses. They emerge from capitalism unenlightened, intimidated and burdened with the stamp of that system. The process of adapting their minds to the new social structure takes a long time and is extremely difficult. . . .

"We want to develop democracy for the people. The scope of democracy depends on the ideological resistance which we can offer to the Right whenever it tries to exploit this democracy to attack the Party and the people's government, whenever it tries to transform criticism into a sharp attack. If we effectively silence the Right a few times, then on the one hand we shall educate the masses to differentiate between friend and foe, and on the other, Rightist elements will have to think ten times before they utter a word. . . ."

This amounted to a bald justification of any means available for

---

* He cited a skit, since censored, about an entrance examination to modern Polish universities. ". . . And what is the Polish radio's best program," the Professor asked. "Moscow. In the Polish program." "Excellent. It always makes me sleep so well. And now the last question 'What is the best road to socialism?" "The one that is the longest . . ."

the suppression of dangerous thoughts. It was reinforced by a deep recognition that the majority of Poland's eggheads were no longer reliable for the Party's purposes. "It would be better," Werblan admitted, "if we had sufficient strength, if we had a sufficient number of Party intellectuals to win this struggle by way of criticism, by way of a free combat between the art proclaiming our truth and that other art, but we do not have such elements; our comrades have taken sides with the adversary. We must therefore win this battle with the force of a workers' state and its monopoly on propaganda instruments, maybe even worse, but nevertheless win."

Viewed by the standards of the free society, this kind of talk could be equated with the basest totalitarianism. Yet it was not exactly so. Even in such a repressive statement as Werblan's, there was a strong element of apology for the method used. This element would have been present in no other Communist country. "There is obviously a definite risk," Werblan conceded, "in all limitations on democracy (this in turn is not understood by the dogmatists). What serves us and what serves the bourgeoisie must be decided upon by well-defined Party collective bodies, i.e. the Party authorities, and these bodies are fallible. . . ."

This sort of bad conscience showed through time and time again, in the Polish drive against "revisionism." It appeared in Gomulka's own statements, as he continued to weigh the need (by Communist standards) for coercive measures against his own reluctance to use them. "We do not reject administrative measures [Communese for 'force']," he said in October, 1958, "but we must not forget that administrative measures are only an auxiliary factor in the line of our political action." Perhaps, he added hopefully, "discussion groups from factories" could visit recalcitrant writers and persuade them to write what the Party wanted.

The task of the confused Gomulka censorship was not made easier by the determined resistance of most Polish writers. In December, 1958, the Writers' Union formally protested the efforts to curb freedom of expression in their country, whether by "administrative methods" or not. The censors, noted the poet Mieczyslaw Jastrun, were now "confiscating not only the thunder but even the cloud." The Party answered with more attacks on "pessimistic black literature." Its own threats of further censorship were reinforced by strong pressure from Moscow. (One can imagine the reaction of the Soviet Central Committee, on hearing that the Polish Writers' Union had boldly telegraphed its congratulations to Boris Pasternak for winning the Nobel Prize for Literature.)

*   *   *

Despite such repression it must be admitted that two years after the October Revolution, Poland still retained a freedom of access and expression unknown anywhere in the Communist world. Western books continued to be translated into Polish, up to the sensitive borderground of George Orwell's *Animal Farm*. By and large, the philosophical and literary voices of Western Europe and the United States had been permitted to penetrate this country. Radio Free Europe might be attacked in the country's press, but the jamming stations were silent. Freedom might be hard-pressed by the instinct for dictatorship, but the tension between them does exist.

Most conspicuously, the freedoms of the October were retained in the Polish universities. Scientists, research scholars and teachers were still given an elbow room which the canons of Marxism, as interpreted by any other group of national Communist authorities, do not permit. Deans and professors, broadly speaking, could say what they think. Whatever the repressions ordered visited on the writers and political journalists, the window had been kept open for an entire new generation of Polish students.

But no amount of official humanism or felicitous comparisons with Czechoslovakia or the Soviet Union, could restore the eggheads' lost illusions. "Would it not be best," *Po Prostu* wrote just before its dissolution, "to dissolve the entire Party? Would it not be better to liquidate the old and begin with the reconstruction of a new Communist Party in Poland? My Lord, how much simpler that would be. . . ."

For two stormy years the angry intelligentsia had occupied the center of the Polish scene, or so it had seemed at least to the foreign visitor or the foreign newspaper reader. Many of the other problems in Poland, e.g. the Church-State controversies, were locked within the people trying to solve them. The intellectuals, however, were articulate, and they liked to talk to foreigners. As a result, a foreigner's sojourn in Warsaw was apt to involve long and

very interesting hours debating the possibility of democratic Marxism with X in the Bristol Hotel or at the Krokodil night club, or
analyzing the significance of the workers' council movement with
Y at the Journalists' Club on Voksal, a roomy resort dedicated to
sometimes startlingly different varieties of food, wine and dialectics.
After some days of this indoctrination, even the hardest-shelled
visitor really believed that the future of the better world was intimately involved with the continued publication of *Po Prostu,* that
democracy had been dealt a fearful blow in the change of editors
at the illustrated weekly *Swiat,* that European civilization would die
if there were any more tampering with the editorial board of *Nowa
Kultura.* Frequently, foreign press reports on Poland reflected this
distortion of emphasis.

There was some truth in the intellectuals' concern. If among the
journalists, poets and others who gathered in the Warsaw watering
places was a liberal sprinkling of opportunists—a peculiarly aggressive chameleon-type was the former Ambassador to France, Jerzy
Putrament—there was a great deal of honest searching after justice.
The Marxist eggheadery was naive and often dangerously unac-
quainted with the life of the world around them. They had after all
been shielded from any direct contact with civilization between
1939 and 1956. To have prosecuted a search for truth, under their
circumstances, required both courage and honor.

Their influence all over the Communist world was and is tremendous. The same restless questioning that began with attacks on
"Stalinism" has been spreading into every guarded corner of this
world. For the conditions dividing the Poles from the other captive peoples, including the Russian, are only a matter of significant
degree. In every House of Culture throughout these countries there
has been debate, and much continuing debate the present structure
of Communism cannot stand. The regime in tightly controlled
Czechoslovakia has had to complain about the "utopianism" of its
youthful writers. In 1957 and 1958 there were serious crises because of literary "revisionist" tendencies in such "safe" satellites as
Bulgaria and Romania. In Russia itself, the questioning of the
youth took shape in a flurry of critical comment, most of it perforce
literary, which was serious enough to require Khrushchev's personal
attention. In fact, the greatest task of Khrushchev and his friends

in the Soviet Union is to keep Party control alive after most pre-
tense at party ideology has been swept away. Hence the intensity of
the crusades against "revisionism" and the movements back towards an effective if less bloody Stalinism. In literature and the
movies, to say nothing of politics, the old ideas of Zhdanov's Socialist Realism have been reinstated. The sectarian lines of Communism have been drawn tighter in every field, thus more or less
proving Kolakowski's point.

In these years of struggle within the Communist bloc, the angry
eggheads of Poland have acted as a focus for the general discontent. A Polish student was the most interesting visitor to any
Communist university, and concurrently, the object of greatest
suspicion by any regime. (Nonetheless, the number of Polish
student scholarships at the University of Moscow was increased
even after the Soviet Thaw ended, in an effort to find conformist
recruits.) Just as Gomulka has influenced the other Communist
leaderships, so the Warsaw intellectuals have powerfully influenced
every intelligentsia behind the Iron Curtain. They have re-introduced
the element of freedom.

They themselves are not very happy—especially the Marxists
among them. The doubts in Stalinism among the revisionists have
increasingly given way to doubts in the whole Communist system.
Since many of them still pretend to be convinced Communists, this
leaves them no respite from their mental gymnastics. Even the
Gomulkist Marxist theoreticians have been men of such proven
elasticity that they could probably justify the establishment of a
House of Morgan branch in Warsaw, on sound Marxist reasons—if
given a day to prepare their briefs. "We are revisionists," said
Gomulka's chief theorist Wladyslaw Bienkowski, "but within the
framework of Marxism." No framework was ever subjected to such
tension and torsion.

The unhappiest of all are the Party intellectuals currently charged
with the revitalization of Communism in their country. Now that
the element of compulsion is gone, no one wants to have any Communist connections, if they possibly can be avoided. The Communist Youth Organization, the Union of Socialist Youth, numbered
3,000,000 when membership was compulsory. It is now barely
80,000. "In the Warsaw Polytechnic," said Minister Zolkiewski,

just a year after the October Revolution, "there are 12 members of the Union of Socialist Youth out of 14,000 students." The university population, he conceded, is "fleeing from politics." Faced with the resolutely apolitical attitude of most Polish youth, the organizers sent out to recruit them are in the position of the hard-pressed movie operator handing out free dishes and chances on a new Cadillac to any patrons who will come.

At the same time, to placate the Russian defenders of orthodoxy, every new step away from the accepted version of Communism must be justified by "the peculiar demands of our country" or "economic necessity" or the often heard argument that "Marxism means change, doesn't it? Marx just couldn't have foreseen this world of today—the world of atomization." Conversely, every step at censoring revisionism must be reinforced by excuses that the pressure of capitalist imperialism is growing or that the *enragés* are shattering the Party mission by their dissension.

The surviving active revisionists continue to stray ever further away from Marx, as now interpreted, without bringing themselves to accept any ideological alternatives. They rightly protested in the beginning against the Stalinist's substitution of illusion for reality. Now they have produced their own kind of illusion. The graceful statue of Copernicus might almost have smiled, standing outside of the Academy of Sciences off Warsaw's *Nowy Swiat*. Not since the Cracow canon's works were pronounced heretical by the Inquisition 500 years ago had so many intellectuals puffed so hard to prove in public that the round world was still gloriously flat.

5

The Cardinal's Country

> "What then have the Christians suffered in that calamitous period, that would not profit everyone who duly and faithfully considered the following circumstances . . ."
>
> —St. Augustine, *The City of God*

O N MARCH 27, 1958 the pastor of the village church at Tomaszowice, near Lublin, was charged by Polish authorities with "anti-state activities" for converting a Communist on his death-bed. Besides producing this gratuitous addition to the Party's current weeding-out campaign, the priest had gone on in his funeral sermon to attack what the official press summarized as "the people's rule," "agricultural reforms" and "the principle of tolerance."

Two days later the same government which brought charges against Tomaszowice's priest held up distribution of a magazine called *Argumenty,* the official organ of the All-Polish Union of Atheists and Freethinkers. The censors' complaint was that the current issue contained an unduly serious attack on the Roman Catholic clergy, for "intolerance" and "hostile manifestations" towards the regime.

On their face, these two official acts are wildly contradictory. The first sounds like one of the commonplaces of orthodox Communist religious persecution, long familiar to the readers of *Pravda, Rude Pravo,* or for that matter Tito's *Borba,* since the heartening eccentricities of modern Yugoslav Communism have never included a relaxation of its war on the independent church.* The second item might have been given a Madrid or a Rome dateline, if some wire service editor had found it headless on his table. It would have been perfectly consistent with the more or less acute regard for Catholic sensibilities in countries where the Roman Catholic Church is a partly protected state religion.

Yet the attitudes behind *both* of these acts became a hallmark of the Gomulka government's treatment of Roman Catholicism. As viewed from Warsaw, the offenses cited would have been equal infractions. Both village priest and big city atheists had overstepped the bounds of the declared truce between the national Communist government and the national Catholic religion, which began with the ascent of Gomulka to power and the release of the Polish primate, Cardinal Wyszynski, from three years of confinement. Even on its face—to say nothing of its relative operating efficiency —the truce is one of the most signal political developments of the Communist era. It is crucial to Poland's "national Communist" government, for it is the fulcrum on which rests the inner stability of the country. It has been broken, or almost broken, many times. But its very fragility is the warrant of its continuance.

Gomulka's mass support in the country stems largely from the tolerance and active support he has given the religion of 96% of its people. The support comes from a population largely anti-Communist or at best apolitical entirely. This population accepts him as a patriot, his government as the best that a trying international situation will permit; but quite justly regards his treatment of religion as the hostage of his good intentions. So for Gomulka the moral is clear. There may be great danger for the physically weaker animal in this latest reenactment of Isaias' prophecy of

---

* Because it refuses to become a state church and remains at least a potential focus for Croatian Nationalism, the Roman Catholic church in Croatia and Slovenia remains in a state of seige. Church persecution in Yugoslavia, in fact, has grown all the more formidable for the comparative refinement of the regime's tactics.

the lion laying down with the lamb.* But the lion is well aware that if anything happens to the lamb in his custody, it will be impossible for him to maintain control of either the sheepfold or the jungle outside.

The exact circumstances enforcing this truce are unique to Poland. They involve a national tradition, an extraordinarily religious people, and an extraordinarily able church leader. The peculiar power of the Polish primate would be difficult to exercise in secularized, if nominally Catholic countries like France or Belgium; nor could it be realized in those intellectually unchurched parts of the world, e.g. certain areas of South America, southern Europe and parts of the United States where Catholicism presents the distressingly overbalanced picture of 98% processions and scarcely 2% St. Thomas Aquinas or Leo XIII.

But in discussing the Polish premises for the Truce, we would be foolish to underrate its universal significance. The Cardinal is a Pole, with an incandescent faith in the power of his country's history. His nationalism has fused itself completely with his religion, although on occasion it has warred spectacularly with religious authority. Several times in the last ten years Wyszynski courted the suspicion and disapproval of the Vatican in his insistence on Polish bishops for the former German territories, or his own way of dealing with the hostile Communist state. He is a man of supple dealings but iron will (what else could make a Pole found a national total abstinence society?), with both a shrewd political sense and a singular grasp of the constant relationship between theology and every-day Christian life. But his accomplishment can and should stand apart from its Polish circumstances. For his solution to Poland's particular religious problem is a brilliant and communicable answer to a universal question that has occupied the priests of all religions since the Illyrian soldier-emperor Diocletian decided that using bishops for lion-fodder was good Imperial policy: how to keep the faith alive, strong and influencing, in the face of the hostile state.

First for the local premises.

Poland is the most Catholic country in Europe. It is virtually

* For the record, 11, 6: "Calf and lion and sheep in one dwelling place . . ."

so even by simple numerical tabulation. Pre-war Poland had a population which was roughly 70% Roman Catholic. Over 4,000,000 of its people—most of the large Ukrainian and Byelo-Russian minorities, belonged to the Orthodox Church, although a further sizable segment of the Ukrainian minority was Uniate, that part of Orthodoxy which is in communion with Rome. There was a small, but healthy and flourishing number of Lutheran and Calvinists, less than 700,000 in all. Polish Jewry counted for some 3,000,000 souls—most of them pious believers, who set more store by the Talmud Torah than the political pronouncements of the emergent pre-war Zionists. The Russian annexations of the East took away almost all of Poland's Orthodox population, and all but a handful of the Uniates. In their terrible persecutions, the Jews were almost annihilated. The Protestants, principally Lutherans of both Polish and German stock, were either decimated by the German occupation or forcibly evicted in the corresponding Polish take-over of the Western territories.* The result is the present population figure of 96% Roman Catholic.

But numbers on census reports hardly tell the story. The distinguishing feature about Polish Catholicism is that most of its baptized are communicants. They work at their religion (in city parishes as well as in the country). Their piety shows itself most ostentatiously in the huge pilgrimages to the national shrines, notably the hilltop monastery of Jasna Gora ("Bright Mountain") that looks down on the otherwise undistinguished manufacturing town of Czestochowa. Each year visiting foreigners are regularly swept off their feet by the spectacle of literally hundreds of thousands, who go there for the Feast of Our Lady of Czestochowa. Up the tree-lined road they march from the factory streets to the sturdy Pauline monastery on the hill, to celebrate the anniversary of the August day in 1656 when King John Casimir dedicated the entire country to the Virgin Mary.

The mass piety is astonishing. In 1956, two months before Cardinal Wyszynski was released from confinement, almost a million and a half people came there in pilgrimage time to renew

---

* The native Polish Lutherans, strongly nationalist, were brutally persecuted by the Germans. Bishop Bursche, their leader, was one of the first Poles to be executed in the Nazi terror.

the king's vows. Even in the worst days of the pre-Gomulka persecution they could not be stopped. The most eloquent witness to their constancy is the organized hand-wringing which annually marks the pilgrimage season in the Communist press. "From time to time mass pilgrimages disorganize the life of the town," wrote *Trybuna Ludu* in October 1957, "disturb the supply system, paralyze public transportation, attract thousands of sharpers and tricksters." An understandably secular view.

It is not too hard to draw a crowd for a pilgrimage, as devil's advocates have been saying for centuries. A more accurate testimony to the faith of the Poles is the constant, everyday use of their churches. Poland is one of the few places in the world where a church is apt to be a populous place in the afternoon of a weekday, when no services are scheduled, simply from the fact of people dropping in to pray.

In their outward appearance, these well-used edifices show a great similarity to the mediaeval and Renaissance churches of western Europe. Originally or as reconstructed—the pure Gothic of St. Mary's in Cracow, austere St. John's in Warsaw, the Baroque interior of the Cathedral at Oliwa—they show the usual overlay of various architectural periods, with the interiors so often showing the classic Catholic combination of great art and gross gimcrackery. The Mass is the same as in Europe or anywhere else, with fewer local peculiarities than in Milan or Seville. The religious orders of the universal church are represented in strength—Jesuits, Dominicans, Franciscans, along with more peculiarly central European orders like the Paulines or Piarists.

There are two major features, however, which distinguish the Polish churches from their counterparts in the West. The first is this phenomenon of constant use. The second is that the sister churches in western Europe are many hundreds of miles away. To the east, in the area between the Bug River and the China Sea, only a handful of Catholic churches are allowed open and those under obvious heavy restrictions. Here in Poland is the half-isolated frontier of Catholicism. It has been so for the last 1,000 years.

The frontier fervency of Catholicism in Poland is the stronger for its connection with Polish nationalism. Czestochowa is not merely a shrine commemorating a pious occurrence or celebrated as the repository of the Black Madonna (which devout tradition insists was painted by St. Luke). It is the site of a famous siege in Polish history. In 1655 the country was overrun by the Swedish armies of Charles Gustavus. Thanks to the chronically centrifugal tendencies of the Polish nobility (some of whose leaders had invited the Swedes to visit), resistance was fractionalized and ineffectual. The reigning king, John Casimir, took refuge in the borderland of Silesia. Cracow and Warsaw had both fallen. Only the monastery at Czestochowa held out, garrisoned by a bare company of troops and its own 85 Pauline monks and brothers.

For forty days the prior, Augustine Kordecki, kept the resistance going. On the day after Christmas the Swedes retreated, and the example of their repulse worked as a catalyst in reorganizing the Polish resistance. Czestochowa was talked of as a miracle. The king, in one of the few laudable acts of his reign, dedicated the country to the Virgin Mary the following August, to signal the act that ultimately liberated his royal republic.

Czestochowa is one isolated example from the long intertwining of Poland's religious and political history. But it is only an appreciation of this intertwining that explains why atheist Communist ministers put cathedrals on a priority building budget, why Army officers and non-coms troop into Sunday services that their counterparts in most non-Communist Catholic countries would shun as a mark of clericalism, why an artistically unprepossessing portrait of the Virgin has been transformed into a Polish combination of Plymouth Rock and the Washington Monument.

The power of the church comes from this old-fashioned identification of a people's character with Latin Christianity, the abiding heritage of a frontier church. In countries of the more protected West, the ideal of the all-powerful nation and the universal church started butting heads very early in the game. The British ideology first grew great and fat by opposing its insular traditions to the appeal of a pan-European Church. The modern French idea of nationhood derives largely, if disastrously, from the opposition of Eighteenth Century logicians and revolutionaries to a French hierarchy which refused to accept the fact that the era of St. Louis IX had died. All these and similar divisive controversies inside Latin Christianity grew in an atmosphere where Latin Christianity was unchallenged at home.

In Poland this was never the case. The Poles were too far east for any Latin premises to get automatic approval. Historically, Poland is the easternmost stronghold of Roman Catholicism. Just as the Poles themselves have been surrounded by physical national enemies, the Polish religion has been beleaguered by opposing faiths: Orthodoxy on the east, Islam to the east and south, and after the Reformation, Lutheranism in the west. The Poles have been traditionally jealous of their outpost distinction. But it has left them for the last 1,000 years in a spiritual and emotional state of siege (when the besieging was not actually a military and political one as well).

The state of siege began almost with the beginnings of the Polish state. The reckless pride of the frontiersman began with it. As the German Harald Laeuen said in his book *Polnische Tragoedie:* "The ambition to be regarded as the forward wall of Europe was awakened before the work of pouring on the concrete was anywhere finished." Poland was converted to Christianity in 966—to use the handy historical date—when the chieftain Mieszko, the founder of the Piast dynasty, accepted baptism in the Latin rite. He thus made himself automatically a controversial figure in Slavonic circles. Except for the neighboring Czechs and Slovaks (and the Croats and Slovenes far to the South) the other Slavic tribes received Christianity from the spiritual legatees of Byzantium. They adopted the Cyrillic alphabet and the Greek liturgy (although translated into their vernaculars). They took over, too, the Orthodox idea of national churches, whose patriarchs were at once officials and servants of the local king as well as representatives of the universal church. The Poles on the other hand developed and never lost a strong sense of submission to the authority of the Supreme Pontiff, higher than kings and councils. Hand in hand with their zeal for the Roman Church went an intense desire to spread its doctrines eastward.

This missionary attitude deserves to be distinguished from the sword-in-hand evangelism of the Teutonic knights, whose potential heathen converts in Prussia and the Baltic regions were so worked over by the knights' exertions that most of them were only able to accept Christianity posthumously. For all its militancy *vis a vis* the East, the church in Poland developed early in its life a certain tolerance which was generally far ahead of its time. At the Council of Constance in 1417 Paul Wlodkowicz, the rector of the newly founded University at Cracow, denounced the sword-in-hand conversion technique as a violation of the natural law, which grants to all peoples, even pagans, the right to possess their own land and work out their own destinies, as long as they are peaceably disposed. Well supported in the Council, his thesis sealed the moral decline of the German knightly orders in the East. Happily they had been physically defeated by the Poles at the battle of Grunwald just seven years before.

The Poles, in fact, had secured by persuasion a far greater harvest of converts than the Germans by attempted intimidation. In 1386 Jagiello, the Grand Duke of Lithuania, accepted Catholicism as the state religion of his country in return for the hand of the heiress of Poland, Queen Jadwiga. By the early fifteenth century the combined Polish and Lithuanian Church, loyal to Rome as few others and solidly led by native bishops (the hierarchy in the first two centuries after conversion had included many foreigners) was sending its priests eastward along with the irregular advancings of the Polish armies.

The Reformation touched Poland and at one time claimed a considerable number of the nobility as converts; but its roots never sank deep. The peasantry stayed fast in their Roman beliefs, as did the kings. Not long after the founding of their order, the Jesuits brought into Poland the revived faith and discipline of the Counter-Reformation. As in Austria, they stamped their seal on the country in the form of hundreds of Baroque churches, and a network of schools. There was some harsh treatment of Protestants and their doctrines. In general, however, Poland was spared both the religious horrors of the Thirty Years War in Germany, and the methodical government persecutions of England or France. Tolerance was the rule more often than not.

There was, however, a notable lack of tolerance in the relations of Poles with their Orthodox neighbors on the east. Here the church remained a fighting missionary organization, with differences of doctrine sharpened by the clashes of territories and ways of government. One of the great martyrs of the Polish church, the heroic St. Andrew Bobola, was slaughtered by Cossacks whom he was trying to convert. The Ukrainians and Russians saw such things differently. The worst apostate in their border history was Andrew, son of Taras Bulba, the hero of Gogol's novel, who betrayed his faith and his country to fight with the Poles. In the last of several battles surrounding his defection, Taras pronounces the famous curse on the Poles, denouncing the West and preaching the coming victory of the Czar.

This border warfare between the Polish Catholics and their Orthodox neighbors hardly ever abated, although it was not necessarily conducted as furiously as inside the Bulba family. In 1596 the Poles succeeded in persuading a number of Orthodox dioceses to accept the supremacy of Rome, while keeping the liturgy and the theological shadings of Orthodox religion. The Uniate churches, as they were called, grew considerably. But their growth was checked by the rise in Russian military fortunes, since the Uniates, considered as apostates by the Czars, were subjected to the worst kinds of persecution.

After the eighteenth century partitions of Poland, the Catholic Church, officially speaking, supped at a lean cupboard. The Czars built Orthodox churches in Warsaw and heavily supported the rise of Orthodox congregations anywhere else. The surviving Uniates were induced to rejoin the Orthodox Church by whatever means at hand. The Polish magnates, who came to have considerable weight at St. Petersburg, shielded Catholicism to an extent, but preaching the Word in the Roman tongue was an uphill struggle, constantly.

In the West the Catholics had an even harder time of it. The Germans have always tended to look on the Poles as a species less than human, possibly because of their recurrently unsuccessful efforts to eliminate the Poles from the human race altogether. Catholicism, as the religion of the Poles, was never favored in the east of Germany, or the annexations thereto—except for several major enclaves like the city of Breslau, where German Catholicism was always very strong. In the latter part of the nineteenth century it was put under attack by Otto von Bismarck, the shark-minded chancellor whose diplomatic and military capacities only gained respectability when historians started comparing them with the deeds of his successors. Bismarck's *Kulturkampf* was directed against all Catholics, on the pragmatically sound grounds that he desired no people in the Kaiser's kingdom with even spiritual allegiance to the outside world. But it fell most heavily on the Poles who lived inside the old Imperial German borders. Bishops were imprisoned; priests proscribed; congregations deprived of churches. In turn the Catholic churches became the defiant repositories of Polish language and Polish culture. Before 1890 the *Kulturkampf* had ended with a tacit admission of defeat. It had not done much to cement either German-Polish, or Lutheran-Catholic relations.

The weight of all this disapproval and persecution had the effect of greatly strengthening Polish Catholicism. At a time when the churches of other European Catholic countries were harrassed by the tensions of nineteenth century liberalism, anti-clericalism, Ultra-Montanism, Darwinism, and almost every other theory worth mentioning, the church in Poland remained the great rallying-point for the submerged nation. Like the Church in Ireland, it grew impressive in the leanness of its strength. It was saved from the corresponding intellectual failings of the Irish Church by the prominence of many of its teaching priests and bishops.

It was thus in the nineteenth century that the union of the church and the nation was sealed. In this Slavic Western country, set upon equally by Orthodox Russians and Protestant Germans, every church became a flag, every sacrament a recital of the national anthem. The Church went into the twentieth century as the living conscience of its country, and the repository of its history. This was true on the broadest level. The peasant reckoned it so, as did the merchant and the count. Thanks to the accidents of history and the stubbornness of a nation's character, the synthesis of mediaeval Christendom marched into the modern era to keep its watch between Breslau and Brest-Litovsk.

*   *   *

The history of the Church in the short-lived inter-war Republic was by comparison with the past blissful. Under the Polish Constitution of 1921 the Church was given many privileges. If not actually acknowledged as the state religion, it was declared to have "the chief position" among faiths with equal rights. Although religious freedom was thus guaranteed, it can hardly be said that life for some Protestant congregations or the Orthodox parishes of the East was an officially prepared bed of roses. In general, however, there were no real hindrances placed in the way of the Protestant congregations. In the east the Orthodox had some trouble. In 1922 the Orthodox congregations were recognized by the state, and organized as an autocephalous national church under their own metropolitan (previously they had been under the rule of the Moscow patriarchate). But many disputes arose over the reclaiming of Catholic churches taken over by the Russians in the nineteenth century. There was a good deal of unpleasantness involved in some of these actions—and the Orthodox invariably were the losers.

The Catholic hierarchy itself did not take part in such violations of other peoples' religious beliefs. On the other hand the hierarchy did not do much to mitigate them. Many of the lower clergy, finally blessed with the resources of a surfaced nation behind them, provoked local outbursts against non-Catholic congregations. Priests and bishops did speak out, however, against the incidents of anti-Semitism that occasionally occurred, more frequently in the closing days of the Pilsudski-Beck government. Cardinal Hlond, the primate, was most prominent in this cause.

After 1926, the Church had recurrent clashes with the Pilsudski dictatorship, which was rather anti-clerical in tone. These troubles were of course dwarfed by the real persecution that accompanied the arrival of the Nazi Germans. Their war on the Church was far crueler than Bismarck's *Kulturkampf,* and the more curious since it was begun by an Army which included Catholic chaplains in its officer corps. The invading Army units were quickly succeeded by the various garrison and security arms of the SS and Gestapo. In due course of time, Polish Catholic priests became the favored occupants of concentration camps. By the end of the war, fully 40 per cent of the Polish clergy had been jailed by the Germans. Of this number half were either killed or died as a result of their imprisonment.

The Communists' seizure of power brought consequences equally as black for religion. On September 12, 1945, the new Polish Communist government abrogated the concordat with the Vatican signed in 1925, which codified the Church's right to nominate its own bishops, carry on religious instruction in the schools, etc. Several months earlier officials of the Soviet M.V.D. had arrived in Lublin to set up a campaign for eliminating religion from the life of the country by subverting it. They attacked the problem with zeal and, at first, with circumspection. The subversion was planned as a long-term project.

The immediate aim of the Communist government was to get itself legitimized, i.e. accepted by the world as the only legal government of the country. The assault on religion was subordinated to this end and for at least two years the government moved slowly. Until 1948 persecution expressed itself merely in number of indirect hindrances.

The first decisive step in the anti-religious campaign was the government confiscation of Caritas, the Catholic relief agency on January 23, 1950. This deprived the Church of its major device for directly improving the material lives of a poor people. With this came a corollary campaign of steady harassment. All large church estates were seized. Shrines would be closed for "repair." Troops and Communist youth groups would be assembled for the exact times normally given to Sunday Mass. In the government-controlled factories and offices, regular church attendance began to constitute grounds for an employee's dismissal. The meetings of Catholic youth groups were steadily curbed with restrictions. The entire social aspect of the Church, in short, was put under heavy attack. It became increasingly obvious, as well, that priests and prominent Catholic laymen were under secret police surveillance. By the spring of 1950, at least 500 priests and religious had been arrested.

For the Polish church, as with the other churches in Eastern Europe, the Communist attack on religion, in itself, came as no surprise. But the tactics were often puzzling in their indirection and subtlety. As the history of the post-war decade shows, many a well-meaning clergyman laboriously brushed from his eyes the sand of state secretariats, peace proposals and patriotic unity campaigns to discover that he had been used by the Communist state while meaning to defend himself against it, that he had been hopelessly compromised by his acts of seemingly harmless acquiescence. In 1950, commenting specifically on the situation in Poland, *Osservatore Romano* cited an apt historic parallel to the Communists' church notice. "The genuine Polish Catholics," it wrote, "are in the same situation as the first Christians during the persecutions of Decius. For tactical and strategic reasons no direct blows are used. Like Hitlerism before it, Communism does not want to create martyrs. In this situation the "regime Catholics" are a new embodiment of the *traditores* of the third century who agreed to surrender the Christian doctrine to the service of the pagan emperor. . . ."

Decius, a candid Communist Religious Affairs specialist would readily concede, had a comparatively easy time of it since he was dealing with only one church. The Communists found all three branches of Christianity—Protestant, Orthodox and Catholic— in their new dominions. Subverting each branch posed special problems of its own, and suggested varying degrees of success.

With the Orthodox, it must be admitted, the Communists had the least trouble. This is not to impugn the real resistance put up by thousands of Orthodox priests and bishops in eastern Europe, as before in the Soviet Union itself. But the very nature of Orthodoxy almost betrayed it. Through the centuries, Orthodoxy, descended directly from the Caesaro-Papalism of the Byzantine Emperors, has tended to shelter beneath the protecting arm of the state in which it finds itself. Each of the Orthodox churches is a national church, historically supported by its particular country. When a state turned Communist, with all its functions and functionaries, the Orthodox were in a sad predicament. Pledged traditionally to uphold—and depend on—the just state that St. Paul described in his Epistle to the Romans, they suddenly found it replaced by what amounted to the Beast of Revelation,* a beast which had succeeded to all the state's offices and laid claim to all of its legitimacy.

The bishops who protested were dealt with harshly. Others were found to replace them. For the Russians themselves had dis-

---

* "And out of the sea, in my vision, a beast came up to land, with ten horns and seven heads, and on each of its ten horns a royal *diadem;* and the names it bore on its heads were names of blasphemy . . ."

covered the propaganda usefulness of a subservient religious body during World War II, when they changed their previously open persecution of religion to a clever infiltration of the Russian Orthodox Church's hierarchy. The satellite governments of Romania, Bulgaria and Yugoslavia took their own behavioural cues from the Russian example, and largely succeeded in subverting their churches. In Romania, only the Uniate Church, that part of Orthodoxy which had returned to communion with Rome, resisted. The imprisonment and mortality rate among Uniate bishops and priests was shockingly high.

Protestantism posed a different kind of problem. Protestant congregations in Eastern Europe tended to include the more alert and intelligent elements of the middle-class population. In some cases their very alertness proved their downfall. Many well-read Protestant church leaders were disastrously impressed by the doctrines of Karl Barth, the moody Swiss theologian whose views on the Christian's attitude toward the state could best be described as a kind of Jean-Paul Sartre pietism. Barth's other-worldly *Sehnsucht* had not prevented him from making a determined stand aginst the Nazis in World War II. Unfortunately, he was never sufficiently impressed with the irreligious militancy of Communism. He seemed to regard it rather as some kind of good social force gone slightly wrong, against which Christians had no business preaching crusades. This ostentatious neutralism, coming from the foremost theologian of Protestantism, considerably sapped the normal anti-Communist fervor of many good Calvinist pastors. So did the sometimes extreme fraternal zeal of the World Council of Churches, which persisted in inviting to its councils Communist-line clerics like the infamous Bishop Peters of Hungary—possibly on the theory that in any truly ecumenical religious gathering the devil's point of view should be heard, too.

The passive attitude of Barth and those like him worked particular havoc among the East European Protestants. They had, however, a few impressive leaders who rejected Barth's version of earthly appeasement. Bishop Lajos Ordass of the Lutheran Church in Hungary will stand out in history as a man who yielded to no one in his opposition to Communism, and possessed more ability to withstand it than most. He was far more intelligent in his opposition than his opposite number, Cardinal Mindszenty. The Lutheran Bishop of Berlin, Otto Dibelius, retained a shrewd and saintly attitude towards the Communists, one which most closely parallels that of Wyszynski. He preached no "crusades" against Communism; but he fought the Communist state whenever it tried to encroach on the Church's ground—which, by Lutheran canons, includes the education of the young as well as the formal ministry. Although most of his flock lives in areas under Communist control, and some of his pastors were arrested, Dibelius was never touched by the puppet East German regime in Pankow. He became too important a leader in the lives of a largely Lutheran population.

Dibelius and Ordass aside, the Communist states of Eastern Europe found it relatively easy to infiltrate the independent Protestant clergy, confused alternately by the theological neutralism of Barth and others and their own traditions, notably in case of the Lutherans, of a dependent state church. With the Catholics the problem was more serious. The arterial link with Rome proved the principal difficulty in every local effort to subvert the Church. The entire Communist strategy, therefore, centered on the effort to cut the artery. Moscow hoped to encourage the rise of national churches, independent of outside control, but by definition dependent on the state mechanism in one particular country. It has often been observed that the Roman Catholic communion is "authoritarian"—a pejorative definition, as the word is generally used. Without entering into detailed explanation of the term here, we must conclude that the very "authoritarian" structure of the Roman Church was what made it difficult for the Communists either to infiltrate or colonize.

The Communists in Eastern Europe did not want to destroy the Church, if for no other reason than that the Russian example had proved this an impracticable, not to say an unattainable goal. Their attempt to *subvert* it was done rather on the analogy of the Japanese *judo* expert whose whole art is based on his facility for using the opponent's own strength to stun him. In every country, therefore, they tried first and always to undermine the authority of the bishops, as custodians of the link with Rome. If they could render the congregations headless, they knew they could control them. Few Christians in fact have paid so much attention as the

Communists to the truism given by St. Paul: "And in proportion as a man sees his bishop keeping silence, let him stand in greater awe of him. For when anyone is sent by the master of the house as his steward, we ought to receive him as him who sent him. Clearly then we should regard the bishop as the Lord himself."

When the Communists arrived in Poland, both the leading bishops, August Cardinal Hlond, the primate, and Adam Cardinal Sapieha, Archbishop of Cracow, were old. At least in the very early stage of the Communist rule, they were also too strong to risk suddenly alienating. Hlond died in 1948. Sapieha followed him in 1951. It was therefore natural that all the regime's attention and the bulk of its energies in this field be concentrated on breaking the authority of the new Primate of Poland, Stefan Cardinal Wyszynski.

The Primature of Poland, it must be explained, is not the honorary office to which Americans and English Catholics are accustomed. In Spain, England, or the United States, the primate is at best a *primus inter pares,* the bishop whose possession of the country's first and oldest see gives him a kind of precedence among his fellows.* Not so in Poland, or for that matter in Hungary. The Primate of Poland is by tradition and by accepted law the head of the national church. In the days of the kingdom the Primate had the power to crown the king or refuse coronation. He was regent of the kingdom during an interregnum.

Thanks to the efforts of Cardinal Hlond, the Archbishop of Warsaw had been given *ex officio* the ancient primatial see of Gniezno, where the first Polish bishops reigned, as well as his own city see. Since World War II, the Primate has also been administrator of the Western Territories recovered from Germany. All this diocesan power, added to his primatial prerogatives, make

---

* In the United States the bishop of the primatial see of Baltimore is no longer made a cardinal (the last cardinal in the Baltimore see was Cardinal Gibbons, who died in 1921). This is the result of the late nineteenth century reactionary Vatican suspicion that American Catholics, due to their distance and different ways of political thinking, e.g. about the problems of an established church and church-state relations, are not quite so reliable as European Catholics and hence should not be given any imposing office around which they might crystallize the idea of an independent church. That this superstition has been apparently codified into unwritten Church law is a sad relic of parochial Italianism.

the Cardinal Archbishop of Gniezno and Warsaw probably the most powerful local prelate in the Roman Catholic Church, outside of the Pope himself.

The selection of Wyszynski for this office was somewhat unexpected. He had been a favorite of Cardinal Hlond's, it is true, but his background and interests would generally have been regarded as too radical for the Primatial see, in a country whose very religiosity was under heavy attack. He had no title of nobility, or particular family distinction. He was born at Zuzela, in the diocese of Lomza, on August 3, 1901, the son of the parish organist and schoolteacher. As far as his father's calling was concerned, he was a conformist, not a rebel. He became distinguished for his piety, enough to earn him an early trip to the diocesan seminary at Wloclawek. He was ordained in 1924.

Father Wyszynski was a scholar, and the Church realized it. He went on to the Catholic University at Lublin to get a doctorate in Canon Law in 1929, whereupon he took the train west to Belgium, Rome, France, Holland and Germany, intent on studying the Church's solutions for modern social problems. He spent some time at the University of Louvain and at the Jesuit college in Rome, the Gregorian, before returning to Poland to put some of his ideas into practice.

Like many young European priests of his day (although unfortunately not enough) Wyszynski was critically impressed by the translation of Catholic morality into ideas of social and economic justice, as begun by Pope Leo XIII, and continued by Pius XI. He took up his headquarters at the Wloclowek Seminary, where he taught. But he devoted most of his time outside of classroom hours to highly active campaigns to keep the Church in touch with the factory worker, who was then posing a crisis in the European Church's handling of spiritual and social problems. He was no stranger to a trade union meeting hall. At one point he founded a Christian Workers University, designed to set up a joint program of discussion and instruction for blue-collar men in the area. He started, also, a Catholic Library for workers in Wloclowek.

Inevitably he addressed himself to the problems of Communism, which represented a growing temptation to the exploited workers in Polish industry. He wrote a good deal, mainly on social problems, trade unionism, and the rights of workers. His output of those years included several books and a stream of articles for the church and university presses. In one article published during the thirties, called "The intelligentsia in the vanguard of Communism," he cited several reasons for Communism's future success in Poland: 1) pauperization of the people as a result of crises and wars; 2) unemployment; 3) mechanization of industry, and 4) defective division of land in the country. Unfortunately few people in politics paid much attention to this.

In the context of his Church, he represented the younger generation which had taken seriously the social gospel of the modern Papal Encyclicals. A poor boy himself, he was appalled by the genuine inequities existing between classes and pocketbooks in the Polish republic. He was aware of Communism and its perennial appeal to people who have been deprived of their share of the world's goods. He studied his sociology and economics hard enough to realize that the pressures of modern Europe were such that no church, however sanctified, could save its apostolate by a mere repetition of the words *Unam Sanctam Catholicam et Apostolicam*. Revolted equally by Communism and a European's idea of cartel capitalism, he set out to take the church to the people, as zealously as any man of his time.

World War II he spent in hiding. His bishop had ordered him to escape from the Germans, who did not fancy the idea of aggressive, socially conscious Polish clergymen running about loose. In 1945 he returned to Lublin, where for a few years he was a professor at the Catholic University. In 1946, he was consecrated Bishop of Lublin, a see he held until his elevation to the primature.

*   *   *

Wyszynski represented a new Europe in the churchly world as fully, if more constructively, as the members of the Polish Politburo in their newly confiscated striped trousers showed a new Europe of politics. He was in roughly the same modest social boat as his cardinal contemporaries, Josef Mindszenty, the son of a farmer at Cehe Mindscent and Aloysius Stepinac, who came from a peasant family in Krasic, near Zagreb.

The image of the lean-fingered prince bishop dies hard, however, especially in American consciousness. The Cardinal Archbishop of an ancient European see can still be conveniently pictured as a cultivated younger son of an old noble house, who plays Mozart on his palace spinet while waiting for the steward's report from the wine cellar. It is true that illustrious members of the nobility continue to find their well-traveled way into the hierarchy, although it is debatable how exactly they would fit the stereotype. Count von Galen, the German Bishop of Muenster was a noteworthy recent example. Poland, in fact, had before Wyszynski's time a long tradition of episcopal nobility. During the years after the Polish partitions the Vatican made a practice of nominating members of the leading Polish families to the heirarchy. It was felt with justice that the nobility represented the social and political rallying point of this nation that had lost its statehood. Since the bishops were in effect the acting representatives of the political nation, the logic was clear. The flowering of this system was the late Adam Cardinal Sapieha of Krakow.

Sapieha was to some the uncrowned king of Poland. A member of an old princely family, he was himself not far from the storybook bishop idea. His assurance and a not inconsiderable wit were effective bolsters to his sanctity, when dealing with two succeeding teams of totalitarian interlopers. In the German occupation he once entertained the Nazi Governor General and his staff in his palace, serving them on his rich china precisely the same wretched ration then being allotted to each Polish citizen. As his power in the country was tremendous, they ate their food.

He was as curt with the Communists as with the Nazis. Shortly after the end of World War II they refused him a passport, on grounds that he might present the government in a "bad light" while overseas. "Why should I criticize you?" he replied. "I have every reason to praise you. The churches have never been so full."

It is doubtful, however, if all the Cardinal of Cracow's wit, courage and sanctity could have prevailed against a whole decade of Communism. He was of the old school in the matter of Church-State relationships. If the state became hostile, he and those like him would resist it with all the weight of their influence, and force the persecutors to desist. For they were very conscious of the church's historic and formidable political power. If the state were both hostile and overwhelmingly powerful, however, the expedient was that of Christian martyrs through the centuries—to stand on the faith and die for it, without compromise or concession to the godless.

This view, as expressed in the extreme, later became the stand of Cardinal Mindszenty in Hungary, although he differed sharply from Sapieha in almost all other respects. In 1945, even before he became Primate and Archbishop of Esztergom, Mindszenty threw down the gauge to the Communists. He organized the Catholics of Hungary in a series of mass pilgrimages and crusades. He preached a gospel of no compromise. He made no distinctions between different varieties of Communist government. He hoped quite openly for the days when the Church could again control its own Catholic Party. After the Hungarian revolution of 1956 briefly liberated him, almost his first act was to found a short-lived Catholic Party in politics.

This was not the stand of Wyszynski. When he was installed as Primate, in the Cathedral of Gniezno, his opening words were carefully designed to preclude any thought either of organizing a new Catholic party or looking back with nostalgia to an age when such a political force would have been possible in his country. "I am not a politician," he said, "not a reformer, not a man of action. I come as your spiritual father." Having made this point, he embarked on a course of what his supporters have frankly defined as "political compromise" with the Communist ruling party. The compromise, as Wyszynski was to show, would stop short of "ideological compromise," i.e. substantive concessions in matters of faith, morals or philosophy. But it was an effort to get along, in the manner of a priest who must minister to a prison of which he is himself an inmate.

The older bishops did not hold back their protests. Sapieha made clear his own doubts about Wyszynski's 1950 agreement with the Communist government. But Wyszynski's idea of cautious conciliation had its defenders, and the defenders included some highly placed men inside the Vatican. For, although necessitated by the Communist conquest of a new Europe, it was an old position in the Church, and there was an old debate about its efficacy.

For twenty centuries Christians have carried on this debate.

During times of persecution it naturally reaches an extreme of intensity. On the one hand, to use a military analogy, are the bishops who prefer like Mindszenty to throw down the challenge to the hostile state and withdraw into a fortress, defiantly at odds with the state surrounding it. They would push St. Augustine's idea of the *Civitas Dei* to a relentlessly logical conclusion—one which Augustine probably did not himself exemplify. Their aim is either to force the enemy to withdraw from the fortress by the quality of their resistance, or die if necessary in the defense.

The other side of the debate chooses the more venturesome, and spiritually more risky course of staying on the plain to maneuver, i.e. to keep the life of the Church going in the midst of the hostile state as long as possible. This way courts the danger that the faithful may be infiltrated, cut off and disposed of piecemeal by the enemy. It demands the coolest leadership and the most disciplined spiritual followers. But it also holds out the reward that with a force in being on the field, the enemy might be either persuaded or forced to tolerate its existence. It takes into account, furthermore, the formidable ideological challenge of modern Communism, which demands itself a formal religious obedience, but whose totality makes it an infinitely more dangerous enemy than the worst of the *Kulturkampf,* the anticlerical liberals, or indeed the pagan Roman statists. It is a role, historically, which is probably less congenial to Augustine's thought than to that of Aquinas, who always set great store on the Christian's injecting himself into the life around him, however unpleasant that life might be.

In modern times the second school of thought has been brilliantly enunciated in Europe, and given brilliant support, notably by the former Vatican pro-Secretary of State, the present Archbishop of Milan, Cardinal Montini. At one point Pope Pius XII himself championed it and one suspects that his successor, John XXIII, is even more sympathetic. The arguments of this determinedly apolitical type of Catholicism have been reinforced by disastrous past experience. Europe is no stranger to the sight of heavily subsidized state Churches, holding very definite political as well as religious positions, wedded to very definite political relationships. As one of the new school, Coadjutor Archbishop Jachym of Vienna expressed it: "We are trying to reestablish the church on a mass basis, which excludes no one because of his political beliefs." In making this statement Jachym went on to cite a maxim of the brilliant Austrian Catholic writer, Frederich Heer: "The church never intended to serve as night watchman for the citizenry."

It is no coincidence that the greatest strides in the post-war Christian Democratic movement were made not by priests, but by old-school laymen like DeGasperi and Adenauer. Many of the brightest younger prelates tended on the contrary to shy away from active Church participation in politics. They felt not only that such participation automatically alienated whole segments of populations, e.g. Socialists, from getting the Church's sacraments. They were aware also that Church political parties, or uncompromising Church opposition to secular parties, had in past years impeded the march of social justice in Europe, like a sleepy hippopotamus (to borrow T. S. Eliot's Anglican analogy) who grumpily upsets the bustling river traffic every time he surfaces. Through Montini's influence at the Vatican, the Church began in the 'forties to look with sympathy on these new socially conscious prelates, who hoped to be the more pastoral for being the less political.

Wyszynski belonged to this group from the start of his episcopate. He had the advantage, also, of an extraordinarily sensitive set of political antenna and a background, both practical and theoretical, in dealing with the Church's social problems, Communism among them. He showed a deep appreciation, on personal as well as technical sociological grounds, of the extensive economic problems of Polish society, which the Communists so loudly set out to correct. His feel for practical sociology and politics carried itself even into the language of his theological pronouncements. ("We are a nation of individualists," he once told a student audience, "but Grace socializes.") Like the bishops who converted the first heathen Piast kings, he was not afraid of putting alien forces and theories into Rome's capacious baptismal font.

*   *   *

The accession of the socially conscious primate coincided with an intensification of the Communists' campaign against religion.

It was no accident that this followed Gomulka's downfall in early 1949; then as now Gomulka's ideas of national Communism included a relatively hands-off policy towards religion. With Gomulka in prison and the last non-Communist internal opposition ended as well, the Bierut government flexed its muscles and proceeded to give the Church a long-promised pummeling. Only a few months after he was installed, Wyszynski wrote a vigorous letter to Bierut protesting the recruitment of "patriotic priests" in the standard Communist pattern. "We are deeply grieved," he told his parishes at the same time, "by so many tragedies of priests' souls that do not withstand the pressure of perplexing circumstances."

In April 1950 Bierut offered the Church an armistice. The state promised freedom of religion, freedom of the Church press, and uninterrupted religious instruction in the schools and government institutions. The price asked was the Church's agreement to do nothing that would hinder "the building of socialism." The offer was part recognition of the Communists' failure to set up anything like an independent national Church, whatever successes they had in recruiting a few score "patriotic priests." It was also an attempt to implicate the Church in the government's activities, through the implicit recognition it gave.

Wyszynski signed the 19 clause agreement, although not only many of the older bishops but the Vatican looked darkly upon it. It was the logical result of his conviction that the church must bend over backwards in the prison atmosphere of eastern Europe, to emphasize its non-involvement in politics. Any ecclesiastical ventures into politics, as Cardinal Mindszenty's experience showed, could be seized on by the Communists and made the excuse for new punitive measures. Wyszynski and other Polish bishops also signed the Stockholm Peace Appeal—a less justifiable participation in international Communist propaganda. He explained this act with the weak excuse that the most diverse elements in the country should join in the "effort."

No sooner had the cardinal scratched these ultimate demarcation lines on the ground than the Communist regime jumped over them. The attempts at recruiting patriotic priests resumed, as did the activities of the spurious progressive Catholic Pax movement (see below). Bierut's religious overseers tightened the pressures against religious instruction of Polish children. They completed the take-over of Caritas, the church's large and flourishing welfare organization.

The Primate reacted. "We gave an irrefutable proof of the church's good will," he noted in a statement to the Communist authorities," [but] since our signing nothing has changed in the government's negative attitude towards agreement. . . . Your asking for new conditions to implement the agreement may be a normal method for Soviet justice, but it certainly shocks those whose ideas of justice are Polish. Soviet justice has been described as a backward step, which goes back to the first lispings of lawgivers, when society was not yet organized on a system of law. Soviet justice despises, distorts, ignores, presses underfoot all that has been acquired in 20 centuries of glorious civilization. Are you a Polish government, with ideas of honor that must perforce be Polish, to countenance this? If you do we the episcopate will be witnesses to this unthinkable fact before the people and before history."

With the advantage of hindsight, such indignation at a Communist double-cross might seem naive. It may have been, in the circumstances. But Wyszynski's concessions had the advantage of giving the Church an absolutely irreproachable position in the eyes of the country. This included Communists of the Gomulka persuasion, for in appealing not to Rome, but to the nation, the Cardinal rubbed quite a few Communists' consciences. He had done his best to make peace, and he had been rejected. In the context of the time it was a very different thing from Mindszenty's action of declaring war on sight, in 1945.

The tempo of persecution then increased to the point of violence. Caritas had been taken over. The schools and religious houses were systematically closed down. The monastery and convent schools, 135 in 1945, had gone down to 50 by 1952. In the period 1952 to 1954, eight bishops and up to 1,000 priests, nuns and monks were imprisoned outright. In 1953 hundreds of priests and nuns of ethnic German stock were forcibly transplanted from the Western Territories to central and eastern Poland, on the pretext that they were plotting to restore German rule. On his visit to Rome in 1951, Wyszynski had gained from the Vatican the concession of appointing Polish titular bishops to the vacated German sees in the West. It was important, in view of the constant regime accusations that the Vatican was plotting against Poland with the Germans. (This was one of the few effective propaganda cards that Bierut had to play.) Bierut turned it down, and refused to let the bishops take possession of their administrative sees.

Through all this the faithful remained so. There were cases of farmers who drove the "patriotic priests" from their churches, or fishermen who severely handled Party officials warning them away from church. Religion went partly underground. A bishop visiting a country locality after the October Revolution was shocked to hear the children deny any knowledge of their catechism. He found out later that they had been rigidly instructed never to discuss their catechism before strangers.

Possibly the most bizarre case of Communist retaliation against believers (but in the era of the money-grabbing New Class by no means atypical) occurred in a Baltic fishing village just before the 1956 October. A man had joined the Party for reasons of opportunity, then repented and confessed his sins to the priest on his deathbed. When the local officials found this out, they retaliated against the deceased's survivors, by confiscating all the black market goods he had been allowed to hoard as the privilege of Party membership.

At one point in the struggle period the Primate received a group of "progressive Catholics," who took great pains to tell him of "the many roads down which the church may march." "There is one road you have forgotten," he added, "the road to prison." On September 29, 1953, agents of the U.B. called at the Cardinal's Warsaw residence at 17 Miodowa. They took him off to the first of several monastery hiding-places, after thoroughly searching his apartments. The formal charge against him was "persistent abuse" of his functions. In the Communist mode it had been preceded by a long article in *Trybuna Ludu* denouncing Wyszynski as an "enemy of the people." The writer, incidentally, was Edward Ochab, the same Central Committee member who later paved the way for Gomulka's return.

The arrest was the final blow in a harrowing year. In January the regime 'convicted' four priests and three laymen employed at the Cracow chancery on the usual charges of spying and black market activity. Arrests, searchings and imprisonments increased, culminating just before the Cardinal's arrest with the conviction of Bishop Czeslaw Kaczmarek of Kielce of "spying" for the United States and the Vatican. It was on this issue that Wyszynski went to jail; for he had followed Kazmarek's sentencing with an uncompromising attack on the government's anti-religious policy.

With this the campaign of the government's new Religious Affairs Bureau reached its apogee. It had progressed much as similar efforts in other Communist countries: first the confiscation of the Church's public charitable functions, then legal invalidation of Church marriages, then the closing of schools and religious instruction elsewhere. The final formal step, a decree of February 9, 1953, required prior official consent to Church appointments; the government also gave itself the right to recall Church officials. All these steps had been taken later in Poland than anywhere else in the Iron Curtain countries. This was not only a back-handed tribute to the peculiar strength of the Polish Church, but to some extent a reflection of Wyszynski's skilfull leadership. He had compromised in every reasonable way, made concessions beyond the point of normal prudence, but resisted only when attack was made on religious essentials. Besides gaining the Church time, this strategy had the merit of forcing the regime into a series of open attacks, where the Communists would have much preferred either one sweeping showdown or the tested joys of progressive infiltration.

After several transfers the cardinal was ultimately confined under heavy guard in a monastery at Komancza, an isolated spot in the extreme southeastern part of the country. He was not badly treated, merely kept in strict seclusion from anyone his jailers did not want him to see. He later called the experience a "rest cure."

The anti-religious campaign, which Warsaw called Operation X, continued with some success during his absence. But the gains in church disorganization were more than offset by the renewed fervor of the population. On November 10, 1954, Khrushchev gave the order from Moscow to turn off the tap, in a party decree denouncing the use of violence against "believers." In Poland there was a sense of relief all around at the ensuing relaxation.

A year later the government officially offered Wyszynski his freedom, if he would renounce his primatial see. He refused, exactly as had Stepinac in Yugoslavia, given a similar proposal. The offer from Gomulka the next year was a genuine one. In the last week of October, 1956 Gomulka's two most trusted advisors, Zenon Kliszko and Wladyslaw Bienkowski, made the first Communist trip to Canossa, by going to the cardinal's jail. He was freed unconditionally on October 28. On the way back to Warsaw he stopped off at Czestochowa for a quiet prayer.

The government met his conditions for the new Truce: basically, release of all imprisoned clergy and compliance with the 1950 agreement, in particular the provision allowing religious education in the schools. In return the Cardinal gave his implicit promise to throw the weight of the Church behind the Gomulka government, to stabilize the freedoms won in the October, but curb the explosive popular feelings that might bring the Russians back in force, as in Hungary. Cheering, praying crowds began to swell around his residence just a few hours after his very unobtrusive return to Warsaw. "The shepherd was lost," he commented, "but the sheep did not scatter."

*   *   *

A truce is a rough equality of forces, codified. Nothing is more characteristic of Poland's strange Frozen Revolution than the cardinal's truce with Gomulka, which has been kept on both sides with relative consistency. Every child in Poland, who requests it, receives one hour a week of religious instruction in the lower schools, two hours at the high school level. The religious education teachers are either priests or laymen. They are paid by the Communist state. Their classes are generally held in the state school buildings.

Similarly all the priests and religious in prison were released. Bishop Kaczmarek was formally declared free for "lack of evidence." A number of religious objects and some properties have been returned to the Church, gradually. In February, 1958, the government renewed the long suspended permission for Polish priests to study in Rome. The massive Party attacks on the Church have ceased, and with them the restrictions against those who participate in religious activities.

The Church has responded by continuing the national equilibrium, through admonition, injunction and example. The Church has been helpful also on an international level. Despite all the German pressures at Rome in the Pontificate of Pius XII, the 1958 Papal Yearbook finally gave Polish names to the dioceses in the former German Western Territories.

The Cardinal's intervention in the crucial 1957 election was decisive. He insured that Gomulka's government would win its unprecedented free election, with his usual tact, by issuing an announcement of the episcopate condemning any boycott of the elections. Bishops and priests all over the country ostentatiously put unmarked (i.e. pro-government) ballots into the boxes. (The cardinal himself voted unobtrusively in an unexpected polling place. He wanted no pictures.) Since then the Church, Wyszynski in particular, has directly helped the government by its continual appeals for abstinence, hard-work, more self-discipline on the part of each citizen, in view of the country's appalling economic problems.

There was striking, if coincidental similarity in the type of appeals for diligence and moderation given to Poland's discontented, hard-drinking working population by Gomulka, the atheist man of ethics and Wyszynski, the Christian man of morals. Gomulka, in one of his speeches to workers' groups, commented on this with interesting indirection. "Today," he said, "I visited the miners in Zabrze, where St. Barbara's feast was being celebrated, and I was told by the comrades that the miners went to church in the morning and a priest gave the sermon, and this priest repeated more or less word for word what I had said yesterday about working on Sundays and feastdays . . . he urged the miners to work, to give the country that coal. It seems to me that if we had more such priests—of course I am not saying literally that they are to be in a cassock—but if we had more such priests with such convictions in our party organizations, or even among authorities, then things would be better in this district we mentioned. . . ."

Soon after Gomulka made his memorable statement at the Ninth Plenum of the Central Committee, on May 15, 1957: "Our party cannot as part of its policy apply administrative pressure to bear on believers without taking account of the fact that the former conflict with the church set millions of believers against the people's government and estranged them from socialism." This has remained the Warsaw government's policy. It is often enunciated by Bienkowski, the Minister of Education, who regularly performs at Party meetings the verbal gymnastics with which Gomulka justifies to his own faithful this apparent breach in the dikes of "Marxist-Leninism."

For all this official and unofficial agreement, the church-state relationship has been a truce in armor. Even in its most tranquil moments, restrictions on Church activities have remained. It is no coincidence that the cardinal's semi-official weekly newspaper, the excellent *Tygodnik Powszechny,* was not able to get a government paper allotment for any more than 50,000 copies (although it sells prodigiously on the newsstands). The faculty of law and social sciences at the Catholic University of Lublin, although taken away by the Bierut government, has not been restored, and there is a rigidly observed ceiling on the number of students the University is allowed to educate. The government has "allowed" publication of *Argumenty,* the official organ of a newly revived Association of Atheists and Free-thinkers, which makes its regular violent attacks on religion (moderated, as we have seen, by the official censor) without implicating any "official" Party paper.

There was always grumbling among the Party activists about the prevalence of religion in the schools. "Why does the religious instructor have a monopoly for moral education and ethics in our lay schools?" asked the Party youth newspaper in March, 1958. Unquestionably the return of religion brought some reprisals against the previously privileged children of Party workers by the great majority of children, who with their parents had suffered for their Catholicism. As the lady of a Communist New Class official complained: "At least under the Fascist government [i.e. the pre-war Pilsudski government] one had a choice about sending the children to religious instruction. Now the social pressure is so great that a child must go to avoid being singled out for punishment." *Trybuna Ludu* from time to time printed similar complaints from its Party readers. ("No child wants to sit beside the daughter of the district Party secretary," wrote a man in

Zamosc, "because the children say she must be in alliance with the devil.")

Such scare stories, as might be expected, were full of exaggerations. In fact the over-literal Party press began to print them even before religious instruction had resumed, which somewhat detracted from the white heat of their indignation. On the whole, persecution and the hard geographic facts of life have brought to the Polish churchgoer an impulse to tolerance rather than reprisal. But religious teaching is nonetheless a constant source of potential truce-breaking. So, to a lesser extent, is the matter of Church appointments. The government began to intervene in a few Church appointments early in 1958. Although it has the right under the terms of the Truce to approve them, it had not previously exercised its veto power. In these cases, the Church declined to submit a second choice, preferring to let the livings lie temporarily vacant.

In the middle of 1958 there was further trouble over the distribution of relief supplies. Gomulka consistently refused to turn back to the Church its previously confiscated relief organization, Caritas. The cardinal imported relief supplies notwithstanding, principally from American Catholic sources, on an informal basis. They were distributed under Church supervision, with unofficial goverment acquiescence. When the Church wished to formalize the system, the government then insisted on official participation. In Communist language this means over 50% of the votes and 99% of the authority and credit. The Church refused, and an impasse resulted. For months relief goods sat in the warehouses, as the argument over their distribution grew more severe.

On July 21, 1958, all these tensions came to a head, when the prosecutor of the city of Kielce, accompanied by a small force of police, invaded the national shrine at Czestochowa and confiscated books and pamphlets which had been printed there. The Polish hierarchy, and the great portion of Polish Catholicism, reacted with shocked indignation. They denied the regime's charge that the cardinal's Institute of the National Vows in the monastery there had been evading censorship.* They accused the Communist

* Since the primate's institute is a social organization, the argument ran, it is exempt from the censor's attentions to the press.

officials of desecrating the shrine, after having entered by force
and making off with Church funds. The cardinal ordered that Au
gust 10 be set aside as a special day of prayer throughout the
country, by implicit apology for the insult to the national patron
saint.

The indignation was justly aroused. For the Czestochowa raid
was only the symptom of a suddenly heightened campaign against
the Church in the entire official press. The regime spokesmen
talked darkly of Vatican influences at work disturbing the original
truce—dating from Wyszynski's 1957 visit to Rome—a testing of
the truce in the worst Communist tradition. Various 'gentlemen's
agreements' between Church and State were broken off. The
government took action to ban all religious emblems from state
school rooms and, more substantively, to forbid any members
of religious orders from teaching the religion classes permitted.
Gomulka himself, on September 24, made the sharpest attack
since 1956 on the Church. ". . . the Episcopate of the Catholic
Church in Poland," he concluded, "not only does not [support]
the Polish government and the Polish state authorities, but openly
and secretly works in the other direction." This speech was a signal
for attacks on the Primate and other bishops in the Warsaw and
provincial press.

The order to remove crucifixes from schoolroom walls caused a
great deal of trouble in this pervasively Catholic country. A few
riots were caused, a few arrests were made—not much by normal
Communist standards, but enough to threaten the whole Truce
edifice. The Church in its turn reacted strongly. If Cardinal Wyszynski shrewdly kept his peace, there was very little restraint in
the sermons of many village priests.

The reasons for this potential break-up were partly Soviet pressure, partly the natural uneasiness of a Communist government
faced with the rising power of a national Church. There is little
doubt but that many of the clergy, noting the Church's rising
power, let their enthusiasm run away with them and forget about
the Soviet divisions in their parish exhortations. On the Communists' side, each instance of a village priest preaching an anti-
government sermon was of course magnified a hundred fold. It was
made grist for the mill of the Party leaders who preferred open

war on religion to continuing the *modus vivendi* that insured their regime's stability.

The breach was healed temporarily as a simple matter of discretion by both parties. Arbitration boards of bishops and Communist officials were instituted, to clear some of the specific points of argument. Relief supplies were finally distributed, by a government commission with three Catholic members. Although the issue of religious orders teaching classes remained unresolved, Gomulka did make some concessions. The press abated its criticism campaign, slightly. The Catholic deputies in the Sejm, organized in the so-called Znak ("Sign") group were given a long withheld permission to open their own publishing house, the first unhindered publishing operation Catholic circles had enjoyed since the post-war freeze.

It was, all in all, a revealing test of strength, which would probably not soon be repeated. Yet the pin-prick attacks on the Church went on. Priests were arrested from time to time, on faked "morals" charges. Although the sentences given were slight, there was little doubt, from this and other portents, that many of Gomulka's followers chafed under the Truce restrictions.

*　　　　*　　　　*

An interested observer of this and all such church-state crises was the self-proclaimed "progressive Catholic" leader, Boleslaw Piasecki. The very existence of Piasecki, a handsome blond demagogue of 46, deserves some explanation, for he is not only anti-Catholic but anti-Gomulka. His "Pax" movement is not only an interesting Moscow Communist attempt to infiltrate the Church; it is also a flourishing commercial operation, dealing in everything from cement to rosaries. It is a highly effective propaganda apparatus, with one daily, two weeklies, a monthly and a huge publishing business. It is a wing of Soviet intelligence in Poland, the largest and most blatantly defended Moscow Polish outpost. At the same time, it is a direct descendant of pre-war Polish fascism.

Piasecki, who runs this complicated mechanism with discouraging competence, is a classic case of the opportunist at large. In a quarter-century of *voltes-face,* changes of identity and chronic allegiance-switching, few other Europeans had bounced higher or more often, while managing constantly to land on their feet. All the old 'shirt men' of the pre-war Fascist days have gone. The black-shirts and the brown-shirts were ripped up in the war days, and few remember people like Francois de la Rocque, the French Croix-de-Feu Fascist, Leon Degrelle, the Belgian Rexist, or the boss of the Dutch green-shirts. It took a really malleable Fascist like Piasecki to show everyone how easy it is for a good, vigorous 'shirt man' to prosper under Communism, given a few simple retailoring directions. It is the index of his prosperity that he now possesses, besides the trust of his Russian friends and a sound organization, the only Jaguar in Warsaw.

His career started out much the same way as other Fascists of his day. A politically conscious student at the Warsaw University law faculty in the mid-thirties had the chance to demonstrate his extreme disapproval of the existing order, broadly speaking, by becoming either a Fascist or a Communist. (Most students tended to join the National Party opposition.) Boleslaw Piasecki took the first choice. By his early twenties, after a brief period of dalliance with one of the National Party's splinter youth groups, he had set up his own organization, the National Democratic Falanga. The Falangists wore green shirts and wanted a pure Slavic Poland as badly as their neighbors the Nazis wanted a pure Aryan Germany. They dug up all the standard formulas of pre-war Fascism: salutes, massed flag-bearings and the provocation of riots against Jews. Despite the crudeness of his "Arm and Sword" bully boys, Piasecki got the support of some official Polish circles at least until the German invasion proved premature his advocacy of a brotherhood between neighboring pure-Aryan and pure-Slavic peoples.

The one original element Piasecki had in his Falanga was a touch of religion. His new cosmos was to be militantly Catholic as well as Polish, the simon-pure nationalism only an agency for a greater realization of "Catholic" principles. The Roman Catholic clergy was not very happy about this gratuitous support. The Falanga got nothing but a cold shoulder from the hierarchy and hardly any respectable followers from the laity.

Early in World War II, according to most good sources, Piasecki offered the services of his Falanga to the German occupying armies. Although the *Wehrmacht* at first accepted them, the SS agencies which followed wanted no part of Polish cooperation, having as their charter Alfred Rosenberg's announced "elimination of the Polish state." After being jailed by the Nazis, Piasecki got out to the east. He led guerilla fighters (made up of former Falanga members and others) for several years against both the Russians and the Germans. He was sentenced to death *in absentia* by the Lublin Communist government and the Russians in 1944. Early in 1945 he fell into the hands of the N.K.V.D. in Warsaw.

At this point the Piasecki saga might have been expected to stop. But in the conversations he held with the representatives of Soviet security forces, both sides demonstrated an impressive flexibility of tactic and identity of motive. After six weeks' imprisonment, he was released, supplied with a printing press, considerable amounts of Russian funds and the nucleus of an organization, called Pax. The man just a few months ago denounced by the Lublin government as a Fascist reactionary, now published a prospectus for a new "Catholic" group. His thesis he put in a nutshell: "Despite the general opposition of view the Catholic can be in accord with socialist progress in a Communist state."

It is a moot point whether Piasecki or the Russians got the idea of his running this soft-shoe infiltration of Polish Catholicism. It is certain that the highest circles of the N.K.V.D., then the Soviet security effort in Poland, were called into consultation. Franciszek Mazur, the leading Moscow Pole, worked directly with him in his projects. In any case, the post-war Piasecki movement was about the most ambitious Communist effort to capsize a Catholic church and turn it to their own purposes.

Pax began slowly, with the publication of a weekly in 1946 called *Dzis i Jutro* (Today and Tomorrow). In the confusion after World War II, when the Communist New Order was still looking for tactical footholds, the frontal attack on religion was withheld. Pax, posing as an interested honest broker between the Church and the Party state, was able to attract some Catholic support that Piasecki's pre-war Fascist movements had never succeeded in enticing. Cardinal Hlond, then the Primate of Poland, even gave Piasecki an audience. Deceived by its loudly stated brand of social-gospel Catholicism, several respectable Catholic intellectuals joined

Pax. In the 1947 elections, Piasecki and his friends put up candidates for a few electoral districts under the name of the "Catholic Progressive group." Although they were beginning to hawk the Party line, they were careful to keep away from any obvious Communist associations. Piasecki's old Fascist friends, who were now incorporated into his new movement, he kept in the background.

After a year or so of Pax's activity, even the best-guarded of Piasecki's camouflaging techniques proved transparent. But in the darkening atmosphere of the Bierut police state, his dubious "progressive Catholicism" seemed at heart a little better than unleavened Communism to many Catholics who had no love for Piasecki.

Pax had its own resources. Operating on the government subsidies initially given him, Piasecki built up a network of publishing operations. His daily paper, *Slowo Powszechny,* was and is the most expensive publishing operation in Poland outside of the Party newspaper, *Trybuna Ludu.* His other organizations produced a torrent of reviews, books and devotional objects—all loudly dedicated to "Catholic" purposes. A Catholic visitor in Poland could easily be taken in by the plausible appearance of one of Pax's "Veritas" book-shops, where Church classics are displayed in the windows along with rosaries, images of the saints— and other publications giving a strange view of Catholicism indeed. All the citations of *avant-garde* Catholicism, the quotations of contemporary Catholic thinkers in France, etc. were dedicated to the overriding proof that Communism and Catholicism were perfectly compatible, especially if the hierarchy could be taken out of the picture.

Piasecki himself is an organizer of considerable efficiency. Like the man who made three more millions on the one he inherited, he ran up the Communist subsidies into a big publishing and business empire. The two Pax firms, Veritas and INCO, set up a variety of factories that had nothing to do with their original religious mandate. These included textile plants, automotive communications factories, trade organizations, the Polish color monopoly and several schemes involving the licensing of Polish patents to Russian firms. They still employ something just under 5,000 people and they generally realize a profit of some 100,000,000 zlotys a year. This Piasecki can plough back into some of his propaganda efforts. The Pax companies operate under the ground-rules laid down for government factories, with the consequent breaks on taxation, insurance and commercial rules. But they are private. The scope of the biggest private industrial enterprise behind the Iron Curtain is an indication of the trust Moscow has reposed in this friendly ex-Fascist.

Within his organization Piasecki exercises absolute and rather secretive control, backed by the well-padded sponsorship which he failed to get from the Warsaw government in the thirties. His own bosses, until the debacle of the Polish secret police, were the fifth department of the Bezpieka and the Soviet agents placed above him. Now the latter call their shots directly.

They have had no reason to be displeased. For his evident talents have given them a secure outpost within Polish society, and better still, an outpost that masquerades as independent of Communism. In a famous article in the illustrated weekly *Swiat,* published in the anti-censorial days following October, 1956, the young liberal writer Leopold Tyrmand made this summation of Piasecki's machine: "What is Pax? It is difficult to give a simple answer. It is not a political party, but it has a political programme; it is not a movement and yet it puts forward Parliamentary candidates. It publishes magazines and books, controls two great corporations with a turnover of zlotys in the billions; it has its own foreign affairs departments, it own real estates, its fleet of motorcars; its own schools and sanitoria. . . . Some police actions within its own ranks indicate that even this attribute of power has been given to this strange organization. . . ."

For a time Piasecki made successful inroads among the clergy. His favorite device for doing this was typically unattractive. Equipped with a concealed tape recorder, he would stop by for a talk with a parish priest, then take the incriminating recorded conversation to the political police. If the priest would agree to "cooperate," he then offered to intercede with the authorities to let him off. Through this and similar means he persuaded a certain number of priests, probably something under 100, to support the Pax movement actively. While the Primate was under arrest, he stepped up his activities, and even tried to enlist Wyszynski. He had scant success. When two informal ambassadors from Pax came to the place of detention at Komancza, the Cardinal heard them out in silence for an hour, as they explained the rewards of collaboration. Then he asked only that they leave.

The Union of Patriotic Priests, organized in Poland under the Pax aegis, never got more than 60 participating recruits. There were far more border-line cases where a village pastor, as times grew harsher, went several steps towards becoming a latter-day Vicar of Bray. Until his death, the Union was led by a renegade priest, Jan Czuj, a theology professor with excessive fondness for politics, who got himself appointed head of a government-sponsored Catholic Seminary, the substitute offered the Church after the theological faculties of Warsaw and Cracow universities had been closed down.

The Polish bishops looked on this seminary, as on Pax, with justifiable suspicion. Through the worst years of the persecution, they kept their ranks unbroken, as did most of the lower clergy. It was one of the conditions posed by Wyszynski for his return that Pax be in no way included in negotiations.

When the Cardinal came back from his prison, he had the eternal problem of Ulysses returning from Ithaca. He solved it in the grand manner, but with caution. With the remnants of the patriotic priests, he had no mercy. They were told to obey the orders of their religious superiors or face immediate deprivation of faculties, if not excommunication. All but a handful of the worst compromised obeyed, and did penance.

But with the Pax movement and the considerable body of respectable clerics studying at the government-sponsored theological faculty, Wyszynski was cautious and patient. He first took pains to reestablish his physical authority as Primate (which had not been questioned *de jure* inside the Church) and to test the sincerity of the government, in fulfilling its part of the truce bargain. He took no immediate action against Piasecki, but there was not much doubt about his feelings. In 1955 the Vatican had placed Piasecki's publication *Dzis i Jutro* on the Index, as well as other writings in which he explained his program. Now that the ban was reinforced by the Cardinal's disapproving presence, a segment of Piasecki's following seceded. They formed a separate organization, which has since drawn further away from Pax 'Catholicism.'

Piasecki had meanwhile shown himself hostile to the Gomulka regime, to say nothing of the liberal Communist revisionists who supported it. In the teeth of the angry October Revolution, his daily paper published a denunciation of "revisionism," attacking just about all the anti-Stalin tendencies which the Gomulka regime was about to crystallize. In succeeding issues Piasecki hewed hard to the Moscow line, and his papers continue to do so. He became one of the most hated men in Warsaw, and he still is. The mysterious and fatal kidnapping of his son in January 1957 slackened the force of the anti-Piasecki denunciations. But the Polish press continued its efforts to smoke him out as a public Russian agent. Only the last-minute stirring of the Warsaw censors prevented the daily *Zycie Warszawy* from running a caricature of Piasecki, well known for his love of finery, under the provocative Latin heading *Ex Oriente Luxus* (Luxury from the East).

After watching the liberal Communist press do part of his work for him, the Cardinal finally acted. Almost immediately on returning from Rome in 1957, he ordered the Polish clergy to cease all dealings with Pax. This included writing in Pax papers, doing business with Pax firms and buying religious articles in Pax stores. This happened on July 6.

The Theological School in Warsaw he dealt with by counter-infiltration. Priests (or seminarians) were forbidden to study there without the express permission of their bishops. In cases where they were allowed, they were to do so under well-defined limits and for specific purposes. The administration of the school, through liberal exercise of this episcopal veto power, thus returned to the control of the Primate.

The Cardinal's dealings with the Theological School ran into no serious government opposition. Not so with Piasecki. His message denouncing Pax was held from publication by the government censors. (*Tygodnik Powszechny,* in protest against the ban, suspended publication for a week of its own accord.) The government, clearly, continues to support Pax with far more liberal rations of newsprint than that given to the small legitimate Catholic papers. Pax receives the same rebates of taxes which it enjoyed in the Bierut days.

The reasons for this are partly tactical. The Gomulka regime wants to keep the old Trojan Horse handy, with its motor running, to subvert the bishops' authority, in case of any further rupture in the Truce. But this does not explain entirely Gomulka's rewarding of a man and an organization which continue to oppose his own policies on "national Communism." The answer is again, as the Poles would put it, *raison d'etat*. Piasecki is Moscow's man. Given the circumstances, he can be cribbed and cabined, but not permanently hindered.

The only pre-war Fascist leader still in business has grown bolder, as the pressures from the Soviet Union on Poland increased. Although effectively discredited as a Catholic movement, his Pax group is forging ahead on another tack, the Front of Moral Regeneration for combatting "harlotry, hooliganism" and other lapses of the citizenry. In a Polish context, this is something like James Hoffa taking over the presidency of the National Association of Better Business Bureaus. The Poles know this; but Piasecki is undisturbed by popular disapproval, as long as he has his friends in Moscow, the Jaguar in the garage at home, and that attractive 100 million zlotys on Pax's annual profit sheet.

*   *   *

Against the future attacks of the hostile state, whether Pax infiltration or a renewal of open persecution, the Cardinal can offer a united front, a Church with a vigor, a resiliency and a capacity for social and intellectual endeavor which one does not normally associate with such a numerically overpowering organization. Its publications are strictly limited and heavily censored. Its people are poor. Aside from the fundamental matters of religious education and church building, it receives no state help. But it makes itself heard. There is no exaggeration in the often expressed view that the Primate's Church in the *pays reel* of Poland, to which the great majority of the country owes its allegiance. The First Secretary's government is merely the *pays legal*.

There are ten Catholic representatives in the Polish Sejm, whose voices far outweigh their numerical inferiority. Znak, their loosely organized Parliamentary club, has branches throughout the country. They are not a Catholic Party, which the Primate, even under favorable circumstances, would doubtless oppose. "As a priest or even as a head of the hierarchy," he once said, "I do not wish to interfere with the Catholic laiety's activities." But they speak as free-minded Poles and they are allowed to present their views on the Sejm's floor, however much the views are garbled in official accounts of the debates. What they say is important to Gomulka, as well as to their hearers. They are the only audible representatives of the *pays reel,* in a country where Communists must still pay some attention to public opinion.

In an interview with western journalists in Paris, the Catholic journalist Stefan Kisielewski (himself a Sejm representative) expressed very well the necessity of this function: "I think that its role is very difficult, ungrateful and ineffective, but necessary. We entered the Sejm almost symbolically, in the small number of eight [two later joined], although we represent a great part of our community—as was proved by the fact that all the candidates from the *Tygodnik Powszechny* group obtained an absolute majority of votes in their electoral districts.

"We are neither Communists nor socialists, we take no part in the government of Poland, we did not form the present reality in Poland, but yet, having entered the Sejm, in a sense we have become responsible for this reality. We are guided by ideas of the national interest and by realism. As the chairman of our Club often stressed, we have no intention to form a demagogical opposition or to take advantage of all the mistakes or unpopular moves of the government. We have entered the Sejm so that we can reach well defined aims in a well defined situation.

"Among other things, it is our duty to struggle for freedom of thought and conscience, both religious and secular thought, to introduce a non-Communist element into the Sejm, but one which can take its place within the frame of the existing system, to express the opinion and indicate the needs of the nation—to express them before the Party, which is often completely cut off from this kind of opinion.

"In our work we are sentenced to unpopularity: as realists we shall often speak about problems which are irritating to the nation, and as Catholics we shall speak about problems which will irritate the Party. This cannot be helped. . . . I repeat: our role is difficult, both toward the Party and toward the community. This role will be still more difficult, because the Polish press, brought up on Stalinist methods, does not publish the stenographs of speeches made in the Sejm. . . ."

At the apex of the Church's educational effort stands the Catholic University of Lublin, which held out through the worst years of the Bierut regime. One of the best educational institutions in eastern Europe, its graduates are regularly sought after in Polish government agencies, despite their ideological differences. It was founded on December 9, 1918, a month after the recovery of Polish independence, and reopened in 1944 after the Germans were expelled—the first university in the country to do so. Its unpretentious, rather grim-looking buildings in the center of Lublin still have the atmosphere of a fortress about them, as befits the only free university behind the Iron Curtain. Before October, 1956, the University accumulated its share of battle honors—both the former Rector, and the present Vice-rector spent several years in jail. Virtually every faculty except Philosophy was closed down by the Communists. A few months after the October Revolution, walking back to town from one of the poor, overcrowded dormitories, a student showed a foreign visitor a neon-lit sign over Lublin's less-than-distinguished Hotel de L'Europe. "We kept looking at that 'l'Europe' sign," he said, "to assure ourselves that we were still really on the same continent."

The scholars at Lublin comprise one of the liveliest university groups on that continent today. They are working on a huge new Catholic Encyclopedia in Polish, and especially active in Sociology and History, reflecting both the taste of the Primate, formerly their Chancellor, and the necessity for some practical apologetics in a harsh Marxist world.

Even more effective in its field is the leading Catholic newspaper, the Cracow weekly *Tygodnik Powszechny*. Taken over by the Bierut government in the crackdown of 1953 and given to Piasecki's Pax group, it was regained by legitimate Catholic editors in 1956. Its editors are close to the Primate, although *Tygodnik* is not officially his paper. (The freedom of ecclesiastical control under which they work might startle the docile editors of many diocesan Catholic newspapers in the United States.) Its articles are often censored. The government distribution agency Ruch cuts down on *Tygodnik*'s allocation of paper; and constant official—and unofficial—efforts are made to curb its circulation, despite the fact that it is the country's most popular paper, because the only free one.

"The cardinal," one of the *Tygodnik* editors observed, "is a realist, who has today in mind." There is a constant awareness of "today" in every manifestation of Wyszynski's spirit—the newspaper, the university, the delegates in the Sejm. He is on balance a superb politician. The Marxists would call him a "political"; his own French-loving Catholic intellectuals call him *un homme d'etat.* He shares with Gomulka an intense Polish nationalism that translates itself into his churchly concerns. "This is the opinion I heard in the Vatican," he told a student audience, "about Polish priests, 'they are very elegant, these Polish priests, but we cannot use them for any work. They talk well, they smile ravishingly, but they do not know a thing.' This I was told in 1951. I should expand this statement to a majority of our countrymen. They are highly cultured, prompt in understanding, but their knowledge is very shallow indeed. There is no tradition of learning in our country, no tradition of honest struggle for knowledge and wisdom. We have too little respect for our intellect . . . and hence the misfortune that though our nation is an intelligent nation, nevertheless, no very great results are achieved and the West is constantly telling us about this Slavonic unpreparedness. . . ."

"We are to throw into the Polish soil new seed. . . . You are thinking perhaps that I will now give you a lecture on dogmatic theology? I am talking to you about groats and everyday bread, about what you most need. . . . But a good economy requires ethics. Economic deeds are good only when the deeds of man are good in general. . . ."

This nationalism and political sense are the things that have captured the world's imagination about the cardinal. In the language of the correspondents who have discussed him, he is the Cardinal who made the deal with the Commissar (and what better deal than one with alliteration in its headline?). Yet this is a monochromatic view of his character. He is on balance an impressive shepherd of souls. His pastoral pronouncements have shown an extraordinary blend of theological wisdom and social instinct, not shared by many members of the College of Cardinals.

He is a man above all who is constantly on watch, lest he be either attacked by or identified with the other party to the Polish Truce. He showed this concern in a letter to the Bishop of Lourdes, refusing an invitation to participate in the 1958 Lourdes Centenary: "The Episcopate (in Poland) pursues its work in difficult conditions and in the face of delicate situations and considers it its duty therefore to remain at its post to stand guard over faith in the Church and God."

*   *   *

Each year, when the pilgrims go up the hill of Jasna Gora, the vows of Czestochowa are repeated. Each year the crowds gather around their bishops to sing the slow assurances of the ancient Polish national hymn, "Great God, Through Ages Protector of This Polish Land." The language of the vows, as the Primate of this age composes them, are no word-for-word archaisms, and they are delivered, incidentally, with a considerable facility of style: "Now, when three centuries have passed since the joyful days in which thou became the Queen of Poland, here now we the children of the Polish nation and thy children, the blood of the blood of our ancestors, stand again before thee, filled with the same feelings of love, faithfulness and hope which had once animated our fathers. . . .

"We, Polish bishops and the royal priesthood, the people acquired by the redeeming Blood of Thy Son, are again coming to Thy throne. . . .

"We appeal humbly to thy aid and mercy in the struggle to remain faithful to God, the Cross and the Gospel, to the Holy Church and its shepherds, our holy Fatherland, the vanguard of Christendom. . . .

"We promise thee to bring up young generations, in faithfulness to Christ, to defend them against impiety and corruption and to extend to them watchful parental care. . . .

"We promise to work assiduously so that in our Fatherland all the Children of the nation should live in love and justice, in harmony and peace, so that there is no hatred, oppression or exploitation.

"We promise to share willingly among ourselves the crops of the land and the fruit of the world, in order that there are no hungry, houseless or weeping under the common roof of our homes. . . .

"We promise to declare a struggle against laziness and thoughtlessness, against wastefulness, drunkenness and dissolution. . . .

"We are handing to you by a special act of love every Polish house and every Polish heart. . . ."

To which the crowds repeat in unison the traditional answer: "Queen of Poland, we promise."

After more than two years of the Truce the Primate could feel just pride at having made more of the promises of Czestochowa than any churchman behind the Iron Curtain, done more in fact to secure the wants of his church on education than many prelates in very democratic countries. His success has not put an end to the argument about how Christians should deal with the hostile State. If he were again imprisoned tomorrow, the partisans of the Fortress school would say that he had failed, that he had made dangerous common cause with the enemies of the City of God, that a Communist state is not even Augustine's Babylon, the meeting ground of bad and good, but rather the ancient image of uncompromising Egypt, the "conspiracy of the evil," as Rufinus once called it, in the days of the early Church.

Against this he would have the demonstrable fact that he has not compromised with either doctrine or church discipline. With the courage of a good commander, he allowed his Church to be infiltrated, confident that infiltrators could be dealt with, once the front lines were secured. The shadowy fate of Pax and the progressive priests' movements have largely justified his risks. And his behavior has a lesson in it for every churchman. It is a prime example of Catholicism's great metaphysical distinction between the abiding substance of things and their often transitory accidents.

It is thus the Primate's lot to be heavily criticized for his actions from both right and left. To be holding the middle of the road is not necessarily an augur of either political or spiritual virtue (although we have seen in Gomulka's case how it can be used as a good Leninist tactic). But the content of the attacks in themselves explain Wyszynski's position. The right began the criticism. Not only emigré circles, but many strong Catholics inside Poland expressed it in the kind of whispering cavils that so often characterize the devout (or bigoted) lay Catholic's strictures against his priest. Wyszynski, the whispering argued, had made a pact with the devil by coming to terms with the Communists. Better for him if he had taken the noble jousting position of Cardinal Mindszenty. Compromise is the death of faith.

This highly conservative line of argument lost strength as it grew evident that the Cardinal knew very well where political expediency stopped and the doctrine of the Church began. It is still heard occasionally, although such is the way of this parish-house criticism that a visitor to Poland has a difficult job hearing it in public. But its force has ebbed. If the Polish Catholics are not 100% behind the cardinal, the figure is at least well in the nineties. The fervor of the affirmative position in any case far and away exceeds the hesitant doubts of the negative.

By the end of 1957, however, the critical torch was taken up by the left. This criticism is more complicated, at first glance, but more plausible to those (whether non-Catholic, a-Catholic, or anti-Catholic) who do not share Rome's religious premises. This argument is based on the fact that Wyszynski's alliance with Gomulka is in actuality a solid front of "reaction" against all the bold, progressive forces in the country. Wyszynski's strictures against immorality, drunkenness, laziness and general lying-down on the job, because they are concurrent with Gomulka's, are taken as virtual annexes of the Central Committee's own statements on the subjects. Why, ask these critics of the non-Communist left—as well as, to split niceties a little further, the anti-Stalinist Communist left—does the cardinal condone the Gomulka censorship of magazines like *Po Prostu* or the still-born *Europa,* published by the courageous leftist *enragés?* Why does the cardinal implicitly support the Communist denunciation of writers like Marek Hlasko, who are trying to tell the plight of Poland in "realist existentialist terms?"

The left critics go on to note that Catholic writers in published articles in Poland defend the Inquisition, and say that there are no "equality of rights for truth and error." The pronouncements of the cardinal, given these starting premises, sound progressively more disturbing.* The most reactionary elements in Polish Catholicism, it is argued, are now allied with the Central Committee in Warsaw to preserve an arid kind of bourgeois nationalism, stern and authoritarian, against the innovators, who are classed as either "Marxist, socialist, liberal or Catholic."

Such an argument may look tempting, but a few cautions are in order. In the first place, the Socialist strictures about the Primate overlook the fact that his actions, like Gomulka's, are conditioned by the presence of Soviet divisions on either side of Poland. Gomulkist Poland does not move the world's tensions. It merely lives because of them. The Cardinal has definitely decided that episcopal silence, with open churches, is preferable to episcopal logorrhea, running the risk of open warfare.

The young Marxist *enragés* of *Po Prostu,* furthermore, had little charm for the cardinal; they are almost to a man atheist and professionally anti-clerical. A Roman Catholic cardinal, granted his premises, can be forgiven for not lending his support to free speech for people whose ideal is to eliminate him and his Church in some half-Marxist Utopia of the future.

Finally, the Left critics of the Cardinal's course, as was their wont in previous controversies, are arguing on a level completely different from his. They prize the support of Catholic "liberals" not because they are Catholics, but because they share a few premises about social justice and social action with the Socialists. Hence they are useful, in attaining an earthly paradise in which the most "liberal" Catholic would feel uncomfortable. The Cardinal is regarded as a potential assistant in this effort. His religious function has no meaning for them. They are understandably irked by the religious instruction in the schools and opening churches concerns them little.

This confusion of purpose will always exist. If the right-wing Catholic disapproves of Wyszynski because he has no wish to re-

* It took a Polish Socialist emigré, K. A. Jelenski, to take this line to its *reductio ad absurdum,* when he denounced the cardinal's 1958 Easter message as "formulated in Zhdanovian terms." That is to say, Wyszynski spoke of things like giving "clear and legible colors" to human actions and he denounced "modern confusion." The conclusion reached is that Wyszynski, like Gomulka, is really "Stalinist" in his methods.

vive the Caesaro-Papalism (or Papalo-Caesarism) of mediaeval
Poland or the Austro-Hungarian Empire, the non-Communist
secular mind disapproves of him because he values God over all
earthly purposefulness. The primate is, however, a Catholic with
a profound sense not only of the Church's heavenly mission, but
of social justice on this earth. That is why he has given his support, despite the Socialist denials, to the genuinely liberal wing of
the Catholic Church in Poland. The ideals of the disillusioned
Marxist liberals do not strike the cardinal as worth fighting for.

In taking the road of spiritual survival, the cardinal's interest in
social affairs has not resulted in worldly temptations to build a
strong Christian Democratic Party. Unlike Mindszenty and others,
Wyszynski never forgot how imperfect is the world in which Christianity must build its house, and keep that house in working order.
If he were put into prison tomorrow, he could argue, the Truce
would have been justified by the very exercise of the faith which
it permitted. There is no sure system for preserving the Christian
faith, and the church, its vessel. But each day a church is kept
open, another baby is baptized, another marriage is performed
before the altar. Each day the religion teacher comes to school,
another child goes further on the way to knowing its faith, and
how that faith may best be defended. Each day an uncensored
church paper continues to publish, a voice for morality exerts its
force on a de-moralized society.

6

Taming the Wild West

> "When I walked about in this city, I noticed that it
> was a strange town in which the past was burned by fire.
> The fire was ignited by those who have built the past not
> long ago. When they left they burned their achievement,
> but when this recent past was burned, the former, the older
> Polish past remained and was revealed in its crippled walls
> . . . our forefathers' land was revealed . . ."
>
> —*Stefan Cardinal Wyszynski to the university students of*
> *Wroclaw*

BRESLAU WAS once a very fine city. Looking at it today, you
need the patience of an archaeologist to reconstruct how this city
must once have pleased the visitor. There were the neat, old houses
along the Oder that made a watery latticework of the city plan,
the spacious square, heavy in *Rathaus* Gothic, and the dark of its
stone churches, but lightened nicely by the soft elm trees that
stretched their branches over the paths to the bridges. For six centuries it was a German city, pride of its bishops and its dukes,
rulers of the eastern marches which brought their grain, their
homage and their unwieldy Slavic accents into the markets and
the antechambers of the old German business houses. It was the
gathering-place of a German landed aristocracy, as well as its nor-

169

mal trading population—good church-goers, noted for culinary delicacies like *Käsekuchen* and *Schlesisches Himmelreich* and a general insistence on *Anständigkeit*.

It was also, in its time, a Nazi city. Hitler had once enjoyed a lavish banquet in his suite at the Hotel Monopol, and the crowds were desolate when he never came back to speak at the *Jahrhunderthalle*. The uniforms were well-pressed in those days, the *sekt* was plentiful and the parks full of patriotic merrymakers. When the uniforms started marching off in 1938, the God-fearing descendants of the Teutonic Knights slept the more happily in their manors along the Oder, firm in the knowledge that, whatever the auspices, the traditional *Drang Nach Osten* was back in business.

Wroclaw is hardly a city at all. It is square blocks of unrelieved ruins. It is a seedy relic of a hotel where visitors are served by drunken waiters and the principal tourist traffic the unpressed, dutifully uncomplaining 'delegations' of the Communist world, thickly repeating pledges of the fraternity they have been ordered to feel, over many rounds of unchilled Polish vodka. It is a place whose most prominent bit of reconstruction, the Cathedral and its surroundings, serves only to mock the dead shells of city life around it. Its most prominent inhabitants seem to be drunks and trollops, the former clustering unsteadily around the beer stands on street-corners, the latter doing their conventional shimmies on their walks past the shells of burnt buildings. The one or two respectable cafés open, and the new department store, are hardly adequate to take the curse off the overwhelming air of decay. They are obviously not used by many, outside of the New Class. The bulk of Wroclaw's population—decent, beaten-looking people— shuffles through its drab daily rounds like a fighter too tired to hope for anything but the bell. Their only visible link with a world of art and abstraction that should exist somewhere is the tasteful, splashy posters which advertise the latest student art show, the most instructive government exhibition, the most interesting theatre.

So it seemed at first contact with this city in 1957. The contrast between Breslau and Wroclaw grows of course less sharp with time and investigation. But it is hard even much later to shake a general impression of chaos superimposed on order, of the ramshackle intruding on the solid and respectable. This is true of almost all of what the Poles officially call the Western or "Re-covered" Territories, the 38,600 square mile stretch of land be-tween Gdansk (formerly Danzig) on the windy Baltic to Gliwice (formerly Gleiwitz) in the smoky industrial triangle of Upper Silesia. Except for the Silesian south, which has always had large Polish populations, the area has the look of a wasteland that has been half re-populated. Even now a drive along the road between Gliwice and Wroclaw is a combination of natural beauty and man-made ruin. For miles there are stretches of flat, good farm-land, broken by occasional clumps of trees and the recurring sight of the placid Oder or one of its branches, meandering down to the Baltic. But, in a country that desperately needs its farm crops, there have been all too many fields lying fallow or obviously poorly used. Where farms, thanks to Gomulka's agriculture policies, have been put back into production, many of the towns remain half-shells, with only the most makeshift repairs for their war-battered buildings. Others are even more discouraging, for there are fairly populous places completely untouched by the war, physically, whose new inhabitants have let them slip into a slow, crumbling decay.

Yet the Western Territories, which the Poles themselves have until recently wryly called "The Wild West," are the hope of the country's future. The Silesian triangle contains a major portion of Polish industry. (See Chapter 8.) The western farmlands have the potential of making Poland once more a food exporter. The ports and the fisheries of the Baltic, notably Gdansk and Szczecin (formerly the German Stettin), have become the indispensable outlets for a balanced trade and economy.

Concurrently, and partly for this reason, the Western Territories are the trickiest political problem in Europe. Until 1945, and for much of the six centuries prior to that, they were all or in part under German rule. Almost 10 million Germans were displaced from them and East Prussia to make room for the new Polish pop-ulation, which now numbers about six million.* Of these only a

* Due to wartime and post-war population shiftings, and sharply different national tabulation methods, the exact numbers are hard to establish. In 1939 there were 9,600,000 Germans east of the Oder-Neisse line, of whom 7,100,000 lived in the Recovered Territories. There was also a considerable

million are indigenous to the territory: the autochthons of mixed Polish-German culture who have tilled the soil or worked there as long as their family memories last. All the others, including the plant directors, the farm planners and the Party organizers, have come from other parts of Poland. Most of these are themselves refugees from the 69,500 square miles of Polish territory which the Russians snipped off in the east. Some are townsmen from the old Polish cultural centers of Lwow and Wilno, people of considerable taste and sophistication. Others are peasant farmers from the former eastern marches of Poland and the western Ukraine, "the sort of people," as a Warsaw intellectual said in exasperation, "who aren't happy unless they bring the pigs into the living room to sleep with them." Through the last twelve years all of them have been poured into their new homes in the west, to build a new life together on highly unfamiliar foundations. A Polish official conceded to a visitor, in what to anyone who has seen the Western Territories remains one of Europe's great understatements: "We must work on many different levels."

The creation of this new Polish territory was one of Stalin's few real diplomatic "master-strokes." Using a combination of diplomatic bluff and military *fait accompli,* he extracted an agreement for Poland's new boundaries from Churchill and Roosevelt at Yalta,* which succeeding U.S. and British administrations were never able to modify—not that they tried very adroitly or energetically to do so. Having seen their farmland in the east go irrevocably to the Russian neighbor, the Poles clung to this accretion in the west with a zeal that borders on desperation. For possession of the Western Territories means the difference between a balanced, economically viable Poland with at least one tenable frontier and a truncated buffer.

---

population increase during World War II. Of these about 5,000,000 fled to the west in the last months of the war. Many of the survivors died in the chaos of the Soviet advance. The remainder were forcibly evicted by the Poles in 1945–1946.

* The atmosphere in which he succeeded can be gathered from a remark of Roosevelt's, as quoted by Stanislaw Mikolajczyk: "Stalin is a realist, and we mustn't forget when we judge Russian reactions that the Soviet regime has had only two years' experience in international relations. But of one thing I am certain: Stalin is not an imperialist."

Realizing this, and having already extracted *their* pound of flesh from the deal, the Russians were quick to "guarantee" Poland's new western border on the Oder. The United States, concerned with German reactions, has never felt itself able to make any kind of a commitment on this score. This has exasperated anti-Communist Poles as much as the reddest of the Party *apparatchiks,* for hanging on to the Western Territories is the one political article of faith shared by all Poles. Politically speaking, the Western Territories is a package of dormant explosives with an apparently indefinite series of time fuses installed inside it.

For three years after the war's end, Wladyslaw Gomulka himself was the Minister for the Recovered Territories. With characteristic energy and realism he set about to put them on their feet as quickly as possible, making concessions where necessary to the mood and habits of the mixed population there, especially the farmers. By 1949, at the close of the first Three Year recovery plan, he had quite a lot to show for his efforts. Four million settlers had been established on the new land, which was demonstrably richer than the eastern territories taken away by the Russians, at least in its potential. There were good harvests, and a considerable feeling of hope and enthusiasm among the resettled farmers.

Then the doctrinaire wing of the Party took over. Gomulka began his five year process of demotion and imprisonment. It was increasingly borne in on the farmers that Party cards counted more than productivity. The Warsaw central administration ceased to bother about the tremendous special problems of the west, concentrating instead on the Russian directive to industrialize the country. The entire Western Territories went into a long period of stagnation. Fields were left idle and whole towns crumbled away into half-ruins. A Swiss correspondent passing through the area in 1957 could very justly write about the ruined streets, the sagging buildings, the cracked foundations of villages or large market towns, then inform his readers, in the many rich turns of phrase that the German language uses for "I told you so," that the places in question had suffered scarcely any damage during the war, but simply fallen into decay from the apathy of their new inhabitants.* Only after the October Revolution has an effort been made to make the Western Territories both profitable and livable.

This is why Wroclaw presents such an appalling contrast to the real reconstruction done in Warsaw, however much Wroclaw's recent rebuilding. Seldom has the total effect of destruction been so depressing. The war damage, admittedly, was great. Thanks to a fanatical German commander, it was fought over longer than any city in Germany. The Russians did not secure Breslau until May 8, a week after Hitler's suicide in the Berlin bunker and one day after the formal general surrender. By this time it had lost most of its resemblance to a city. Bomb damage had been overlaid by the more dramatic destruction of artillery fire, leaving the city a landscape of jagged walls and dead rubble. The death toll of civilians was staggering. Thanks to a cruelly belated Nazi evacuation policy and the confusion of the time, some 200,000 of Breslau's original 625,000 population remained in the city during the last siege. Not too many of them escaped. Almost the last patch of old buildings in the city's heart was razed by the *Wehrmacht,* to provide a landing-field for observation aircraft. It was only a few days later that the members of the Soviet Army filed into the city to collect the watches and rape the women.

In Breslau, as everywhere else in the recovered territories, the Poles acted swiftly to expel the Germans. All classes and political elements of the country were for once united in this move to confiscate the territory of Poland's old destructive enemy. The Catholic Church, for example, was as swift as the Communists in effecting the hasty Polonization process. Just nine days after Breslau's surrender, Bishop Adamski of Katowice told German churchmen in Breslau, long a German Catholic stronghold, that it would be better if Polish priests took over their cures; Cardinal Hlond, Wyszynski's predecessor, ordered Polish vicars for the old German dioceses in the territories, a step to which the Vatican gave con-

---

* "In a trip across country," wrote *Die Weltwoche's* correspondent Peter Schmid in March, 1957, "one meets at every step houses gaping with empty holes for windows. Very seldom is this the result of bombs or enemy looting. They were quite simply cleaned out by thieves, who could sell the windows at a good price. If you come back in a week, perhaps the whole house will have disappeared and the site leveled."

ditional approval only after years of negotiations by Cardinal Wyszynski.

After the German excesses in Poland, the Poles did not, understandably, use kid gloves in the expulsion process, and thousands of Germans died as a result of the often brutal measures taken to evict them. Looking backward a decade later, the Poles wished they had not been so hasty or so drastic in their deGermanization program. The loss of skilled workers and farmers in the area still shows its crippling effects. Many Germans, with legitimate Polish family connections, might have stayed on at their jobs, with great profit to their new underskilled Polish neighbors from the east.

As it was, there were barely 25,000 Germans left in the entire area by 1957, mostly old people and a few miners and technical workers. These were occasionally reinforced by "fraternal delegations" of Germans from the East German satellite. It was one of them, on one occasion, who forgot his feeling for "socialist unity" long enough for a characteristically German comment on a "new" Polish city. Walking down the faded carpet of the Hotel Monopol's stairway, on their way to a dinner of aged cutlet and brand-new Hungarian wine, two American visitors commented in English about the former elegance of the decor. "Wroclaw," they said, "must have been a great town in its day." "That day," the fraternal German voice answered anonymously from farther down the corridor, "is long gone."

Given an interview with some of the competent Polish officials there, a foreign traveler could feel more encouraged. In 1957–58, the governor of the Wroclaw voivod (officially the chairman of the Voivod National Council) was Bronislaw Ostapczuk. Like many of Wroclaw's new civic and cultural leaders he came from the vicinity of Lwow. (More of the Wilno people, he noted, tended to migrate to the city of Szczecin.) Only 35, he had arrived in Wroclaw just after the war, and worked in the administration ever since, a pleasantly kinetic kind of man whose obvious gift for transmitting enthusiasm was particularly handy in this territory.

Ostapczuk had started working under Gomulka and he seemed to have a similarly pragmatic approach to both political and economic problems. Once more, this time in his fast, serviceable German, came the refrain of the ideological Warsaw Concerto

that every visitor comes to know: "Marxism is only good when it
develops. Every people must develop Marxism in its own way. We
don't reject what the Soviet Union does, but we want to develop
the theory on our own soil. We are against others doing as we do
and our being forced to do as others do. . . ."

In Ostapczuk's office in the large provincial office building, the
half-tired justifications had a truer ring than elsewhere. (They
made, at least, a happy contrast to the Party-line armor-plating
of the local newspaper editors.) The Marxism practiced in the
agricultural part of the Western Territories appeared to be an
even more original variety than elsewhere. It had proved hugely
successful. After the October Revolution Ostapczuk and others
like him had been able to continue the originally happy policy of
Gomulka in concentrating on production rather than Soviet orthodoxy. Nowhere in Poland had the farmers been allowed to scuttle
off the collectives in quicker time. Out of 1,750 collectives in the
Wroclaw voivodship, only 83 were still in business by mid-1957.
Of these 83, party activists would point out with haste, 20 were
composed of people who went back to the security of collectives
after disastrous experience with private farming. The evidence of
a "counter-trend" thus suggested was hardly convincing.

The consequent increase in the farmers' yield, loyalty and dis-
position was huge. On April 1, 1957, Ostapczuk could say confidently that there were only 5,000 hectares still lying idle in his
territory—and they were of poor quality. Every day farmers were
asking for more. The average holding was 12 hectares, double the
former figure, and increasing, since farmers were no longer taxed
progressively more heavily according to the size of their plots.
Everywhere in the Western Territories, and the eye could confirm
his statement, the land that had lain unused and devastated for years
was by 1957 being returned to cultivation, even if the farmhouses
still showed signs of long neglect. The 1957 crop was far better
than the year before, and the 1958 crop turned out better still.
"You will find no piece of land here that is not worked," Ostapczuk
boasted.

The classic complaint of farmers against totalitarian governments is the forced quota of crop deliveries and the fixed pricing,
neither of which provides much incentive for increasing a farm's

yield. Both of these are being whittled away. By June, 1957, the compulsory government quota had been reduced to 35% of a farmer's total product. The rest he could sell on the free market, where the price, then 360 zlotys for 100 kilos of grain, was considerably more rewarding than the fixed quota price of 120 zlotys. In two or three years, the government hoped to eliminate the entire quota system. Thus by a process with which Adam Smith would hardly have been offended, these modern Marxists would have restored their area's agriculture to a flourishing market economy.

Later restrictions and brakings of this bold policy slowed its momentum, as the presure of Soviet disapproval made itself felt. But nonetheless, a visitor could not help thinking that, at this particular moment in history, these Communist bureaucrats were showing far greater faith in the workings of a practical free enterprise system on the farm than the United States Congress in its own farm dealings.

This turn of events gave a new stability to the Western Territories. After 12 years of Polish occupation, barns were being repaired and houses put in order. The aimless surgings of people from town to countryside and countryside to town were ending. In Wroclaw itself, so long sacrificed while the country put its directed energies to the re-building of the capital, a new building program proceeds. It is thus far not very visible, the government people say, because they have concentrated on putting up workers' housing in suburbs. First things first.

Ostapczuk was not abashed, all the same, to admit that a staggering job still faces them. It is a social job as well as an economic one, and here "construction" rather than "reconstruction" would be an apt description. "One can say," he noted, "that in this province live Poles from all over Poland and from the entire world."

This number includes people who have never lived in a city before and city people who have lost their former urban livelihoods. There are Polish refugees from the Ukraine who hesitate to go into a village, because their only image of this social form is the drab and dirty Soviet peasant settlement. There are highly skilled workmen from northern France, attracted to Poland after decades of living abroad, who sometimes still wonder what made them end up as farmers in a crumbling German manor on the Oder. There

are returned soldiers from the wartime Polish Army in the west
suspicious, bewildered and—until 1956, objects of continuing
Communist harassment. There are, finally, the half-German
autochthons, the only indigenous people remaining in the Western
Territories. After in some cases centuries of life under German
rule, these ethnic Poles often speak German better than Polish
They have a resentment towards the new settlers from eastern
Poland which is made all the stronger by their considerably higher
level of culture and material progress.

*   *   *

Only a few hours of travel through Poland's "Wild West" are
needed to feel the heady effects of this strong population cocktail
On a farm outside Wroclaw, in the course of a tour there in the
summer of 1957, I found an entire settlement of French-speaking
Poles, who had returned to the home country in 1946, attracted
partly by nostalgia and more than partly by the energetic lobbying
of Communist Party members among them. Some had come from
Lyons, a few from Paris, the majority from the coal mines or the
textile plants of the industrial north of France. At least one of
them, a young man who spoke perfect school French, had been
brought up in France. He was a former electrician on the Paris
metro. Their farm, still loosely classed as a collective, was hardly
an ornament to Communist agricultural policy. The crumbling
yellow manor house that served as its headquarters was in utter
disrepair. There were still traces of its long-vanished German
owner—an odd sign scattered about the courtyard, an iron gate
with an early 18th century inscription—and of its Soviet 'liber
ators,' notably several whitewash signs in crude Cyrillic letters with
their interminable *Slava* ("Glory") slogans: "Glory to Stalin, glory
to the Soviet Army, glory to the peoples'. . . ."

The boss of the collective, whom I met briefly in his sugar-beet
fields, was a tough, decisive-talking man who looked like what he
probably was, a former worker in the French Communist Party
I suspected he would have felt more natural overturning a Citroen
in the middle of a coal-field strike, even after all these years. He
and eleven others had remained in the "cooperative," as he called
it. (There is little difference in the Polish context between the

two terms, although official spokesmen made much of the "co-operative" as a kind of middle way.) Eighteen others had stayed outside, once the element of compulsion was removed. By the boss' testimony, the "cooperative" people were doing vastly better, but it was quite clear that, short of staying in the village for months of investigation, one would have difficulty checking the truth of his statement.

The others to whom I talked were diffident and guarded in whatever they said. One had to make conclusions, political, economic and spiritual, from the nervous laugh, the downcast glance, the pursed lips or the shrug. It was the same everywhere a visitor shook loose from the free-talking intellectual, the eloquent plant foreman or the indignant student. The freedoms of Poland's October seeped down slowly to the bulk of her people. A consciousness of freedom was even slower to come. The stored memory of ten years of rigid Communist rule, with its heritage of apathy and hopelessness, was very strong indeed.

The men of that *produkcja* were then earning something like 20 zlotys a day. One can only hope they have got a raise since. They had food, but very little money with which to buy clothing. They could get "a little wine," as one of the old men said in his broken French, "but not of course what we'd call wine." Some of them had done service with both the FFI in World War II and the Polish Army since. Of their reasons for coming to Poland they were reluctant to speak. I suspected they might have agreed with another former Polish worker in France, whom I saw in the south. "Propaganda," he said, "propaganda brought us here."

Forces more complex than simple propaganda had brought Herr Rudolph Fest to Bytom, the black and bustling mining city in Upper Silesia, which until 1945 had been known as Beuthen. When I visited his house, on a short tour of the very acceptable workers' housing developments at the Szambierki Mine (formerly the *Hohenzollern Werke*), I was surprised that this polite, middle-aged man and his grandmotherly wife spoke such fluent German. Presuming that he was a local Pole who had originally lived under the German rule of this traditionally half-Polish area, I suggested sympathetically that the Germans must have given him a rather bad time. "Not too bad," he said, "not bad at all." Had he been in the Army? "Yes." Was he taken prisoner? "Yes, but the treatment was all right. It was in an American camp." Fest, it developed, had been a wartime member of the *Wehrmacht*.

His story, if weird by ordinary standards, was normal life history among the people of modern Poland. He had come to Beuthen just before the war from Nürnberg, when Germans were being encouraged to settle in the border areas. He faithfully did his war service, then went back to Bytom and tried working as a cab driver. But he had trouble, he noted, "because I didn't know much Polish." So he got a job at the large mine, brought up his children and has lived there in harmony ever since. Is he a German or a Pole? "You go," said Herr Fest, "where your bread is."

The road from Bytom to Wroclaw winds steadily northwest, through the center of what was once German Silesia. From Upper Silesia, with its long established industrial population, it passes into the farmland of Lower Silesia. From Opele to Wroclaw, the road runs closely parallel to the Oder, which with its western tributary the West Neisse (to Poles the Nysa) forms the water boundary between Poland and East Germany. Few of the villages and towns along the way have escaped either outright devastation or slow decay. I stopped in one of them, quite unexpectedly, attracted by a battered monument in what was once the town square. It was the remains of a German *Denkmal,* its Maltese crosses and Gothic lettering bearing half-forgotten witness to the villagers who had done their bit for the Kaiser in 1914–18 and before. The old Lutheran church nearby was in ruins, but the Catholic church, although damaged, was still evidently used by the Polish population. Large and apparently prosperous houses ringed part of the square, roofs now open to the rain. It looked like a place that was invaded yesterday.

At one side of the square, I met an old woman, who spoke good German. Like the farmers, she was reluctant to talk. She was, she said, a Pole, and she had lived in this place all her life. It had been a nice town. The Russians had smashed it. What more they had ruined she would not care to say. There were many people here who had come from the "East," and she conveyed a world of resentment and contempt by the way she said the word. They had, I gathered, taken over the village administration. The farms were a little improved, she admitted, in the last year or two. For the rest, she was reluctant to speak: "One must be careful." As a few people came by to watch us, she grew more embarrassed. "Had anything been done to repair the damage of the war?" I asked her. "Nothing." She was one of the Western Territories' original inhabitants, it was clear, rewarded by history with more than her share of misery and confusion and the picturesque Greek name of autochthon.

The 1,000,000 odd autochthons are not an accident of history, but its logical byproduct. Silesia is a name that occurs to Americans only fleetingly, generally when they are taking a college history course involving either the efficient aggressions of Frederick the Great against Maria Theresa, or the "significant" upheavals of disturbed populations after World War I. In central Europe it has spelled trouble for the last thousand years. It is a melting pot for which the ethnic and political ingredients were always either too hot or too cold.

It is by no means a German country, having been originally peopled by Czechs and Poles. The first Germans were invited there by its Polish dukes, who had established their primacy early in the twelfth century—an invitation which no Pole will ever duplicate. For centuries thereafter it was governed by a branch of the Piast family, the first hereditary Polish kings. But they governed it within the framework of the Holy Roman Empire, a polity that was never overfond of its Slavic components. Frederick the Great marched his troops over it with such frequency that he finally decided to stay. He laid the foundations for Upper Silesia's industrial development. The outside world has since tended to regard it as German. There are certain parts of Silesia which still suggest the designation, notably Breslau, which since its re-founding in 1250 was a solidly German community. But even a casual visitor could observe the strength of the historic, as well as recent Polish claims.

The small city of Opole, known in its last political incarnation as Oppeln, is in the process of reconstruction. With painstaking care, as is their wont, the Poles have been putting together its high-roofed houses and gilding the damaged Teutonic gables. The Oder flows through its midsection and enough of its riverside houses are left standing to conjure up the impression of what a graceful town it must have been in the old days. But were the old days Polish or German? Straying into the Franciscan church in Opole, a visitor can give himself an interesting object lesson in history. On several plaques and signposts the church's career is written out. From the thirteenth century to the Reformation, it was the stronghold of the Franciscans in Opole. From the fifteenth century on, it had its troubles—from fires to theological differences, until it emerged early in the eighteenth as the Lutheran, and hence German parish church. So it stayed, until 1945, when the Communist armies superseded the Nazis. Polish became the reigning language once more, and the church was given back to the Franciscans. In a side chapel of what is now a well-used parish church lie the tombs of long-dead dukes named Bolko I and Bolko II. These were among the hereditary Piast, hence Polish rulers of the Silesian borderland. It was only after a catastrophic war, a muddled and disastrous peace conference and the ethnic aggressiveness of a Communist government that these two Catholic Polish dukes were returned to the original sponsorship of their resting-place. It took Stalin, among other things, to give Bolko back to the Franciscans. A complicated world for an overseas tourist to investigate.

North of Wroclaw, Opole and the resettled farms of the Western Territories is the great prize of Poland's geographical changes in the west, the new 300 miles of coast along the Baltic. The Oder, with Szczecin now under Polish control, gives the Poles a riverway far more valuable than the Vistula. Szczecin, whose Polish spelling is another monument to the Poles' originality in keeping their Slavic words corseted in a Latin alphabet, is an invaluable port city. So is Gdansk (once their Danzig). Its possession now renders half-superfluous the artificial seaport of Gdynia, which the Poles built out of a marsh in the days of the prewar Polish Corridor. I had the good fortune to visit Gdansk for several days, traveling in a 20-year-old Chevrolet whose driver was profoundly concerned about gears and brakes. (Some sailors returning from Belgian ports, he loudly hoped, might bring him some spare parts.) Here, as in Wroclaw, there are constantly encountered relics of a centuries-old German occupancy. Here, even more than in Wroclaw, there is constantly encountered resentment—an enmity towards the Russians that has temporarily dimmed the long hatred of the Germans.

A mile or two outside of Gdansk, in a barren stretch of parkland surrounded by the characteristic stone steps, stands the familiar embalmed tank of the Russian war memorial. It is the loneliest spot in town. No visitors come there of their free will. Poles commuting to Gdansk from the barely touched cities of Gdynia and Sopot sometimes look at it angrily, or avert their eyes. The more concrete Russian memorial they are thinking of is a large patch of crumbled stone and rubble in the center of the city, which the Poles are still trying desperately to reconstruct. The heart of old Danzig, a rarely beautiful complex of high-shouldered Renaissance buildings, was deliberately burned out by Russian soldiers in an orgy of violence following their expulsion of the Germans. The Poles in Gdansk, like Poles everywhere, will never forget it.

Gdansk today is a city alive, industrious and in a way as bracing as the Baltic air that cools its summers but leaves the winters never so cold and bleak as the plains climate of Warsaw and the Polish south. Its shipyards turned out their first 10,000 tonners in 1956. By 1960, the local planners hope to have an 18,000 ton tanker sliding down the ways, almost too large for the narrow canal which gives the yards and all Gdansk its only outlet to the sea. The work of reconstruction goes on in the same boldly impractical way as at Opole, Warsaw and everywhere else in Poland, gable by gable, the ornamental gold ornament being finished before the next building is begun. New housing is meticulously built in the old Hanseatic style. After a few years, the first examples of this have already taken on the color of history, and the rooms inside them, crowded though they are, have the added advantage of interior heating and plumbing.

But it takes more than industry and reconstruction to make a happy city. The re-building is only a small part of the devastation. Arriving in Gdansk 12 years after the war, anyone would have been overwhelmed by the expanse of smashed stone and skeletal walls. A few old buildings, like the Victorian station, have remained standing. The new Orbis hotel across the flowered station square is brick, clean and functional, doing its job sparely but nicely. Just two steps beyond it stretches the wasteland of ruins. Another lunar landscape, peopled early each morning, at fire thirty a.m., when the workers start shuffling to the shipyards, for the first eight hour shift.

It is still hard to think of Danzig as Gdansk. But as more people come filling up the ruined streets with their traffic, pouring by the trainload from the efficient commuting trains, their speech and faces leave no doubt in anyone's mind that the only German thing left in Gdansk is the architecture. The change of population is a standing shock to anyone brought up to think of the city as the classic Hanseatic stronghold of the history-books, the hometown of Schopenhauer and many who thought like him, the origin also of the hundreds of diverting stamps marked *"Freie Stadt Danzig,"* which made the civic coat of arms so familiar to junior philatelists in the 'thirties. It is not much of a shock to the Poles. Although here, as in Wroclaw, most of the new inhabitants come from the dispossessed Polish east, there are enough to remember not so much the venerable narrow buildings of the German area, as the huge Nazi flags which hung from most of them. They recall not so much the quaintness of the vanished German street names as the fact that it was physically dangerous for anyone to be overheard speaking Polish in the streets in that pre-war period, although for centuries the city had a large Polish population.

There is something neat and homelike about the buildings of Danzig and the former German enclave, set in their groves of disciplined trees above the windy Baltic. One can imagine the ponderous German vacation family life of the Grand Hotel in Sopot— the flaxen-haired children playing on the sands, the latter-day imitator of Thomas Mann torturedly walking the boardwalk wondering whether he is a *Bürger,* a *Künstler,* or just a plain Nazi. It was while walking along this Germanic seacoast, with a Polish lady from Warsaw, that I heard the tragedy behind the problem inherent in the Western Territories, and in fact, all Poland, given an expressive voice. "When they came here first, between the Germans and the Russians," she said, shaking her prematurely greyed head, "our Polish ancestors had to walk thousands of miles. What a pity, as long as they were about it, that they couldn't have walked just a few hundred miles further west."

7

The Pond at Oswiecim

> "How do you expect me to understand someone like Françoise Sagan? Do you know what has happened here?"
>
> —*A Polish lady in Cracow, during a literary discussion*

SOME 15 MILES southeast of the city of Katowice a small round pond lies festering in a grove of trees. From the banks a rickety bridge or footwalk runs out to the middle of the pond, its boards now old and rotting. The hum of insects rises from the shrubbery around the water, and an unhealthy haze spreads over the whole spot, inseparable from the miles of marshy meadow that surround it. Since the pond is shallow, it is possible to observe the peculiar surface of the bottom, a speckling of thousands of white, gritty fragments mixed with the dulled metal of what seems to be chipped tin.

The white fragments are bits of human bones. The grayness of the bottom around them comes from the tons of ashes that were dumped into this still pond between the years 1940 and 1945. The dulled metal in the water is the remains of spoons and razors, hairpins and curlers, thousands piled on thousands, carried into the German concentration and extermination camp at Oswiecim by the people who came to die there. More of the same lies around the

185

pond, which has been very little interfered with since its part-time
German proprietors abandoned it on January 18, 1945. There
are rusted razors with the trademarks of every European country
rotting on their surface, burnt spoons of every shape and design
and the not inconsiderable quantities of bones and ashes that somebody spilled.

The Polish government now maintains as a museum the fenced
enclosures of Oswiecim concentration camp, more formally known
as *Konzentrationslager Auschwitz*. The pond is itself but a tiny
part of the huge complex, which in its heyday embraced not only
the camp at Oswiecim proper, but 39 sub-camps scattered over
a large expanse of Upper Silesia and Czechoslovakia. When the
SS guards left for the last time in 1945, they attempted to burn
the most obvious evidences of their activities along with their camp
records—and some hundreds of sick prisoners who were roasted
in their huts. But the pond, in its ultimate caricature of a village
water hole, has an evil immediacy to its sight that cannot be supplied by the seried barracks, the ruined crematorium, or even the
warehouses which originally contained some seven tons of plun-
dered human hair.

No imagination can stand still looking at that pond. In its shallow depths, through the broken fragments of people that pave
them, one can see the Europe that can never be put together again.
There are the large white houses, and the angry people who grew
tired of supporting them, the banks that failed and the bread that
gave out, the armies that marched but never fought, the gangsters
that learned the secret of marching. There are the disillusioned le-
galities of Woodrow Wilson and Franz Josef, the temporary triumphs of Goebbels, Chamberlain, Pilsudski and the senior Henry
Cabot Lodge. There are the active seeds of Communism. Each
clean white bone is a reminder that Stalin's anti-morality could
grow so great, because the Germans' immorality had been so awful
and any successor to this immorality would seem at first to be good.

I arrived at Oswiecim* to take advantage of the best Communist
protocol. When our car pulled up to the large gates, it was enough
to describe my companion and myself with the magic word *"Dele-
gatcja."* After even a few years of Communist rule, people realize

* On a visit to Poland in mid-1957.

that the only tourists to be reckoned with are the ever-present "delegations," whether from "trade unions," neighboring countries in the "socialist camp" or groups of interested visitors from the West. An American *"delegatsiya"* was especially attractive, and we secured a private guide without any trouble. As it happened, he spoke only German.

The world will probably never see an example of premeditated cruelty that would compare with Auschwitz. Heinrich Himmler selected the camp site himself, and its meticulous organization bore every mark of his warped school-master's mind. It was purposely sited in an area where health conditions were poor. The damp, marshy atmosphere catered to the ravages of malaria and typhus. A German SS medical report stated very early in the business that the water in the camp was not even suitable for rinsing the mouth. The triple or quadruple-tiered bunks, still visible in a few of the buildings, lacked even straw for bedding. There were no floors and most roofs were made of tar-paper. Special sanitary and building precautions, including concrete flooring, new roofs and improved drainage systems were necessary when the Germans converted one or two of the flimsy barrack buildings for the use of cattle.

In its heyday in 1943 the base camp at Oswiecim held over 30,000 prisoners, and the larger adjoining camp at Brzezinka (part of the Auschwitz complex) had as many as 150,000. Those who survived their preliminary treatment were not expected to last more than six weeks. If a man were there longer, the SS authorities suspected him of stealing food or somehow extracting special privileges just to gain the slight additional time. During the days, the prisoners worked in labor camps or factories in the area, interspersing their toil with a brutal program of enforced exercises, drills, and systematic persecution by either the SS guards or the "Capos," the cadre of trusties who kept order among the prisoners. All of the Capos were originally long-term German criminals transferred from their permanent jails to put a stamp of professional bullying on the camp organization.

Regularly, mornings and evenings, the prisoners marched through the gates of the base camp on their way to work details, forcibly tramping to the tune of a prisoners' band, which played

appropriate German marches. Over their heads the SS had written
their ironic motto in huge Gothic lettering: *"Arbeit macht frei—*
work makes you free!" Men who faltered on the march were at best
cruelly beaten, more generally freed for good by shooting, for the
SS guards received a bonus for each prisoner killed "trying to escape." The daily "sports" periods were euphemisms for orgies of
beatings by the guards and the trusties, done while the exhausted
prisoners obeyed an unceasing series of commands to run, jump,
dance or march—all in a crouching position. Food was cut to below a bare minimum. There was watery soup and a coffee substitute once a day, which was all that any prisoner got. Whatever
extras even the SS commissary had chosen to include in the prison
ration were gobbled up by the SS men for their own bulging mess.

Jews and Roman Catholic priests had the highest mortality rate
among the labor camp prisoners. They were, among other things,
harnessed daily to huge rollers designed to smooth out new paths
inside the compounds, kicked and beaten as they fruitlessly tugged
at them and fell in tracks. When a man died, his corpse was laid
alongside the living for roll-call. The camp administration was
most meticulous about the numerical tallies on its rosters.

All this was within our guide's immediate experience. A quiet,
good-natured man, he was a student in Cracow when the Germans
packed him off to Oswiecim in one of the periodic round-ups of
able-bodied Poles in the streets. He had spent a year there and
survived, just how he was not exactly sure. As a souvenir of his
experience, like thousands of other Poles I saw—the manager of a
factory, a journalist union official in Warsaw, Prime Minister
Joseph Cyrankiewicz—he carries with him an indelible blue tattoo
on his arm. His number is written on it. The Poles do not notice
these tattoos any more. For a stranger they are objects of horrified
fascination.

As we walked down the carefully lined rows of long barracks
and huts he gave us a faithful, but chatty resume of their former
uses. ("Here the baggage of over ninety thousand prisoners is still
stored . . . In this one the German doctors performed their experiments . . . In that cellar they killed most of the Russian prisoners . . ."). Quite a few foreign visitors come each year, he explained, and they are all shown around with this inevitable lack of

passion. Before the October Revolution in 1956 the Communists larded the tour with constant propaganda explanations and charges. Now, to the considerable relief of the local "museum" staff, they leave it alone.

No propaganda is needed, and very little conversation. It is all the unaided human intellect can do to grasp the fact that all of this actually happened. Eerie enough are the housefuls of clothes, artificial legs, glasses and suitcases—from every corner of Europe. The pictures are even worse. Lining the corridors are the photographs of what seems to be an entire generation of Poland (and it was virtually that). There are students, electricians, farmers, professors, housewives, priests, carpenters and clerks. They are almost all young, with eyes luminously sad. Each has a date in 1942, '43 or '44 written under his or her name.

Across the fields from the work camp, past the grisly pond with the ashes and the spoons, lies a grassed-over railroad siding and the remains of a few buildings. Here the horror reached its apex. It is the scene of the mass exterminations. For two years the Germans drove Jews from all over Europe into this very siding. Most of them had been told they were being resettled. Thus encouraged, they sold their houses, land and possessions and moved into the railroad cattle cars that clicked their way to Oswiecim. Many were promised they were to be exchanged for German prisoners of war then in England. When they detrained at Oswiecim, they guilelessly asked other prisoners how many miles it was to the English Channel.

As the unfortunate of Europe later found out, this kind of "English Channel" had many tributaries. A few days before I visited Oswiecim, I had the chance to see another monument to the German occupation, the smaller concentration and extermination camp at Majdanek, not far from the old city of Lublin. The horror of Majdanek rivals that of Oswiecim, the more particularly since the Majdanek camp, undisturbed like Auschwitz by official gates or a museum souvenir shop, comes upon the traveler without warning, in the middle of the flat, peaceful farmland. The wooden watchtowers of the SS guards still stand as they were on the day of liberation, their timbers sagging a bit from the weather and the decade-long carvings of souvenir hunters.

When we drove up there, we found only a few Polish tourists wandering through the old compound, with the guidance of a state caretaker. Unlike the larger camp, there was no corps of interpreters; fortunately a Polish student friend was with me. During two hours inspecting the camp, I was able, however, to exchange a few direct words with our driver, who turned out to have been a concentration camp inmate himself. His German stemmed almost exclusively from his mastery of German songs. At Dachau, his particular alma mater, the camp proprietors had felt strongly that the prisoners should occupy themselves with singing. As a result, this Polish cab-driver kept with him the forcibly received legacy of a whole *Liederkreis*—marching songs, funny songs, and the kind, sentimental songs for which Germans are famous.

Time has given its healing perspective to the camps at Oswiecim and Majdanek. The Russians have long since replaced the Germans, with Poles as with Americans, as the popular enemy.* The Polish guide at Oswiecim cheerfully shows visiting parties of Germans around the precincts, not without some creditable embarrassment, at least, on the part of the visitors. No less a psychical authority than Carl Gustav Jung has pointed out, in his *Essay on the History of the Time,* that the Nazi sickness was the sickness of all Europe, of which Germany served merely as the focus. It is certainly true that the alacrity with which others participated in the German atrocities gives few Europeans the right to speak for an unblemished community. Yet for anyone who has passed through these camps, even now, a return visit to Germany will never be quite the same.

There were more than three million Jews in Poland in 1939. At the end of the war there were less than 80,000 remaining. The great majority died in the crematoria of Oswiecim, Majdanek and elsewhere, or perished in the streets of Polish towns. Polish writers on that period recall incidents where starving Jewish children, temporarily escaped from the ghetto, were shot down by German patrols, and died where they fell. Others were systematically killed

---

* Although the Gomulka government, for obvious reasons, tries constantly to remind the Poles of Germany's wartime horrors with the implication that Adenauer's followers are constantly on the verge of marching east with a veritable SS Army, to recreate the experience.

by SS execution squads, which in time were inextricably attached
to the impeccably traditional units of the German army. "I want
to look the century in the face, sir," says the perceptive German
soldier to his commanding officer in Hans Scholz' post-war novel,
Am Grünen Strand der Spree. With these words, permission
granted, he goes off in fascinated horror to watch the execution
squad do its work.

There is an uncomfortable feeling of looking the century in the
face, however long after the fact, when one stands on the site of
the Warsaw Ghetto. The spare stone monument to the Jewish dead
here is tasteful, and crushing in its simplicity. Housing developments are going up around it, and another generation may know
it differently. But as of now the site of the ghetto is bare. The
sounds of the city come up in the distance around it, but in the
center it is quite still.

It was in the 13th century that large numbers of Jews began
coming to Poland. They were the advance guard of a eastward
movement, the result of growing persecutions in England, France
and Germany, where the Jewish colony was already large. Mediaeval Poland, with its mixture of races already bubbling, was a
rather tolerant place by contrast with the rest of Europe. Edicts
of the Piast dynasty guaranteed freedom of religion to the Jews
who came to Poland. They prospered. At one time Poland contained four-fifths of world Jewry. Culturally, the Ashkenazi Jews
built up an imposing inner civilization of their own in Warsaw even
more than in Prague or Cologne. At the same time Jews began
to pass into the mainstream of the Polish community, as they did
in Germany. In time the Jews comprised some of the brightest,
most advanced and cultured elements of the Polish state—as well
as a majority of the village money-lenders.

The Jews in Poland were at first better treated than in Germany
or most parts of Europe. Various royal decrees not only protected
them, but gave them certain special privileges in the community.
As early as the twelfth century, fines were imposed on Christians
who molested Jews, a nicety of feeling rare for that time. Yet as
more Jews came fleeing to Poland from German persecution, the
old incubus of anti-Semitism fastened itself on the backs of the
Poles. The most obviously alien among them became the perennial

scapegoat, the more fiercely persecuted for being devoted to his own ways and beliefs. Gradually, economic discontent added its teeth to spiritual disapproval, for the Jews, however poor the majority of them were, became identified with a definite prosperous merchant class. Phenomena like the *pogrom* of Russia were not unknown in Poland. The first recorded attack on the Jews in Poland occurred in Poznan in 1367. It was not to be the last.

There were anti-Jewish disturbances in eight Polish cities in 1919, just as the country was regaining its independence. Through the ensuing years of the Polish republic, anti-Semitism became an unpleasant part of some party platforms. This could not have happened had not anti-Jewish feelings already been popular among large sections of the population. Their virulence was exacerbated by the old vicious circle of discrimination-breeding-isolation-breeding-more-discrimination. Admittedly the Polish Jewish community was far more religious, more homogeneous and more distinct from the rest of the country than in any European nation. In language (most of the Jews spoke Yiddish) and costume as well as religion, the Polish Jew tended to set himself apart from his countrymen. He lived almost exclusively in cities and tended to concentrate in commerce and the law—partly through inclination, partly because other channels of endeavor were closed to him. There was no future for Jews (unless they were converted Christians) in government, for example.

But Jewish "apartness"—and Jewish energy—of course only intensified the anti-Semitic mood. By the 1930s virtually half the country's trade was conducted by Jewish businesses; over half the lawyers in Poland were Jewish and one-third of the doctors. These facts were constantly drummed into the electorate by "patriotic" rabble-rousers, and they had their effect. By 1938 there were rigorous quota systems in all Polish universities, and Jewish students refused to sit down at lectures in protest against the virulent anti-Semitic agitation of student political groups. In 1938 there was a notorious race riot in Brest-Litovsk, in which two Jews were killed, sixty injured and several million zlotys worth of property destroyed. The following year the Germans marched in to give anti-Semitism their own ultimate codification.

It is true that thousands of Polish Jews managed to survive the war, because Christian Poles hid them and took care of them, with great courage. (The penalty for sheltering a Jew was death.) One lady I met in Warsaw owed her life to the monks of a monastery near Lwow, who hid her for years inside a sliding panel in their library. There were other Jews with similar stories. But the Poles who gave protection to the Jews were in a minority. When the Ghetto in Warsaw finally rose against the Germans in April, 1943, its less than 40,000 survivors fought alone. They were all who were left of the 430,000 Jews once confined there. The others had long since been killed.

In 1945 there was a chance that the few Jews remaining could find peace after their horror. More than any people in Europe, the Poles knew the extent of the Nazi liquidation. The smoke from the crematoria could hardly have been concealed. Like the rest of the world, they felt remorse for what had happened, but in a far more immediate way. Then the vicious circle of misunderstanding began again. Its superficial cause was the large numbers of Jews in high-ranking Communist circles, and particularly in the new state's secret police. Jacob Berman, the most Russified of Poland's Stalinist directorate, was Jewish, like Matyas Rakosi in Hungary; so was Hilary Minc, the clever Communist economic dictator. The U.B. leaders Romkowski, Rozanski and Fajgin, later tried for their crimes by the Gomulka government, were Jewish. So was Josef Swiatlo, who spilled the beans on his U.B. associates over the broadcasting network of Radio Free Europe.

It is not hard to find an explanation for the frequent appearance of Jews among the Communist leadership. The origins of discontented people like Minc and Fajgin can be traced to the isolation which so many educated Jews were made to feel in the intolerant Polish society of the period between the wars. For the secularized Jewish intellectual, once he fled the religious orthodoxy of his own Jewish community, was not welcomed generally by the Christian Poles. All too often, it was the far left-wing groups that gave him his only social and spiritual hospitality. If anyone ever had a good social excuse for going Communist, it was a Polish Jew.

Ironically, it was the Communists who fanned the flames of anti-Semitism, when they appeared after 1953. When Khrushchev paid his celebrated Warsaw visit in October, 1956, and during Bulganin's earlier Warsaw trip, the Russians quite baldly suggested to Polish Communists that they blame the whole of the "Stalinist" excesses on the Jews. This was the origin of Khrushchev's cruel remark that there were "too many Abramovitches in your Polish Party."

Gomulka and Cyrankiewicz, to their credit, resisted this pressure; but on a popular level, the damage was already done. It did little good to remind the Poles that young Jewish intellectuals played a leading part in the October Revolution which had gained for the Poles their measure of freedom. The old stirrings of anti-Semitism were enough to decide most of the Jews left in Poland on emigration to Israel, as it did those who had the good luck to be finally repatriated to Russia. In the first year after the October Revolution some 40,000 Jews left Poland for Israel.

I remember dining with an entire family of able, sophisticated Polish Jews, temporarily resettled, to whom this represented the only solution. Everyone in the family had suffered terribly during the war. The wife had managed to work and support the entire family, on the strength of the fact that she looked like a Gentile. The husband, a doctor, had since reestablished himself, and his waiting rooms were full of grateful Polish patients. But even the hints of further persecution are more, understandably, than these people can bear. They applied for their Israeli visa, driven by no particular enthusiasm or hope. Nothing more than the impelling need to escape once again.

8

Pillage and Patriots

> "All of us in Poland know that this country has been pillaged by methods at which every honest man would shudder . . ."
>
> —*The Grand Duke Constantine, 1822*

T HE HISTORY of Poland, as distinguished from tradition and archaeology, begins in the tenth century, 963 to be exact. Fittingly, in view of its troubled course, the date noted the attack of a German margrave on the Polish prince Mieszko, who was traditionally fourth in the dynasty of what later became the Piast kings. When Mieszko accepted Christianity three years later, it was as much from political urgency as religious faith. (In the early Middle Ages, particularly among the German princes, it was always open season on pagans.) Why had Poland as a nation entered so relatively late on the stage of European history? The answer lies in its position at almost the center of the Slavic peoples. Other Slavic peoples had hitherto been a buffer to the west, against the rising Germans; and there was no danger of attack from the south or from the as yet disorganized Russians in the east. Most European nations had their boundaries and their political systems forged in battle. The Poles had at least the advantage of a few extra centuries of peace.

Once Poland came to the notice of history, it did so with a

vengeance. The first Piast to use the title of King—Boleslaw I—
greatly spread the boundaries of his sovereignty. The Polanians,
as the Poles were then called,* were a vigorous and compact people, easily able to make their way against the advancing Germans
to the west and the scattered Russians and Lithuanians to the east
of them. By the eleventh century, the kingdom of Poland had
pushed its boundaries to the Baltic on the north and the Carpathian
Mountains on the south, the Oder River on the west and the Bug
on the east. In other words, it enjoyed much the same boundaries
as the Polish state of 1958.

Between 1138, when Boleslaw III died, and 1958, however,
the Poles and their boundaries did a lot of traveling. They traveled
most wisely, perhaps, during the reign of Casimir the Great, who
made the Polish kingdom one of the strongest and most forward-
looking countries of mediaeval Europe. Casimir restored much of
the kingdom's boundaries and its morale, both damaged by the in-
vasions of German Teutonic Knights and the same Tartars, under
the descendants of Ghengis Khan, who made mincemeat out of
mediaeval Russia. It was he who founded the University of Cracow
(1364) and attracted scholars and merchants to his country from
all Europe. Under Casimir, the Poles for a time brought close the
two traditional antipodes of their history—Great Poland, the home
of the Piasts, centering around the cities of Gniezno and Poznan,
and Little Poland, the area of the southern Poles, with its capital
in Cracow.

Barely a decade after Casimir died, the Poles were in trouble
again, principally with the Teutonic Knights on their northern and
western flanks. It was to strengthen the kingdom that Casimir's
successor, the 13-year-old Queen Jadwiga, married Jagiello, the
pagan Duke of Lithuania. When Jagiello accepted Christianity
as a condition of union, he brought his countrymen into the Roman Catholic Church as well. He defeated the Teutonic Knights
in 1410 at the Battle of Grunwald, one of the great fighting dates
in Polish history. Besides being monarch of Poland, he retained
control of Lithuania, which in those days covered huge territories
in what are now the eastern republics of the Soviet Union. As

---

* The name, meaning "field-dwellers," makes its own comment on the
Poles' exposed geography.

such, he necessarily turned his face eastward, to confront the rising power of the Grand Duchy of Moscow, which even in those days had begun to live by conquest.

From this time on, as inevitably as the progress of a three-act tragedy, the Poles found themselves the prisoners of their no-man's-land geography. Two ideals lived side by side in a very uneasy coexistence: that of Piast Poland, which saw the territory and the energies of Poland concentrated in the west, a powerful if not governing factor in German Imperial politics, and the new Jagiellonian Poland, whose spokesmen looked to the east, past the stronghold cities of Wilno and Lwow towards Kiev, Novgorod, and even further, past Romania to the Polish-held territory on the Black Sea. The Jagiellos at varying times controlled huge stretches of land between the Dnieper and the Dniester, northward through the Ukraine to the upper Baltic. At one point in the almost constant border warfare, the Poles captured and garrisoned the Kremlin. With what later generations of Poles could have told them was an excess of magnanimity, they later retreated from Moscow, leaving the place intact.

For almost two centuries, the Poles juggled these two ideals successfully, and the frontiers that went with them. But the job was a taxing one, requiring continual skill and vigilance. In time of trouble, there was no safe fastness for the Polish armies to retreat to, no respite in which to regroup. Steadily the German and the Russian pressures increased, although not yet acting in concert.* The Polish state was an enlightened ornament of mediaeval and early Renaissance civilization. It admitted the New Learning to its courts, in line with the old Polish tradition that had already produced geniuses like the astronomer Copernicus and the humanist statesman Cardinal Olesnicki. But circumstances and the impetuosity of the Poles themselves militated against the erection of stable, defensible borders. In the end it was a combination of internal disunity and the unrest of the subject peoples in the east

---

* In the mid-sixteenth century Poland had its last chance to destroy the rising power of the Moscow czars, and missed it. When King Sigismund Augustus told the Crim Tartars that he was negotiating with the Russians, at the moment of their greatest weakness, the Tartar Khan, a political realist, sent him the caustic question: "If you did not profit now from the plight of your enemy, when will you?" The date was 1542.

—Cossacks and Ukrainians—that shattered the Polish kingdom.

Sigismund Augustus, the last of the Jagiellos, died in 1572. After him the Poles resorted to the device of electing their monarchs. There was a certain democracy about this. In many ways, the Poles justified their national designation of the Royal Republic. But what began as a search for a new and continuing royal dynasty ended in a recurrent caterwauling debate over royal candidates which made the modern proceedings of the French Assembly in the Fourth Republic look like models of unanimity. The increasingly powerful neighbors of Poland—Prussia, Austria, and Russia— began to have an increasingly visible hand in Polish national policy. And all three hands were rather dirty. The last great military exploit of the Poles was the relief of Vienna in 1683 by King John Sobieski, who revenged a series of past defeats at the hands of the Turks. It was a magnificent grand-stand gesture for a country already exhausted by continual wars. The Austrians repaid it by participating in Poland's partition less than a century later.

By 1772, when this first partition was made, Poland had neither the strength nor the unity to resist it. The moving spirits were the Russia of Catherine and the Prussia of Frederick the Great. Empress Maria Theresa of Austria, bound at least by ties of religion to the Poles, was less eager for the spoils—although, as Frederick said sarcastically later, "she took them."

The Poles meanwhile had finally suspended the long spiritual debate between Piast Poland and Jagiellonian Poland to put their house in order. A series of reforms was begun under Stanislaus Poniatowski, who was fated to be the last Polish king. In 1791 a Reform Constitution was promulgated, savoring of the recent French and American revolutions. But the reform that had been forgotten in a middling strong Poland was too late to help a weak one. In 1792 the Russians marched in. The Polish Army was surprisingly successful in several engagements, but before a united front of enemies the king and his advisors lost courage. Russian troops marched into Warsaw, looking to the Poles just about the way they looked in 1945. The Germans quickly got together with the Russians to cut the tired Polish melon a second time. History calls it the Partition of 1793.

Thaddeus Kosciuszko, who had gone overseas to help Washington's army in the American Revolution, now led one of his own. He united the whole country behind him, peasants and gentry equally, and the Russians were expelled from Warsaw and most of the occupied territory in two months of fighting. At this point, the Prussians threw an army on the Poles' backs. They captured Cracow, then joined the Russians in another siege of Warsaw. After Kosciuszko had been defeated and captured at the battle of Maciejowice, the Russians sacked the Warsaw suburb of Praga with great slaughter. It was the same suburb from which the Soviet army in 1944 watched the Germans suppress the Warsaw Uprising, without lifting a hand to assist the Polish victims.

In 1795 the last partition wiped Poland off the map of Europe. During the Napoleonic era, there was a brief seven years of independence for a truncated Duchy of Warsaw, and hope for much more. Napoleon was a great promiser, especially in the middle of a campaign, and he promised so effectively that Polish cavalry units led his army's advance into Moscow. But Poland after Waterloo was reduced to a semiautonomous kingdom within the Russian empire—not to speak of the territories absorbed in Prussia and Austria. Twice the Poles rose against the Russians, in 1830 and 1863, each time to be suppressed with great bloodshed. In the Austrian territories things were not so bad. The Poles in Cracow had some degree of real autonomy and could exert an influence on their own governing. But the people of Russian-occupied Warsaw and German-occupied Poznan lived a subject life.

*   *   *

At the beginning of World War I, the Poles found themselves in the half satisfying position of Cinderella being asked urgently to dance by the wicked sisters and all their friends. The unity of the partitioning powers finally broken, both Russia and the Central Powers started vying for the affections, and the military services, of the greatest possible number of their Polish subjects. The result was a bitter merry-go-round of shifting loyalties. The Polish Legion of Marshal Pilsudski, the socialist-turned-soldier, started out fighting for the Germans with a successful two year campaign against the Russians. But by 1917 Pilsudski as well as many of his legionnaires had been imprisoned by the Germans, and effective action against the Russians closed. Other Poles, following the lead of the statesman Roman Dmowski, cast their lot with the Allies from the beginning. In the last battles of the Western Front, after the Bolshevik Revolution in Russia, a Polish army under General Haller was fighting with the Allies against the Germans.

All of these shifts were done for the one object of securing Polish independence, not out of love for any of the Great Power adversaries. It was in the end President Woodrow Wilson's insistence that insured a resurrected Poland. (Lloyd George, among other European leaders, kept sniping away at the Polish claims until the last.) To set up an "indisputably Polish state" was the thirteenth of his Fourteen Points.

The borders of this state, once everyone had finally agreed on the principle of its existence, proved the same headache as Polish borders always had been. In the end, disregarding the insistence of Wilson on having a state with purely Polish populations, the Versailles map-makers accepted a border that went part of the distance back to the Jagiellonian Poland in the east, without regaining the historic eastern borderlands of pre-partition days. This sowed the seeds for future trouble by splitting the Ukrainian and Byelorussian peoples between Poland and the new Union of Soviet Socialist Republics. The new Polish state had at least 30 per cent of its population composed of non-Poles—Ukrainians, Ruthenians, Germans, Lithuanians among them.

In the west the new borders satisfied neither the Poles nor the Germans, and were set up in a steady rain of haggling plebiscites and local uprisings. Sizeable national minorities were stranded with their suitcases and their lands (as long as they could hang on to them) on both sides of the border. The famous Polish Corridor came into being with Danzig (by now German although historically Polish) a free city in the middle of it. It was the uneasy border system of the days of the Teutonic Knights all over again. In less than two decades the very unknightly regime of Adolf Hitler was loudly demanding its "rectification."

At the very beginning of their new life as a nation, the Poles had to fight for what borders they got. The Russians marched westward under the command of Generals Budenny and Tukhachevsky, and fought their way to the gates of Warsaw, where Pilsudski's armies threw them back. It cannot be said that the Poles were a wholly innocent invaded party. Before Budenny's advance Pilsudski had previously charged into Soviet territory and captured Kiev, in his attempt to set up an independent Ukraine. But the militant Red attacks had the effect of confirming the Polish suspicion that a Russian is a Russian—whether Communist or Czarist—as far as Poland is concerned. The Bolshevik scare was certainly a contributing factor to Pilsudski's repudiation of all his former socialism, the moment peace was restored. "I left the red carriage," he said in a famous aphorism, "at the station called Independence."

Behind Pilsudski's military front, a constitutional government was set up in Warsaw and the Poles tried their hand at parliamentary rule. But 123 years of national suppression had left Polish democratic processes a little creaky at the joints. In 1926, after destructive inter-party bickering, Pilsudski ran off a *coup d'etat* and ruled as a semi-benevolent dictator until his death in 1935. After him came Smigly-Rydz, who was also given the title "marshal," and his ill-starred foreign minister, Colonel Beck. In their foreign policy, Pilsudski and his colonels played a desperate and not very wise game between the Germans and the Russians, or, more frequently, between the new power of Hitler and the post-war understandings with the French and the British.

Domestically, their program did not have much better luck. Although much progress was made in reconstructing and creating parts of the new nation-state—the ground-up construction of the new Baltic seaport, Gdynia, was an example—the government of Pilsudski and his successors was too spasmodic in its activity to do much permanent work. The economy needed some pump-priming and this, unfortunately for the Poles, was before the time of ECA. The economy was largely agricultural, and very disturbed by the political troubles of the post-war period. A great national effort was needed to integrate it. Whenever it was attempted, it foundered because of political disunity and inexperience.

For all its faults, however, the Pilsudski regime was not the base tar-baby that Communist propagandists have since kept conjuring up, by way of justifying their own excesses. If the rule could be described correctly as "authoritarian," it was a kind of authoritarianism which did not have either gas chambers or a Communist

secret police, which permitted, in fact, a huge amount of personal
freedom among its citizens compared to the Nazi and Communist
vises that were subsequently fastened upon them.

Pilsudski and his successors were known later by the rather
derogatory name of *sanacja,* or "healing," regime. They deserved
derogatory epithets principally because they showed a gross lack
of realism, political and economic, that contributed heavily to their
country's terrible sufferings in the decade and a half beginning
with 1939.

*   *   *

Less than a century before the *Wehrmacht* sent its *Panzer* across
the Poznanian plain, Otto von Bismarck, in a moment of characteristic candor, set forth the German attitude towards Poland. "I
am full of sympathy for the Poles," he conceded, "but if we are
to exist we can do nothing except root them out; the wolf cannot
help having been created by God as he is, but we shoot him all the
same when we can." Ever since Frederick the Great got his palms
on Silesia in the eighteenth century, the attitude this expressed
was stated German policy. In this sense Hitler, like the Soviets in
so many cases, was only doing utterly and brutally what his more
civilized predecessors had done partially.

From its beginning the German invasion was characterized by a
hopeless lack of realism on the part of everyone except the Germans and their Russian partners. In Jan Karski's *Story of a Secret
State,* one of many Polish reminiscences of those days, he men-
tions going off to the colors, when the pre-war Polish government
finally mobilized, in a half holiday spirit. He was particularly
pleased that his artillery regiment was to assemble at Oswiecim,
because there in the flat meadows he could see many opportunities
for pleasant off-duty riding. He ended, like most of his fellows in
the army, surrendering to the Russians in demoralized and hopelessly fragmented parts of an army. Others were killed or captured,
division by division, by the Germans, at a time when the British
and French sat quietly behind their 'phony war' defenses in the
West and military experts in the U. S. still talked confidently of
'General Mud' slowing down the mechanized German advance
(which could then be cut up by the "brave Polish cavalry").

Brave they were, but to little purpose. At that, those captured were fortunate. The Germans, with their penchant for obeying rules in one direction and practicing regulated bestiality in others, treated the captured Polish troops as prisoners of war, as the Geneva Convention stipulated. Many of the 1939 prisoners got off far more easily than their helpless families who were picked off the streets of Poland in later years for forced labor or worse in the German camps.

Militarily speaking, the campaign was enough to delight the most pessimistic of German General Staff planners. In conditions resembling those of a classic field exercise, the Germans threw 42 first-line divisions, backed by strong reserves, into a clever mobile campaign against a total of 30 Polish divisions. These were not only organized as World War I anachronisms, but committed as well to a hopelessly impractical yard-by-yard defense of a long, straggling border that made one wonder how the Polish Marshal Rydz-Smigly had ever got his Army commission.*

It took the German Army less than a month to demonstrate the military truth of General Hans von Seeckt's long-standing observation, following Bismarck's wolf-shooting lead, that "Poland's existence is unbearable. It must vanish through its own inner weakness, and through Russia . . . with Germany's help." This time the successors to General von Seekt's *Reichswehr* got there first. In his post-war memoirs, written with the élan of the fastidious butcher-shop proprietor that characterizes so many German staff reminiscences, Field Marshal von Mannstein noted the *reductio ad absurdum* of the tragic Polish defeat. At Kielce, the officers of the German Army Group South messed in a small room decorated with a huge oil-painting showing Rydz-Smigly, marshal's baton clutched firmly in hand, before a background of attacking Polish cavalry. By the time the military art fanciers arrived on the scene, the Marshal's cavalry was virtually destroyed. Rydz-Smigly himself was posting hard for the Romanian border

---

* In justice to the pre-war Polish planners, it should be noted that the border defense had some political motives, which seemed logical at the time. It was widely believed that any armed action, if it occurred, would be quickly followed by an armistice. In that case the Poles wanted to hang on to as much of their own territory as possible.

—"not without having carefully sent his own household furnishings to a safe place," as Mannstein was careful to observe.

That the battle was so swift was in fact a blessing. "If we had been stronger," wrote the perceptive Polish journalist, Stefan Kisielewski, 19 years later, "and if our war with Germany had lasted not three weeks but three months, then not only all the bridges would have been destroyed, but not a house would have been left."

As it was, the Germans made their destructive intentions abundantly clear. The houses damaged during the 1939 bombardment of Warsaw were conspicuously left unrepaired. The Nazi leader Hans Frank was appointed governor general of the truncated central and southern regions; the entire western part of the country was incorporated bodily into Germany. Frank's domain was designed as a subsidiary colony of the Germans, with less rights than any other occupied country. Poles and Jews in the areas incorporated into Germany were bodily moved in to the Government General, to exist at a closely defined level of wretchedness. All valuable industry was ordered removed to Germany, or what was now regarded as Germany. Colonists from Germany, or whole settlements of *Volksdeutsche* from elsewhere in Europe were moved into the territories as fast as the trains could carry their household effects.

The next four years represented a systematic effort to follow Bismarck to the letter. By comparison with some later Russian achievements in this extermination line it was amateurish; and there were Germans who could never overcome mixed feelings of shame and guilt at the horrors they were perpetrating. Horrors they were though, and of a sort that would never have been visited on western Europeans. The word "Pole" to a German persistently represented something inferior and somewhat unclean. Once such a notion is fixed in people's minds, cruelty becomes more fluent.

Everything conceivable was done to abolish the Poles as a nation. Mass corruption was encouraged and codified by the Germans. The Warsaw black market in time grew famous, the venality of its German customers exploited by the fighting Polish underground as well as the seedier elements in the population. Education in Polish was virtually done away with. A thorough and lasting effort was made to root out the intelligentsia. Priests, professors, lawyers, journalists were prime targets. "From the old Warsaw press corps," one of its survivors later estimated, "and I would say this is true of all Poland, there are barely 20 per cent of us left."

Well over one million Poles were deported to Germany for forced labor. Some were taken into the German army. Many more others got the fate of the prisoners in Oswiecim or Majdanek. Else they were shot out of hand, sometimes totally without cause, as hostages or simply elements that the Germans wanted to get rid of. "If I wished to order that one should hang up posters about every seven Poles shot," Frank once boasted, "there would not be forests enough in Poland with which to make paper for these posters."

On September 17, 1939 the Russians marched into eastern Poland to complete the dismemberment of the country, or, rather, to reestablish the dismemberment of 1795, when Russian and German sentries had met in similar circumstances at their new common frontier. With the entire country occupied, the Poles did their work of organizing an underground resistance. General Wladyslaw Sikorski was a fortunate choice as Premier of the government-in-exile. A long-time opponent of the late Marshal Pilsudski and his friends, he guided it with spirit and skill, politically and militarily, until his unfortunate death in a Gibraltar airplane crash in 1943.

Now that the war effort of the London Poles is again officially recognized, Sikorski can be talked about in Poland. Although others in the wartime governments have varying reputations, there is no doubt about the honor and respect Poles still give to his name. Even in the painful negotiations with Stalin for the release of imprisoned Polish soldiers for the common war effort, Sikorski was the one Pole who could make some little headway.

The Polish underground, operating under Sikorski's direction from London, became the most formidable in Europe in an amazingly short time. It operated its own schools, newspapers, welfare services and small munitions plants throughout the German-occupied territory. Its clandestine military arm, the Home Army,* was

* Known generally by its initials of A.K., for Armia Krajowa.

echeloned and distributed almost as efficiently as the Polish armies fighting in Italy, Narvik and the Middle East, and the Polish Navy and Air Force flying out of Britain. The Resistance hampered the Germans in many ways, and kept the population remarkably united against them as well. Couriers went back and forth from the underground to the outside world. Wireless stations, constantly operating just about a half step ahead of the German detection crews, were in daily communication with London. There was a system of courts—and executioners, to pass and fulfill sentences against conspicuous collaborators with the Nazis. Everything was prepared for the final moment of rising, when the Poles would unite with the victorious allies and fulfill the promises that the slightly overconfident cavalry officers had been making in August 1939.

Unfortunately the liberator was to be the wrong ally. By 1944 it was all too clear that the Russian armies, now thoughtfully motorized by U.S. Lend-Lease, would arrive very shortly at the Polish border. It was in that year that the fateful decision was made to stage an uprising of the Home Army in Warsaw, in the hope of seizing the capital from the retreating Germans, helped by the threat of the advancing armies of Marshals Zhukov and Rokossowski.

On August 1, 1944 the Home Army began its fight for Warsaw. Promptly at five p.m., firing began at the Germans from the windows of houses, street corners and at barricades thrown together. The Army Commander, General Tadeusz Bor-Komorowski, had calculated that his 40,000 troops could capture and hold the city for a matter of days, given the steady pressure of the Russians, now only eight miles away, and continuance of what looked like the beginning of a German collapse. He had small arms and machine guns for half his troops, and medical and food supplies for a week.

The decision for an uprising was a calculated risk on the part of the London Poles. In the face of continued Soviet advance, and the presence of a Soviet-sponsored puppet government, waiting in Lublin for the expected take-over, both London and the Home Army leaders on the spot realized they would have to make some show of strength themselves—if their legitimate government was to survive. They hoped that the example of the Uprising would work powerfully on Allied public opinion, if not the judgments of the Allied military leaders, and bring both renewed pressure from the Russians and air reinforcement from the West.

In this hope they were badly deceived. To begin with, the Germans reacted against the Uprising with a speed and force that the Poles had not imagined. Five divisions were thrown into the battle for the city, after the Poles had made some striking initial successes. Reenforcements were taken from the front to assist them, both ground and air forces. Despite this overwhelming strength against it, the Home Army put up an amazing fight in the city, still confidently expecting help from the outside. One of Bor-Komorowski's messages to London, dated ten days after the revolt's beginning, shows the dawning feeling of abandonment, as help did not come:

"These are our conditions of fighting: we have received from you but one small dropped supply. On the German-Russian front, lull since the third. But for the exception of a short speech by the Deputy Prime Minister from London on the eighth, nothing to comfort us. The soldiers and population of the capital look in vain to the skies, expecting Allied help. They only see German aircraft against a background of German smoke."

Allied air drops were in fact planned to a considerable degree. But the long distances involved tested the ultimate ranges of the aircraft then in operation. Incapable of defending itself properly, the air drop operation was a tragic failure. Losses were huge, and the material which actually got through to the Poles negligible. The hope of ground pressure from the West, or paratroops, was completely visionary. The chances of a quick Allied victory in the West had already been muffed by the SHAEF high command's apparent determined aversion to concentrating its forces at any one point for a breakthrough.* With the front virtually stabilized, it was clear that General Eisenhower, who then as always regarded caution as the supreme virtue, would risk no aid for a militarily dubious operation in the East.

Much argument has since raged over whether the Russians could have reached the capital in time to bail Bors' troops out. It is true

---

* Chester Wilmot's "The Struggle for Europe" gives the best summary of this major command failure.

that the headlong momentum of the Soviet advance had been halted on a line running just east of Warsaw. But stubborn German resistance and the Russians' need for logistical regrouping are hardly enough to explain the victorious Red Army's four and a half month delay before Warsaw. All evidence points to the fact that had the Home Army been Communist, Warsaw would have been relieved. As it was, the Russians were all too eager to let the Germans deal with the independent Poles. Advancing with the Russian armies were the Communist Polish units of General Berling's Kosciuszko Division, who were to establish Communism militarily in Poland. The Communist committee at Lublin, backed by Communist underground units throughout the country, was already engaged in setting it up politically. In Moscow, the Soviet leadership first brazenly ignored the plight of Warsaw, then discussed aid efforts with studied and skilful procrastination. The Russians clearly did not want a desperate resistance movement to interfere with their plans for Poland's occupation.

So the Poles went through the last act of their military martyrdom in weeks of steady fighting, hopelessly ill supplied with weapons and food, constantly pushed back by the unexpected arrival of German reinforcements. German tanks again made a battlefield of Warsaw, blazing out clear fields for fire along the large avenues like Marszalkowska and Nowy Swiat. The Home Army was reduced to communicating with its scattered strong points through the city sewers. No meaningful air assistance was to be had from the allies, for the immediate reason that the Russians refused to permit American shuttle landings on Soviet fields. (A shuttle system would at last have permitted large-scale air drops.)

As far as the pressures of the big picture were concerned, President Roosevelt was too engrossed with his illusory hopes about doing business with Stalin, to do much more than deprecate the situation. Churchill ventured more, but was held back both by Soviet and his own military staff opposition. On October 2 Bors surrendered. Just four months later the armies of Rokossowski marched in. "You wanted to fight the Germans," said a Russian officer to a woman member of the Home Army, "Well, we thought we'd watch and see how you did."

Before Warsaw surrendered, survivors of the Home Army

were being hunted down all over Poland by the newly formed
security police. Sixteen Polish underground leaders, including General Okulicki, the Home Army's last commander, were enticed to
Moscow, then quietly taken off to imprisonment elsewhere in the
Soviet Union. Okulicki died in prison in 1955.

The Warsaw uprising, with its more than 200,000 killed, was a
national revolt that came straight from the main stream of Europe's history. It was founded on the traditional pull of nationalism, made bolder by oppression. It was a foretaste of Budapest
more than ten years after it, as it was a reflection of many uprisings before it in Polish history—1831, 1848, 1863, 1904. It
was frustrated by a mechanism that earlier nationalists had not
reckoned with: the cool-headed oppressor who moved the more
efficiently because he was untroubled by the necessity of pretenses
at morality, or excuses of expediency. In Warsaw, 1944, the
Soviet armies waiting across the Vistula did even deadlier work
than the Asiatic tank battalions in Budapest twelve years later.

Yet the very savagery of the Russians in 1944 made the Poles
in 1956 discipline their impulses to active revolt in a way quite
extraordinary in history, especially Polish history. They knew
the depths of implacability. They knew the futility of courage.
They knew the undependability of allies. They had a mass sense
of the possible that is rarely given to groups of people—let alone
a whole population. They took their step, then they stopped. They
were prepared to go the limit, but they forced themselves to halt
just before it was reached.

Seen from the perspective of recent history, the struggles of the
Poles through World War II and its aftermath suggest moves on
a cruelly tilted chessboard, their every bold or clever stroke either
cancelled or obliterated by a sliding of the piece in the opposite
direction. The diplomacy involved is interesting in itself as a study
in various forms of Allied self-deception, and hardly a happy
record. For if the London Poles were too unbending for their own
good in diplomatic negotiations with the new Soviet power, they
were more than matched in their unrealism by the wishful thinking of the Roosevelt diplomacy. The French revolutionist Lamar-
tine was at least being frank in his self-interest when he denied
aid to Poland in 1848 with the words: "We love Poland . . . we

love all the oppressed nations, but most of all we love France."
In their handling of the Polish question in and after World War
II, the American statesmen, from Roosevelt through Eisenhower,
only deceived themselves with their Micawberish altruism.

Far more immediate to the visitor is the palpable effect of all
these reverses on this country's people. The Poles, admittedly, have
learned through centuries to cope with adversity in their own way.
No race anywhere has a more impressive, if often exasperating
capacity to live and feed on its illusions, to excuse away the actual
present by concentrating on the implausible future. Like mountain-
climbers, pure disciples of Ghandi, and the U.S. Marines, the Poles
have made adversity an essential part of their morale equipment.
Never was this quality so put to the test as during the double-decade
1939 to 1958.

In 1939 there were 35 million citizens in the Polish republic—
of whom almost one-third were admittedly not Poles at all, but
Ukrainians, Byelo-Russians, *Volksdeutsche* or Lithuanians who
were either passively unhappy or actively discontented at being
placed under Polish rule by the Council of Four at Versailles.
In 1945 there were 23 million Poles left to make up the population of the new country. Six million Poles (including the three
million Polish Jews) had lost their lives in the war. Those who
survived could hardly say that they were alive exclusively because
of their bravery or virtue, although there were many brave and
virtuous among them. Nor was it always the tough ones who came
through. There were a lot of tough ones killed in Oswiecim or in
the battles of Warsaw. There were tough ones in the lime pits which
the Russians dug for the corpses after the massacre at Katyn.

In 1957 I asked a prominent Polish manager with a four digit
Auschwitz number tattooed on his forearm just how he had seen
the experience through. Survivors with low numbers are conspicuously rare, since the German camp commandants had made it virtual policy that prisoners should not be allowed to live after four
months. "Luck," he said thoughtfully.

In many cases it was something worse than luck. Especially at
the home front, the survivors were as often as not the people who
had developed the fastest footwork in a society where law had all
but collapsed. The footwork might have involved getting an illegal

ration card, or hijacking a food shipment, or informing on a friend. The awful legacy of both Nazi and Communist occupations is the fact that they made criminality into a virtue, or at least a necessity. Even the brief experience with the inconveniences of wartime rationing between 1942 and 1945 was enough to make lawbreakers or downright crooks out of thousands of Americans. In Poland, where people have had to *live* on the black market, not had the choice of dabbling in it, the spread of basic chicanery was multiplied almost to an infinite degree. Almost unconsciously, its effects have seeped into the country's soul. A government official would solicitously ask a tourist whether he is getting a good rate for his dollars on the black market. A promising Warsaw student could quote in an instant the going rate of exchange, and goods, on the local black market anywhere. Such people were not what one might call black market types. They were and are honest, constructive citizens of the community, merely grown used to facing the realities of their existence, where the moral distinctions between soldier and robber, merchant and smuggler have long since grown vague in the popular mind.

This tactical struggle for existence, bad enough in itself, must be played out against the ever-fresh background of Poland's three great disillusionments. The first was the failure of the Allies to help Poland in 1939. The second was their inability to liberate Poland after World War II, with the consequent complete betrayal of the underground Resistance. The final false liberation was of course the October Revolution of 1956 itself. Every Pole, inside Poland and abroad, knows and appreciates the reasons underlying Gomulka's frustrating course of compromise, constantly swinging the wheel between liberation and repression. The fact of Russian power is inescapable, and it is there. But realization is hardly enough to blow away the frustrations of a people who had their revolution frozen into curious immobility, just when it seemed within reach of success.

The result of this recent history is widespread apathy, a desire to escape conditions as they are, even if only in one's mind. The only really active force in Poland today is religion, and even that is not enough, as the constant exhortations of the Primate and other bishops confess, to restore a tattered morality. Drinking is obsessive.* The vodka barometer is always falling—whether with a miner struggling along a street corner in Katowice in early afternoon, or a prominent journalist in Wroclaw to all intents and purposes comatose in the hotel dining-room by two p.m. Or it can be the crowd at the Kameralna, one of Warsaw's weird night clubs, where the customers stage their drunken fights with something like boredom, as if they were wearily trying to live up to a conception of what a lively night club drunk ought to be.

In vain, newspaper editorials constantly remind their readers that vodka consumption—now over 70 million quarts a year—has jumped two or three millions each year, steadily; or that, in 1958, the money spent on vodka virtually cancelled out the total amount of the national wage increase. In vain Gomulka makes his warning moralistic lectures. All too often the pupils are not vertical enough to notice that they are being rapped on the knuckles.

A country that uses vodka as a spiritual Alka-Seltzer is not a happy phenomenon. But given the circumstances of this country's recent history, the wonder is that the Poles, drunk or sober, have managed to survive at all. No visitor could pass even a few days in Poland without taking off his hat to the tremendous guts of its people. No American, in particular, could spend any time there at all without pondering, with sadness, the appalling gulf of unshared experience that divides Poland and the rest of Eastern Europe from the calm and comfortable legal minds in the U.S. State Department and elsewhere who devise their philosophies of "liberation" or "retrenchment" or "massive retaliation" or worse in the wholly deceptive safety of a nation that has yet to taste horror in person.

---

* I recall the night of a friend's arrival in Warsaw, at the inevitable Hotel Bristol. The porter was too unsteady to offer anything other than moral support with his baggage. The female clerks at the desk had clearly been dipping into the vodka font recently. One had the feeling that admission was less the result of a reservation than a chance—and momentarily favorable—whim. The elevator operator came down in his old-fashioned grillwork cage in answer to his bell, one hand at the controls of the elevator, the other adjusting a bottle to his lips. When the tourist moved to the bar, by the power of suggestion if nothing else, he found the bartender liberally quaffing his own wares behind the counter. He ordered a vodka, but admitted that he had no Polish currency to pay for it with. "It doesn't matter," the barkeep said and poured him one. And then, "Have another."

Books can be written about the sufferings of Europe's body and spirit, movies and plays seen. But the experience cannot be measured, let alone felt by anyone who did not live it. Most of the available witness about the Nazi period, at that, comes from Western Europe, where the privations were at least on a level comprehensible to American experience. They thus could not be compared to the country where the ghetto and the gas-chamber were commonplaces, and the cities were destroyed not once, but two or three times over. "In 1939, when I first saw the Marszalkowska burning," a Polish woman relates, "I stood and wept, watching everything that was familiar to me being strangely destroyed. In 1944, when it was all smashed again, I could not even cry. I was beyond tears. We just watched it and tried to save ourselves. I know they have rebuilt the city, but I never want to go to Warsaw again."

The wartime experience of the Japanese was in some ways similarly awful. Even the Warsaw Ghetto in 1943 might have been preferable to Nagasaki or Hiroshima. Certainly the people of the Polish countryside never had to undergo anything like the concentrated horror visited on the people of Guam or Okinawa during the bombardment and the subsequent ground fighting there. But Japanese, Okinawans or Filipinos were the fortunate possessors of stable and unified social structures, based on an unswerving traditional cooperation; their very society was an efficient if temporary cushion against the accumulation of physical horrors.

Not so in Poland. There one found a society crippled with its own confusions, pockmarked by its own peculiar talent for disunity in all but the severest times of crisis. Within the space of 15 years this society was subjected, helpless, to every destructive and demoralizing artifice of the two great thuggeries of modern times —each one determined through ancient traditional nationalism, as well as modern "ideological" reasons, to exterminate Poland. Both thuggeries, especially the Communist, stubbornly masqueraded as forces for good and/or inevitable standard-bearers of progress. Each managed to appeal to certain elements inside Poland itself. Allies failed. Leaders were chronically found wanting. When peace finally returned, it was only to replace the fire of the war years with the steady cauterizing work of a puppet Communist government, determined to sear away the last bit of freedom. Only the church remained to the Poles. At times, if we rule out the supernatural, even this consolation survived by a narrow margin.

Heard against the sound of history, "Poland Is Not Yet Lost" makes an apt title for the country's national anthem. The very survival of these 28,500,000 people renders the flamboyant prayerful words of the anthem almost prosaic.* Is the Black Virgin of Czestochowa a true and real presence, as the peasants in the crowd believe? Was there some truth in the claim of Mickiewicz in his poem that Poland was the "Christ of nations"?

Faced with the unbelievable national resistance of this country, no foreign observer would be polite to disregard these ancient nationalist traditions. And few people outside his country would be in a position to criticize or moralize extensively as Wladyslaw, aged 40, Polish worker, father of four, hope of his country, survivor of Bismarck, Pilsudski, Majdanek, Hitler, Stalin and the prisons of the Bezpieka, walks down to the *kawarnia* on pay day to get plastered on a half-litre of bad vodka.

---

* "While we live she is existing,
   Poland is not yet fallen;
   We will win, with swords resisting,
   What the foe has stolen. . . ."

9

The Plan and the Jungle

> "For some persons think that the right regulation of property is the most important, the question of property, they say, being universally the cause of party strife."
>
> —*Aristotle,* Politics

IN THE CENTER of the Lenin works at the Polish steel town of Nowa Huta there is a huge heap of iron ore. It sprawls dull and dirty in the well arranged disorder common to steel mills, giving of its mass to the heavy cranes that hoist the ore on tracks leading to the modern furnaces. It is the food of the industry. Without its constant bulk to devour, all the brains and power of this new artificial steel city will go idle, and with them much of Poland's national investment.

The ore comes from Krivoi Rog, far east in the Soviet Union, where faceless workers take it out of the ground. Or, to be more specific, 75% of it comes from Krivoi Rog. A similar proportion holds true, if in varying degrees, of the basic materials for almost every major factory in Poland. The miles of track leading back into Russia hold each segment of the economy in their steel grip. When the cars do not come west on the tracks, the wheels in the factories do not spin; the furnaces light to no purpose.

At the time of the October Revolution, the cars stopped at

Nowa Huta. The huge grey-black heap beside the tracks sank lower with unmistakable meaning. After Russian-Polish relations were resumed, the cars from Krivoi Rog started coming again. Now there is generally as much as a month's supply of ore on hand.

In October, 1956, the workers at Nova Huta led the people in their area in the national protest against the Soviet Union. They knew far better than the rest of the country what that protest might have entailed. For the spectacle of Poland, as every other country in eastern Europe, is that of a nation made a colony by deliberate disruption of its economy, arranged so that everything in that economy flows into and out of the Center in Moscow.

The complement to colonization is the spectacle of "Marxist-Leninist principles," with or without overt Russian help, at work destroying a country's economy. In the beginning, Poland's national Communist proprietors were revolted by the havoc and the waste of Communism's own untrammeled "planification." That is why, mindful of the ore heaps at Nowa Huta, they have still tried, with guilty courage, to right some of the wrongs done.

*   *   *

During the years of foreign occupations, the Poles developed the idea of the "two Polands." One Poland was the country of reality as it existed under whatever foreign occupation happened to be current—poor, downtrodden, angry, but forced to keep its wishes passive by the unpleasant strength of the occupation. The other was the nation of plans and hopes, as they were fostered by the patriotic Polish emigration outside the country's borders, aided by their agents within.

Although the "two Polands" idea continued through 12 years of Moscow Communist control, the relative freedoms of the early Gomulka government took away much of its force. Politically and socially, the nation of plans and hopes was allowed to invade the country of reality. There is now, as the First Secretary of the Party keeps thundering, only one Poland. And to a great extent he is right.

But the concept of the "two Polands" had meanwhile transferred itself from politics to another field. It has become the most convenient framework for describing the Polish economy—or for that matter the economies of Czechoslovakia, Communist China or the Soviet Union. There is now the Poland of the Plan, and the Poland of Reality, a double image which no amount of post-October patching has been able to unify.

The first image is Poland as it appears on the charts of the current Five- (or the new Fifteen-) Year Plan. It is a land of constantly advancing industry, of burgeoning farmland, of surging trade. Led by keen-eyed ministers from Warsaw, assisted by the lean-jawed committeemen of the industrial trusts, put into practice by dedicated plant managers and unselfish patriotic workers, the new economic Poland is if anything the statistical economic recreation of the mythical central European kingdom where all the women were beautiful, the men fought like lions (but rarely had to) and the wine sat on the palate like the distillation of a thousand summer nights.

If Poland of the Economic Plan has its troubles, they appear invariably as moral failings or temporary circumstantial difficulties. Raw materials may be lacking. There may not be enough trained personnel. Or, most sad of all, the workers or sometimes even the plant managers may not be dedicated or unselfish enough. But this, as every schooled Marxist-Leninist can say, is merely a matter of insufficient indoctrination. If the workers are shown the need for sacrifices, the Plan says, they will understand the glorious goal. Temporarily, they may need discipline.

The Poland of the Economic Reality is far different. It is a feral place of constant, tired struggle, where everyone has his price, but the price is seldom enough. It is a jungle of interminable queues for some of life's necessities and haggling or pilfering for others. Its water-holes are the black-marketplaces in every city, like the Ciuchy in the Praga district of Warsaw, where scuffed shoes are haggled for and the prices of crushed American cigarets are never low. Its dwelling places are plastered ruins where four families must share a four room apartment. Its most available commodity is the zloty, that curious fur-bearing financial animal which changes its pelt with annoying irregularity—now 100 to the dollar, now 125, now 140.*

* The official foreign tourist rate, inaugurated in 1957, is now 24. Until 1957 it was 4.

The jungle has its show-places, given it by the Poland of the Plan, and there is some hope in them. A new high-speed electric railway runs from Katowice to Warsaw. A large new ship slides off the ways at the Gdansk shipyards. The miners' houses at the privileged Szambierki Mine at Bytom sit, neat and attractive, not too dissimilar from some company towns in the coal belts of the United States. A large new Orbis hotel opens in Warsaw. But such monuments of comfort and triumphs of industry have to most of the jungle's inhabitants the appeal of a viaduct super-highway running through a slum. When people in the Other Poland see them, they may feel more anger than pride. This does not belong to them, no more than does the very well-furnished apartment of a New Class journalist in Warsaw. The jungle's hero is more likely to be the man who smuggles and gets away with it, the worker who goes easy on the job to do another one, the housewife who finds a little bacon to bring back to the communal kitchen. The jungle's principal relaxation is vodka Saturday afternoon and Saturday night, before it goes to church on Sunday.

These two Polands have existed side by side since 1945, although they were not at first irreconcilable. But they grew steadily more distant from each other, so that by 1956 there was open war between them. The Gomulka government, when it emerged from the debates of the Eighth Plenum in 1956, in effect pledged itself to bring the two images together. In some fields, notably agriculture, it succeeded in doing this, with a correspondingly good influence on both Plan and Reality. In others it merely tried, or half tried. The bumpy history of the country's economy between 1956 and 1959 is the story of this interestingly public effort.

Gomulka and his followers set out to make their economy efficient because on its stabilization rested the government's and country's hopes of survival. They set out to appease the just demands of the workers, which Gomulka recognized as just. For well over a year idealistic economists, many of them the angry young men of the October, preached that the images of the two Polands would at last be brought together "under socialism" (without of course admitting that they were ever really apart).

As his political dealings with the Sejm and the intellectual opposition made plain, however, Gomulka refused to sacrifice Party control to economic efficiency. A thousand circumlocutions were therefore invented, a hundred different expedients tried, to fit Reality into a new Plan. They all foundered on the immovable facts that a good Party *political* plan is almost by definition uneconomic, that workers want primarily to work for themselves and their families, that they will work hard only if treated fairly and given incentives. A young mining official in the coal country, discussing the latest quota system in 1957, said it all: "People do not work for these artificial things. They work for a house, for something they own, for something concrete."

It should be said nonetheless that the effort has been unique among Communist rulerships, in that it was made and to an extent made sincerely. The New Economic Policy in the Soviet 'twenties was lined with deceit. In the minds of most of its proprietors, it was used as a calculated stop-gap until the regime became strong enough to enforce planning with police. The Yugoslav experiment of workers' councils was equally a stratagem, done by *fiat*. In Poland, on the other hand, the two worlds of the government's Plan and the people's Reality tried hard to come to an understanding. This is something which has never been attempted in the closed satellite economies of Czechoslovakia or Bulgaria, to say nothing of Communist China, where the advertised economic concessions of 1956–57 turned out to be mere provocation, paving the way for the 1958 communes.

In the Soviet Union the Plan has long since made Reality in a sense dependent on it. Its people, wise in the ways of Communist living, have themselves formalized the differences in the two worlds as they have long experienced them. The Soviet Union of the Plan is the outer world which they learn about in school and read about in the papers, in which Soviet citizens believe. It is the world of documents and officials, norms and Marxist explanation. But beneath it is the Soviet citizen's private world of Reality. They call this, familiarly, *Blatnoy Mir,* the world of bribes, chicanery and wholesale corruption. Without *blat* it is difficult to live.

Occasionally the world of *blat* breaks surface in the official press, with the *Pravda* story of the crooked athlete or the wicked factory manager so beloved by the feature departments of American newspapers. But in practice the two worlds live together and separately. The incongruity and immorality of their joint existence does not disturb many Soviet minds. The modern Russian in this respect is like a man who has lived next door to a dragon all his life, regularly feeds it and struggles with it, and equally regularly reads official proofs and assurances that by all the standards of truth the dragon cannot possibly exist. So after a while, he gets indignant, if its existence is pointed out to him.

This double life, which the Soviet Union exemplifies, is made inevitable by the premises from which modern Communist economics proceed. As Djilas said in *The New Class*, Lenin's idea of politics as "concentrated economy" has been inverted in modern Communist practice: "economy has become concentrated politics; that is, politics play an almost decisive role in the economy." It is safe to take out the 'almost' in his statement. In the world of the Plan ideology disguises every motive as an economic one. Yet actually all economic motives and plans are only disguised systems of political control.

None of the satellite countries has yet grown grey enough under the Soviet system of economics to accept it wholly. Even in such an obedient satellite as Czechoslovakia, the government has had to make concessions to popular feelings, based on the memory of past standards, which would never be granted within the borders of the Soviet Union. In Hungary, economic rebellion insured the complete solidarity of the country behind its short revolutionary government; even the Kadar government has had to make concessions on this front in the last two years, long after the rebellion itself was smashed. It was given to the Poles to bring their protest against the Plan world out into the open. There it has stayed.

The Communists started their experiment in Poland with potential advantages which Pilsudski had never imagined; for, from a strictly economic standpoint, Poland's enforced move westward was a large net gain. The territory annexed by the Russians contained one-third of pre-war Poland's arable land, and half its forest areas. The territory gained from eastern Germany, by comparison, had an industrial potential two-thirds as large as the entire industrial output of pre-war Poland.*

* This is based on the 1938 figures for the area's actual industrial production.

Poland was put in a position to double its coal production. The move greatly increased the potential of zinc, lead and the small supply of iron ore—to say nothing of existing electric power facilities (and potential) and industrial plants, serviceable despite all the wartime destruction. The principal industrial raw materials lost in the rest were the entire supply of potash, much salt and almost four-fifths of the crude oil deposits (like the long colonized Zistersdorf fields in Austria, another testimonial to the Soviet fondness for oil diplomacy). The agricultural losses were outweighed, at least in potential, by the fact that the yield of the smaller German farm lands was in some cases, notably that of wheat, almost twice as great.

The development of the new western territories had been commercially as advanced as the lost eastern territories had been retarded. The 38,600 miles of ceded German territory was veined with 11,654 miles of railroad lines. The lost 69,500 square miles in the east had contained only 6,121. The development of roads, canals and other means of communication was proportionate. The disciplined waterways of the Oder network made a superb substitute for the sluggish river Bug. The bombed remains of Danzig and Stettin, awaiting their Polish rebaptism into Gdansk and Szczecin, were still great Baltic ports, the like of which Poland had not enjoyed since the modest medieval commerce of the Piast kings.

From this impressive new economic potential one critical element was wanting: people to run it. The losses sustained during the war years amounted to over 6,000,000 people. There was added tragedy in Germany's systematic liquidation of the Polish intelligentsia, the manager and in the skilled worker class. But pre-war Poland to begin with had been a largely agricultural country, its industry limited principally to the Silesian areas in the southwest. In 1937 over 60% of the population earned its living in agriculture, forestry or fishing.

The Poles quickly drove all Germans but a handful of miners from their new land. Besides the overweighting problem of resettling the old German areas, the Communist economic catechumens faced the fact that most of the people to settle in the west had come from precisely the areas in eastern Poland that had been least industrialized, least developed. [See Chapter 7.] To start the German machines going again, to say nothing of producing new Polish industry, virtually an entire new technical generation had to be educated. Czeslaw Bobrowski, the "liberal" economic planner who became Vice-Chairman of Gomulka's advisory Economic Council, described his central personnel problem very neatly, in a 1957 interview. "The proportion of engineers," he said, "is just the same as you have in the United States. Except in Poland they are all 25 years old."

But here the Communists had another factor in their favor. The very lack of an industrial tradition made the population less critical of their mistakes. Pre-war Poland had also had a great deal of centralized government control of industry, communications and utilities—if for no other reason than that a country rebuilding itself from scratch in 1918 had little time to develop organic capitalist traditions by 1939. Most Poles agreed, as they faced the reconstruction problems of 1945, that a large amount of state ownership was inevitable.

The first plans for economic reconstruction looked reasonably hopeful. The primary objectives of the new Central Board of Planning, to put roofs on the country's factories and shirts on the backs of the citizenry, were to say the least unexceptionable. They were powerfully helped by $481,000,000 worth of UNRRA assistance, which Poland continued to receive until 1947. Direct loans were made from several foreign countries, including a $90,000,000 U. S. credit. (There were difficulties about the latter from the very beginning, as the late Arthur Bliss Lane recalled in his book *I Saw Poland Betrayed,* especially when the Americans discovered that part of their money was going to support a security police apparatus.) Thus pursuing the first needs of reconstruction, doctrinaire Communism kept its inner thoughts to itself. For the first three years after World War II, Poland's economy remained a compromise between Communist ideas of statism and European socialist or peasant ideas of private, government or group enterprise. (Since most of the businessmen had been killed during the war, there was never much concern for them in the new order.)

The nationalization laws of 1946, while sweeping in their confiscations, were by comparison with later years almost apologetic in their excuses for needed national ownership. Other ordinances turned the new "march towards Socialism" into what was apparently to be an interesting three-legged race. Three sectors of the economy were defined and delimited: the nationalized sector, the private sector, the cooperative sector. The former included all the new 'socialized' industry; the second took in some of the farming population, small handicrafters and artisans and retail stores; the third included both agricultural elements and 'small production.' To any capitalist (who had the courage to admit it) the government offered a place in the middle private sector. He had only to set up a plan for a privately owned industrial plant and, subject to certain restrictions on private property, he might get it.

The prospect of the three-legged march to socialism delighted the Socialists, who still in those early days retained their independence from the Communists' United Workers Party. Private and cooperative business were encouraged, and they did much to reconstruct the country's economy in the early reconstruction period. The government, after the usual delusory plans for Communist land-reform, kept a wary hands-off attitude towards the peasantry. To many farmers, workers and small businessmen—who had not received much comfort from pre-war Polish governments—the Communists looked not at all bad.

While this period of cooperative reconstruction went on, which some Poles recall as the Party's NEP period, the planners in the Central Committee were busy inside their offices. Their leader was Hilary Minc, the very clever, soft-spoken Minister of Industry & Trade, who later became economic dictator of the country, and by consequence one of its most hated men. He had studied at the Sorbonne and worked for a time in the pre-war Polish Ministry of Finance. As early as 1928 he was deported from France for Communist activity, which he continued in Poland thereafter. He was an orthodox Moscow Pole. In 1939, when the Soviet troops moved into Poland, he marched back east in their rear and remained in the Soviet Union until the end of the war.

Neither Minc nor his friends on the Central Committee had the least intention of permitting their three-legged march towards socialism to gain momentum. Late in 1946, the first of a series of decrees rolled off the presses, restricting the newly given concessions to private business. The economic tightening that followed kept pace with the political. The share of the capitalist sector dropped from 9% of the gross value of industrial output in 1946 to not quite one per cent by 1950.* The cooperatives began to fade in 1948. Shortly after Tito defected from the bloc—a signal for general economic Bolshevizing, Minc announced that the farms would be turned into collectives, but gradually.

The following year Minc had the Central Board of Planning abolished. Bobrowski, who headed it, was packed off to become Ambassador to Sweden. Bobrowski's first Three Year Plan, by Minc's and Moscow's reckoning, had been a base concession to the consumer. A new State Commission of Economic Planning was established, Minc presiding, and a shining new plan came off the drawing boards. This, the Six Year Plan, was in Minc's own words, a copy of "the Soviet Union's Bolshevik methods." So began the now familiar cycle of absurdly high goals, production norms and fixed targets. Building and consumer goods were all but forgotten in the new, ruthless drive to put a fat new assembly line and an expanded mine shaft everywhere the Soviet Union wanted it.

*　　　　　*　　　　　*

In discussing the failings of the Six Year Plan, a highly placed Polish economist once noted, in what may have been conscious irony: "We went too fast. The theoretical capacity of our industry grew faster than our capacity to assimilate." The most superficial post-mortem shows how completely this theoretical capacity divorced itself from real facts. Even setting aside the strategical political purposes of the Plan, i.e., to complete the Communization of the people and the Russification of their industry, the tactical blunders committed were prodigious. Although higher mathematics has never been put under a Marxist anathema, the Planners in Warsaw demonstrated what has become the traditional ability of their kind to misunderstand anything but simple arithmetic. The goals of the Plan were set and fixed, as were the ratios of achievement for each year. But there was little or no effort made to establish any relationship between sectors of the economy.

* As reported in *Polish Postwar Economy* by Thad Paul Alton.

If one sector failed, its interdependent neighbor was supposed to go on as usual. It was the spectacle of a man who buys a machine, expecting each part to run for exactly the same time, at the same pace, without the need of a single repair.

The Planners found out in addition that there was something called cumulative damage, which they had neglected in their calculations. The old nursery rhyme about kingdom, battle, rider, shoe, etc. all lost for want of a nail may not be politically sound, but it is certainly true in economics. Lack of sufficient investment in a coal mine one year can mean an alarming decrease in production three or four years later. This in fact was the fate of the Polish mining industry, under the Six Year Plan.

The goals were also steep. Agriculture, positing a level of 100 in 1949, was expected to reach a level of 150 by 1955. Industry had to hit the 236 mark, while some sections of industry, like the machine-building industry, were supposed to find a lofty production level of 364.

Having thus set the goals, Warsaw's human calculators made no effort at coordination among them. As a Polish economist exemplified, writing in 1957,* "As compared with the Six Year Plan provisions, the outlays for construction (referring to centrally planned investments) were fulfilled 123.5 per cent. The other outlays, consisting of the purchase of machinery and equipment, reached only 74.5% of the planned level. In this way the execution of the investment program was constantly strained by the demands of construction and presented much greater difficulties than foreseen. . . . The scope of many investments was inadequately defined, with a tendency towards narrowing it. Thus, for example, the preliminary planning of a factory did not provide for the installation of such facilities as water, electricity, connecting roads or the construction of auxiliary installations necessary for production . . . the costs of investment were [also] underestimated. This meant that in order to complete many projects it was often necessary to spend half again or even twice as much as planned."

Little thought was given to plant obsolescence. In their faithful pursuance of existing Soviet models, the Planners ended by building

* Alexander Szerwentke in *Gospodarstwo Planowa,* January, 1957.

a number of plants which were out-moded and already economically inefficient by the time they were finished. They had no flexibility, except that required to revise the goals upward. The Planners' answer to any difficulty was to repeat in their own words the old injunction of *King Henry V:* "Once more unto the breach, dear friends, once more. . . ."

The result was as horrendous as expected. Profusions of unwanted items piled up, while kindred shortages magnified themselves, e.g., if production of automobile motors fell to a standstill, the manufacturer of headlights, inflated by the thought of higher norms and Marxist-Leninist promotion, went on overproducing his useless headlights. A small but typical case of this was published in the Warsaw press in 1956. An increased production of soda water and beer demanded 40 million metal bottle stoppers. Yet something went wrong at the bottle stopper works. The plan called for only 25 million, and it was at that only 56% realized. The breweries and the bottle factories had to cut down accordingly, and hastily. So, for want of bottle caps, the Poles had their fill of thirsty Saturday nights.

There was, finally, the neglected human element. While Hilary Minc (who quite possibly knew better) was calling for ever more enthusiastic production quotas, the condition of the worker grew desperate, and the Poland of reality began its slide downward to a real jungle existence. Even the first published estimates of the Six Year Plan allowed only 24 per cent of the investment for consumer goods and light industry. In fact, only 15 per cent was spent on light industry and the consumer. The consequent shortages in clothing and housing more than cancelled out any paper wage increases. The black market grew constantly stronger. While tens of thousands were drawn off the land to work in the swollen factories, the farmers left to work it showed a marked disinclination to produce more. They produced less.

The grumbling of the workers was hardly satisfied at the photographs of a new Polish automobile, the Warszawa, coming off the assembly lines of the hopelessly uneconomic Zeran plant in Warsaw—particularly since the finished cars had to travel in convoy from plant to their places of use, so many of them broke down in transit.

Here was another aspect of the vicious circle, one from which Polish industry has conspicuously not recovered. Since the only way to get any extra money was to increase one's output, speed became the only factor. A new expression called *"brakorobstwo"* (faulty production) entered the language. Defective machines, wet-down grain deliveries, bad or missing parts became the standard. The workers had stopped caring.

By 1955, with the crumbling of the U.B. police apparatus, the government lacked the mechanism to attempt the Soviet type of production-by-coercion. The devices used to mollify the public had long since been exposed as just that. The loudly announced price cuts in essential items did no good, since the items thereupon had a way of disappearing from the shelves, to be replaced by similar articles bearing different names, but with the old prices restored. The next year official spokesmen even began to admit that the announced real wage increases were incorrect due to a "mistake" at the accounting office. The Poland of the Plan and the Poland of Reality had never been farther apart.

Still, the Warsaw bureaucracy was beyond appeal. Wladyslaw Bienkowski noted this in a speech to a Communist discussion group (June 1957): "The system of authority and leadership has led in the past to this, that 20 millions of citizens were crippled.

"You could not sweep up the street nor fill up the hole in the pavement until this item appeared somewhere in the state commission on Economic Planning, or somewhere in the voivodship or local committee. This is the tragedy of the past period, in which we slowly and gradually paralyzed normal social life. . . ."

*　　　　*　　　　*

The ubiquitous poster of the happy worker, the masses of regularly cheering crowds, the centrally written pronouncements about the undying-vigor-of-the-working-classes-in-their-struggle-for-socialism: these are the centerpiece in the fake flower arrangement of every modern Communist economy. One of the most shriekingly denounced theses of the heretic Bukharin was his suggestion that the workers are in principle hostile to the state. For the myth of the Happy Worker is the prop justifying everything in the servile state from secret police systems to socialist realism in the arts.

Bukharin, the last Bolshevik theorist with either brains or honesty, never discarded the first Bolshevik premise that all the pain and shooting of Communism existed to pave the way for Marx' eventual withering-away of the state. Since the workers were naturally hostile to any state organism, realizing that all states were repressive, the transitional Communist state, he argued, must above all reckon with their hostility and placate it. The state must satisfy grievances, not exacerbate them. Only by so doing will it justify its existence.

June 28, 1956 was a great day for Bukharin, from whatever vantage point his shade may have viewed it. The Poznan revolt, which began then, finalized the three years of turbulence that began with the East Berlin riots and the Pilsen riots of 1953. Unlike the later October Revolution, Poznan started as a half-planned economic protest exactly like Pilsen. The Czech workers had gone out in the streets over the economic dislocation of the regime's currency reform. The incidents that set off Poznan were less spectacular, but of the same order. Overpaid taxes due the workers had not been returned. In addition, a slide-rule increase in their production norms, performed in the offices of the Warsaw bureaucracy, had decreased the actual amount of wages received. This was involved with the reclassification of the Cegielski factory from its formerly privileged position as a plant producing armaments. To finalize the indignities, the local administrators had forbidden any overtime work. They thereby forced a great number of workers to the practice of 'moonlighting.' Extra jobs were becoming almost routine for workers who wanted to feed their families.

Two days before the riots, a delegation of 30 workers had gone to Warsaw to see the Premier about their grievances. They had got as far as the Minister of Motorized Industry, one Julian Tokarski, who to his everlasting regret dealt with them brusquely. They came back to the factory equipped only with promises, and those on only a few of the points at issue.

The workers' meeting on Wednesday was not happy with the results, and they decided to show their feelings. By nine a.m. Thursday an orderly protest march was under way, headed for the square in front of the Town Hall. Speakers got up to address them, local Party officials included. There at first seemed no danger of violence. Foreign visitors staying in Poznan, sampling the official enthusiasm of the Trade Fair, saw nothing unusual.

But at the very time it seemed most orderly, the march of the irritated workers was generating violence. Since the workers' delegation had gone to Warsaw, rumors had started circulating that they were detained, as well as rebuffed. The people of other factories, hearing about the march, started to join it—notably the railway workers, who had been spectacularly abused. There was no recognizable leadership other than the encouraging power of community feeling. But this was enough to uncap the resentments of ten years' aging. Police militia took no steps to hinder the marchers. Many of them joined, and guns started to appear in the marchers' hands. There was little looting or actual disturbance on the way, even later in the afternoon. One of the most remarkable things about the demonstrators was the way they policed themselves. The few times that hoodlums in the crowd tried to disturb a store or a house, others pulled them out, with severity.

Flags and placards began to appear. Rumors spread. Shopkeepers and business men and students joined the march. It changed itself from several columns of factory workers into the spectacle of half a city moving through its own streets. When word passed that the original workers' delegation had been arrested, the crowds stormed the jail and freed everyone inside it. The original placards asking for higher wages gave way to new ones attacking the Russians and the Communist government. The chemical transformation was working which turns protests into angry shouts and gives one man the strength of ten because he has a hundred more behind him. At eleven a.m. the first shots were heard near the headquarters of the Bezpieka.

The resulting siege of the entire U.B. compound was accomplished in a most unprofessional way. Gasoline was clumsily put into beer bottles, and most of the improvised Molotov cocktails did not explode. It was only by chance that the demonstrators managed to set up a machine gun, which cut off the defenders of the headquarters into two sections. The U.B. at first fired over the heads of the crowd, then into it. By this time parts of the crowd were fanning out to attack other public edifices of Communism, like the radio jamming station.

The first troops arrived at three, called out by a panicked city government. They argued with the populace from the vantage point of their tanks and trucks; then they either stood idly by or actively joined the people. If the first tanks had any ammunition, they showed no inclination to use it. The second group of tanks and troops arrived about 5:30, and were equally ineffective. The crowds, which had then begun to organize, drove the tanks around the city, but they were too unskilled to use them.

At seven p.m. reinforced Army elements took over. They were careful about injuring demonstrators, and did their most effective work with tear gas. By the next day the Army was in general control, and the scared survivors of the U.B. free to resume their nasty work. By Thursday afternoon the fighting, where it occurred, had grown bitter. The picture of the marchers carrying a flag dipped in blood has become world-famous. There was no question about the universality of sentiment involved. One witness recalls the spectacle, extraordinary in a Europe so long spiritually divided, of the crowds lifting a picture of Our Lady of Czestochowa to the top of a captured building, while they were singing the old Socialist revolutionary song, *Na Barykady Ludu Raboczy* ("Workers, to the Barricades").

The complete spontaneity of the demonstration caused its failure as a military effort. But its lesson fell like a ton weight on the hardest-shelled Stalinist in Warsaw, as an example of how the whole country could well explode. That it all began with a dispute about overtime and back taxes, coming after long economic oppression, was on its face an ironic vindication of Marx' powerful inaugural address at the First International slightly over a century before: "That the emancipation of the working class must be achieved by the working class themselves . . . that the economic subjection of the man of labor to the monopolizer of the means of labor . . . lies at the bottom of servitude in all its forms of social misery, mental degradation and political dependence. . . ."

*   *   *

The Poznan Uprising killed any hope of proving the new System's superiority, or of faking it. Deception had already been ripped aside. Even the works of official economists could no longer hide the fact that the economy was not only broken but shredded. Even the straightest-faced spokesman could no longer evoke that reassuring phrase, "the economy is advancing on all sectors towards the building of socialism." The government in some cases was reduced to questioning the records of its own (already heavily padded) statistics. That knowing correspondent of *Le Monde,* Phillipe Ben, visiting Poland in August 1956, wryly discussed in his paper an interview with Premier Cyrankiewicz about the swollen numbers of the institute of "head accountants," a brotherhood charged with administering the records of nationalized enterprises. After reading in the Party paper that the brotherhood was then 150,000 strong, Ben continued: "This figure seemed so remarkable to us that we interviewed the premier about the matter. He seemed very surprised and was rather satisfied when someone of his suite suggested that perhaps *Trybuna Ludu* had made the mistake of adding one zero to the figure. Unfortunately, this had not happened. . . ."

The hopeless planification of too many accountants and not enough work could still have been blanketed by outright coercion, as in the Soviet Union. But besides being squeamish about this, the Warsaw government realized after Poznan that coercion was only to be achieved at the cost of revolution. The anger of the people had long passed the point where it could be contained by secret police surveillance and arrest. The only road left to the Party rulership was for it the most difficult—that of coming to terms with the population, of explaining the errors and trying to correct them. It was on the issue of how much to explain and how far to go that the decisive phase of the October Revolution was fought, inside the Central Committee's meeting rooms at the Belvedere Palace.

Gomulka's victory inside the Plenum was the signal for an honesty never before known in the economic statements of a Communist government. The bulk of his October 20 speech to the Central Committee concerned itself with the detailed admission of past failures. They included the building program, where only 370,000 rooms were constructed in the Six Year Plan, though 900,000 would have been needed even to maintain the level of housing current in 1950; the deception of the statisticians ("The juggling of figures which showed a 27 per cent rise in real wages during the Six Year Plan proved a failure. It only exasperated the people even more . . .”); the disasters of collectivization; the types of uneconomic investment. ("At the cost of tremendous investment, we built an automobile factory at Zeran. New industrial establishments have come into being, establishments which produce at disproportionately high production costs only limited numbers of automobiles which today hardly anyone produces in the world. Can the construction of an industrial establishment of this kind be called a contribution to the productive capacity of our industry?").

Even the accomplishments of the Six Year Plan turned sour the moment they were left standing. "These figures indicate," Gomulka cited, "that coal output went up by over 20 million tons, and this could really be considered a considerable achievement if this rise meant an increase in the mining industry's productive capacity. But statistical data reveal that in 1955 the miners worked 92,-634,000 hours overtime, constituting 15.5% of the total number of hours worked during this time. Calculated in terms of coal this amounts to 14.6 million tons of coal extracted outside of normal working hours.

"Let us go further and see what labor productivity was like in mining at that time. In 1949 coal output per working day per worker throughout the industry amounted to 1,328 kilograms. In 1955 it dropped to 1,163 kilograms, that is by 12.4 per cent. . . . In relation to 1938, which for various reasons cannot be taken as a basis of comparison, but illustrates the present state of the coal mines, output per working day per person employed in the mining industry dropped in 1955 by 36%.

"It emerges from the data quoted that coal mining not only has no achievements to its credit in the Six Year Plan, but even fell below the level of the year 1949. . . ."

As Gomulka himself conceded, and others spelled out, the problems of coal and other national resources were not exclusively domestic. A great many details of the arrangements made by Poland with the Soviet Union came out in the October wash. In a speech to the Central Party *aktiv* of the PZPR in December, one of the veteran economists, Eugeniusz Szyr, discussed in some detail the arrangement whereby the Poles had agreed in Moscow in 1945 to ship coal to the Soviet Union at prices about one-tenth the world market price. Between 1946 and 1953 the Poles shipped some 49.5 million tons of coal to the Soviet Union, for which they received about $57 million in payment. According to the value by world market prices, Poland lost some $525 million on the deal. Szyr added, hastily, that the coal sent to the Soviet Union was of a rough, unsorted variety.

A negotiation of this claim with Poland was one of the staples of the October, 1956 agreement reached with the Russians. But, Szyr warned the members of the *aktiv,* they should not expect any cash payments. "The Soviet party recognized the justice of the Polish stand and on this basis completely renounced the payment of debt which Poland incurred with regard to the Soviet Union up to November 1, 1956. This debt will be precisely described in the protocols of the ministries of finance of both countries. For the time being, according to the opinion of experts on both sides, the amount of this debt to November, 1956 will come to over 2,100,000,000 rubles." The sum of 2,100,000,000 rubles was, curiously enough, just the amount of Poland's coal claims.

As it further developed, the Poles had supported the upkeep of the Soviet Embassy in Poland, and not on the basis of anything like an American-style ECA counterpart fund agreement, either. The Russians had paid only token amounts for their use of the railroads in troop movements, or other communication lines.

All this the Russians promised to rectify as practices, to use Szyr's delicate words, "improper for cooperation among socialist countries." Nobody spoke out loud of the amount of goods looted from the former German territories at the end of World War II. There was also no hope of reclaiming those parts of the Polish economy which had gone to support the war effort of North Korea or the war chests of Communist parties in the West. In a series of articles which the censor never allowed to be published, *Po Prostu* had uncovered some interesting facts about Polish trade relations with France. The French trade had all been channeled through two French banks. Both of these banks were at the disposal of the French Communist Party, which had exacted 30% of each transaction as its fraternal socialist discount.

Gomulka had no automatic solutions to turn all these liabilities

into assets. It was one of the planks of his platform that the day of
the pat explanation, with solution added, had ended. He made
definite points about restoring a theory of real value in pricing
goods and setting goals. He left no doubt but that he would restore
a large measure of private enterprise in agriculture and small
business. But he made also the inescapable statement of honest
government, faced with economic chaos: before getting better,
things might have to get worse. "In the circumstances," he said,
"we must tell the workers the painful truth. We cannot afford at
the present moment any considerable increase in wages, for the
string has already been stretched so tight that it can break. Every
further increase of wages is indissolubly linked with the stepping
up of production and with the reduction of unit costs. This is by
no means pleasant either for us, or, especially, for the working
class."

Gomulka is not an economist. The world of the 'fifties has seen
enough wreckage of economists' mistaken predictions not to hold
this fact against him. Possibly because their respective publics expected too much of them, the economists, like their equivalent
wire-mesh professionals, the lawyers and the psychiatrists, no
longer have the agreed status of successful problem-solvers. Yet
the head of a planned state economy such as his is automatically
dependent on the economists who work for him. As a good political, Gomulka could see the broad problems he faced. He must restore the confidence of the workers; try as a stop-gap to ease restrictions on consumer goods; get back a feeling of initiative in
production, at the cost (for a Marxist) of returning some significant
areas to private enterprise; inject a feeling of realism into the planning, by which actual capacities for once would be taken into account. Since his areas of action were bounded not only by Russian
pressure but by his own limited Communist canons, he had to seek
help from the Communist economists whom he found around
him in the ministries. If they were demonstrably bad technicians,
they were still technicians. And technicians he had to have to
translate broad wishes into detailed directives.

The Warsaw economists took the cue. With what sincerity only
Providence can judge, there ensued among the corps of Planners a
mass rush to the public confessional, on a scale so sweeping as to

beggar description. The pages of *enragé* journals like *Po Prostu, Nowa Kultura* and *Zycie Warszawy* looked after October more than ever like economic editions of 'confidential' magazines, while the Party paper *Trybuna Ludu,* as befitting its more official character, took on the aspect of *True Confessions.* "Now it can be told," most of the articles would run, "I was a Stalinist economist (but I was working for the people and the true theory of values all the time)." Criticisms of government economic policy abounded before October, if they did not help precipitate it, e.g. it was no news to Polish newspaper readers that there was something drastically wrong with the Zeran automobile factory. But the flood gates fell apart thereafter.

It took only a few months for the percentage-pushers to recover from their initial shock. As men schooled in Communist procedures (and living very well by them) they grasped the fact that some deeper explanation than inefficiency was required to explain the economic wreckage around them. They emerged from these reflections with a highly imaginative Communist myth, well furnished with villains, heroes, innocent bystanders and extenuating circumstances. A few excerpts from a February 1957 speech of Dr. Oscar Lange's, the new Chairman of the Economic Council (and a faithful worker throughout the pre-Gomulka period) are enough to show the direction of the excuses: "The changes which took place in the following period, from 1949 to 1954, which we now refer to as the Stalinist period, were based on the narrowing down of this circle of allies (in building working class socialism). As is known, during that period we mechanically copied the methods of socialism accepted in the Soviet Union, and the basic elements of this imitation, which decided other things as well, was limiting ourselves to the worker-peasant alliance and squeezing out the petty bourgeoisie as well as sections of small capitalists.

"There were a number of reasons for this, the most important of which was the cold war, a time when the capitalist powers attempted to undermine from within the social basis of the proletariat in the People's Democracies. . . .

"As regards the sources of distortions in our country, one of the most important of them was actually the cold war situation and the desire for rapid industrialization, especially industrialization that had as its main aim the strengthening of our defense potential. Simultaneously there was a desire for a speedy elimination of capitalist and petty-bourgeois elements, dictated not by economic considerations. . . .

"During this period the opinion prevailed, perhaps rightly so, that these people could not be trusted too much because they lacked training, experience and so on; hence they should be allowed the least possible freedom of decision. . . .

"All this led to a system which today we call bureaucratic centralism. After a time this system became, to some extent, an independent factor, growing beyond necessity by its own inertia. . . . In time a social stratum was created with marked interests and opinions. . . .

"Bureaucratic-centralist methods in our country were methods of building socialism with the help of a war economy, technical means which are also used during war by capitalist states, for other purposes, to be sure. . . .

"It is, however, obvious that these methods of war economy which replaced economic stimuli with administrative decisions and moral-political appeals, which may be necessary and beneficial during a certain period, cannot be permanent methods for administering the national economy. That is why we are gradually departing from them. . . ."

*   *   *

While they were shoring up their past record, the Polish economists were also dividing themselves into two rival schools of thought, which thanks to the new freedom of discussion, could now advance and be recognized. One group, led by Stefan Jedrchowski, chairman of the Planning Committee and Eugeniusz Szyr, were orthodox Communists who had survived the changes brought about by their own abuses. They came to be known as the "Party economists." The others, loose-construction Communists and former Socialists, were known as the "liberal" group. Their spokesman was the same Oscar Lange who had produced the convincing explanations for the failings of the Six Year Plan.

Lange is the former Socialist who had spent some time before 1945 as a professor of economics at the University of Chicago.

After initially serving the new Polish government as Ambassador to the United States, he returned home to pitch into his specialty. He was a leading planner in the 'three-sector economy' program of the first Gomulka period; but by 1948 he had already discovered that it was far easier to be a sophisticated Marxist at the University of Chicago than it was in Warsaw. Like his fellow ex-Socialist, Cyrankiewicz, however, he trimmed his sails before the new Stalinist wind. He participated in the dissolution of the free Socialist Party and faithfully worked for its Communist successor. It was only in 1956, when the winds had noticeably shifted, that he again revealed himself as an active liberal.

In Lange's efforts he was assisted by Bobrowski and some others of like persuasion. Their vision of Gomulka's "new economic model" was an economy in which bureaucratic centralism could be eliminated by a drastic revision of Marxist economic thought. They proposed to give autonomy to individual factories, in a system whose central unity would be not the planning bureaucrat, but the director, guided by a workers' council. Their views on agriculture were similar. With this purge of bureaucracy would go a determined plan to give workers both material and (although they would have preferred not to use the word) spiritual incentives for working hard and efficiently, e.g. profit-sharing plans and a real voice in factory management. They were concerned about the human element, at least insofar as it affected productive efficiency. As Bobrowski said in a 1957 interview: "Another kind of worry is the dishonesty of the workers. Just as once the bourgeoisie discovered, from their point of view* the social-economic value of honesty, thus producing the example of a 'solid businessman,' so we must formulate the generally accepted habits of correct conduct within the framework of our institutions. . . . The institution of the establishment fund [a profit-sharing device] can become a dam, which will prevail over the famous 'disappearances' of goods at the bottom of the economic system. . . ."

The liberal economists were visibly affected by the Yugoslav experiments of workers' councils and individual factory autonomy.

---

* Hedges like "from their point of view," or "as it seemed to them" are indispensable tools of the liberal Marxist economist who wants to avoid trouble.

Nor were they averse, as veterans of the 1946 "three sector" days, to a considerable amount of private enterprise, or private cooperatives in agriculture and small business. In short, they advocated as much sensible economics as the traffic would bear.

The Party economists opposing them had no definite plan, outside of not liking the liberal one. As it later appeared, some of them were frankly nostalgic for the old days of the Plan. In the guerilla struggles across the conference table, Szyr and his followers, in particular, did their best to impede reform. They looked on it all with the horse-blinders' view of the drilled Party percentage-pusher, convinced that there was nothing wrong with the economy that some upward revisions of the Plan—and tighter police surveillance—could not cure. Thus began a struggle that would last as long as Gomulka's Poland. In a sense it was open warfare between the Poland of the Plan and the Poland of Reality, insofar as housebroken Marxist liberals like Lange were capable of representing the latter.

*   *   *

In agriculture the liberals carried all before them. The wreckage of the Planners was nowhere more complete. In every East European country, Bulgaria excepted, the program of farm collectivization had ended in disaster, a casualty of its own cruel inefficiency. Poland's damage was probably most severe. After distributing some 5.5 million hectares among small farmers in the land reform of 1944, the Warsaw government started the steps towards collectivization. At first they were made covertly inside the offices of Hilary Minc's Planning committee. After Gomulka's fall in 1949, the regime repudiated its promises and began to collectivize in earnest.

Every device of the Soviet model was brought into play. There was first the persecution of "kulaks," i.e. almost any independent farmer with a reasonably prosperous holding. They were discriminated against in the purchase of equipment and fertilizers, which is to say they virtually were barred from getting any. An onerous system of forced deliveries was begun, in which they were obligated to turn over to the government the great part of their crop yield, at unprofitable prices. Every avenue of social and economic pressure was used to dragoon farmers into the new collectives. A system of machine tractor stations was instituted—those political watchdogs of agriculture which Khrushchev himself abolished in the Soviet Union in 1957.

The only expedient the Warsaw government overlooked was wholesale killing, of the type which Stalin had ordered in the Soviet Union in 1929, after Yagoda, the head of the O.G.P.U. had warned him that the peasants' loyalty under collectivization could not be counted on. (*Razkulachivatj*—"kulakize"—a modern Russian synonym for "liquidate" resulted from the struggles of this period.) It never entered the Polish language, possibly because the Bierut regime was humanitarian in this respect, more probably because the Poles could not afford the wholesale human wastage possible in the Soviet Union. At all costs, the peasants had to be kept producing.

Produce they did, but in a manner well removed from the Planners' expectations. From 1949, when the intensive drive at collectivization began, the crop yield leveled off or dropped. Through the years, in fact, the yield came to vary in inverse proportion to the amount of forced collectivizing. In 1950/51, for example, when the record number of 2021 additional collective farms were instituted, the yields of the four major Polish crops were seen to decrease by 478,000 tons. The following year, the collectivization drive eased. The increase was only 228. There was a net gain of 225,000 tons.* The system of compulsory deliveries had a similarly discouraging effect, from the Planners' point of view.

"When you go among the crows," a Polish peasant proverb advises, "you must caw as they do." Insofar as they made little active resistance to the government's policy, the peasants were true to the old motto. What they did was to practice a stubborn passive form of subversion. Independent farmers juggled their deliveries, cheated on land records, or used judiciously placed bribes to keep local officials from becoming too curious. The years of oppression after the eighteenth century partitions had given the Polish peasantry an impressive kind of underground solidarity, a

---

* The figures are based on collectives founded between October and April only, which, due to the seasonal nature of the crops, affected the year's production.

tradition easily revived to deal with both Nazis and Communists. The ideas of class warfare introduced by the campaigns against "kulaks" served principally to unite the well-to-do farmers and the poorer class as they had seldom been united before. Communist officials from the cities came, grew exasperated and went, unable to cope directly with the deceptive acquiescence of the Peasant Resistance.

The collectives had been set up as showplaces, in the world of the Plan, where Marxist-Leninist shock brigades were to perform prodigies both in achievement and example. To that end they received almost 85% of the government investments in farm betterment and twice the amount of artificial fertilizer per acre. In the Poland of Reality the collectives performed very poorly for all this assistance. Their output remained far below that of the private holdings. They became a refuge for the unsuccessful or even the criminal elements of the population. By the end of 1955 they numbered only 8.5 per cent of the total farmland.

The most immediate effect of Gomulka's October 20 speech was the disintegration of the entire collective program. Three months after he announced official permission to decollectivize, the 10,582 collectives had been reduced to about 2,500. By January 1958 only 1,728 were left.

The "new economic model" that emerged in agriculture was just that. In effect, the farms were restored to the private enterprise system. Compulsory deliveries were scaled down, on their way to being abolished. Private persons could acquire and dispose of property, with only certain restrictions. Farmers were given credit, and purchases of agricultural equipment were no longer fenced in by paper restrictions. The remaining state farms and collectives were made subject to some efficient investigation.

Without waiting for government license, the more enterprising members of collectives had scattered to their private plots, carrying off just about everything but the name-plates with them. What was true of farmers was equally so of fishermen, who had also suffered from collectivization. All along the Baltic coast, fishermen broke up their old organizations, parcelling out the nets and boats (oftentimes illegally) between them.

The Party theoreticians, already puffing hard to justify some of the October's political scene-shifting, have since performed prodigies of ideological somersaulting in their explanations of the farm changes. Lip service is still paid to the collectives. "In a few years or more," said Edward Ochab, now Minister of Agriculture, in mid-1957, "the peasants will see for themselves that collective farming is better, because it ensures greater labor efficiency, larger crops . . . etc." The return to private ownership is justified by the argument that it doesn't really matter who owns the property, but how it is used—a theory with which many capitalists would agree.

But the results have justified any amount of Marxist-Leninist embarrassment. The harvest for 1957 was a record for the postwar period, a good 700,000 tons greater than 1956. The winter grain crop for 1958 has been assessed as higher still. Sugar production went up by 250,000 tons. Land that had lain fallow in the Recovered Territories has been snapped up by private purchasers. The increased income of the farmers, after prices were raised to fair levels, has not even become inflationary. A gratifying percentage of it has gone into capital investment for machinery, fertilizer, etc.

It is safe to predict that agricultural private enterprise, if allowed to continue, will in a few years eliminate Poland's need to import grain, which the country has done for the last 13 years. It also may concurrently restore the country to its pre-war position as a grain exporter. Gomulka is well aware of the effect this will have on his economy. Agriculture has already helped the general economy powerfully, by reducing the unfavorable balance of payments, by alleviating the cost of living problem in the cities, as food grows more plentiful. It will continue to provide a powerful amount of stability, political and social, in half the population. (When Gomulka saluted the peasantry, in his Whitsuntide address of 1957, as "co-masters of the country," he meant what he said.) This is not at all a bad price, a non-Polish economist can argue, for this profitable piece of Marxist exploration into the world of free enterprise.

*   *   *

In their struggles with the industrial economy, Gomulka and the liberal economists have not enjoyed such good fortune. In fact it became increasingly evident, as new plans and counter-plans were proffered and pigeon-holed, that the First Secretary and the liberal economists were not even on the same side.

The problems involved were admittedly far more intricate. Where the country's agriculture could be straightened out by the relatively simple expedient of righting wrongs and correcting mistakes, industry was in a far deeper mess. The over-industrialization of the past decade had given Poland surplus and uneconomic capacity in steel and machinery. This not only meant an increasing dependence on foreign sources, i.e. the Soviet Union, for ore supplies, but it had taken away energy and output from industries like textiles, chemicals and coal, which would normally be Poland's strong suit. "Coal is currency," a mining executive in Katowice said to me once, and he did not exaggerate.

Yet new plants and projects, once advanced, could not be thrown out the window like discarded blueprints. Selection and rationalization were essential. Consumer goods had to be released to the workers—even if it meant more loans and imports—to alleviate discontent and take up the slack until more production could be resumed in light industry. Plants had to be modernized. Most importantly, the workers had to work harder and better.

As an emergency wages had to be raised and consumer goods obtained. But wage rises were such an inflationary gesture, where goods were so scarce, that Gomulka froze them barely six months after he took power. The rule thereafter (often easier to enunciate than enforce) was that productivity had to rise before wages could. The workers' answer to this was not encouraging. "The government pretends to pay the workers," ran a slogan current in 1958, "and the workers pretend to work."

The liberal economists in the new Economic Council put through a plan for major industrial overhaul in May 1957. They documented a system of worker incentives, including forms of profit-sharing and a detailed plan of decentralization for industry, which would put industry in the hands of the workers at least partly, after they had already returned the land to the farmers. The Party economists added revisions with the zest of an American Congressional committee putting extra amendments on a Rivers and Harbors appropriation bill. When it emerged, the "new economic model" was hardly a victory for the liberals. Instead of giving factories some independence, their direction was put under a system of trusts, "independent units endowed with a corporate status" which would direct the production goals and operations of groups of factories or industries. The trusts were to be "financially," not ideologically interested in the industries working for them—in itself a major step forward. Yet their officials would be appointed by the ministry concerned. This more than hinted at continued political control.

The reform, as finally evaluated, fell critically short of the independent management the liberals had advocated. The odds were that in the end bureaucratic centralism would die, only be replaced by a form of bureaucratic decentralism.

The fate of the workers' councils was more discouraging. At the time of the October Revolution, Oscar Lange called the workers' councils "the cornerstone of the political, social and economic changes sweeping the country." Along with the "independence of socialist enterprises," the councils, in his view, were one of the basic premises of the new economic model.

The workers' councils had sprung up spontaneously even before the October. They had been a major source of Gomulka's strength. Their ultimate economic efficiency was debatable. But they were economically efficient in their context in that they gave thousands of Polish workers the will to work, by letting them in on the decision-making of their factories. A workers' council meeting in a Polish factory was not exactly an orderly process. In a very typical meeting which I saw at Nowa Huta, there was a minimum of polite agenda-raising, a maximum of table-pounding, angry voices, and quick protests seasoned with a lot of rough and ready humor. But generally the council's decisions were determined by what was good for the factory. The men the councils approved as directors and plant officials were largely the people who could do the job well, with little regard to their politics.

This is precisely what bothered Warsaw about them. The problem had not come up in Yugoslavia, where the workers' councils had been set up by the Party, and have always remained under

Party control.* But among Poland's 5,000 workers' councils there were many in which Party members were consciously given a back seat. This clearly ran counter to Gomulka's plans for rebuilding a shattered Party organization.

As early as the Ninth Plenum, in May 1957, Gomulka began to reassert the Party's control, when he ordered Party members to capture the workers' councils in self-defense. "The Party," he said, "should exert political guidance over the work of the councils through systematic consultation and instruction of comrades who are also members of the Councils, but without issuing orders or giving administrative guidance to the Councils."

In April 1958 he went further. The Central Committee announced a new charter for workers' councils, by which their autonomy would be effectively shattered. The Party secretary in a plant was made *ex officio* a member of the Council. Going further, the council itself was merged with trade union representatives—these are of course strictly controlled—and Party representatives into a new workers' conference. In line with Communist doublethink, the new organization was ironically called a "Workers' Autonomy Conference."

At the same time, the Party came down hard on the right to strike, the right which Gomulka had himself so eloquently justified in his comments on the Poznan revolt in 1956. In May 1957, although denouncing wildcat strikes, he had said flatly, "We do not want to apply administrative sanctions in cases where workers walk off their jobs." Strikes had happened in the meantime—like the Lodz transport workers' strike in August 1957 and the Wroclaw electrical workers' strike in January 1958. They were dealt with cautiously and the workers received some support in the public press. Accordingly the official attitude had changed.

At the Eleventh Plenum Gomulka said: "In a socialist state the working class can always defend its rights, through its own organi-

---

* During a visit to Yugoslavia in 1953, I was given an interesting explanation of the council's working processes by an enthusiastic young Party member. "We have complete democracy here," he said, "for example, suppose there is a debate in the workers' council about how much of the factory's profits we should give back to the government and how much we should keep. Suppose the Party members say to give back 70% and others say better 40% or 30%. Well, we compromise at 60%."

zation, if someone encroaches on them, without resorting to a strike.
. . . Therefore any strike which is not approved by the trade unions is contrary to our idea of order and socialist legality. Strikes of
the kind which arise from time to time are signs of anarchy under
the conditions of socialist freedom. In Poland they are manifestations of the activity of the class enemy." To punctuate the statement, two dozen workers were conspicuously fired from their jobs
for "trouble-making." Their fellow-workers might have reflected
that they were just about back where they started from two years
before, and in the same place, for the scene of the firings was the
Cegielski railway equipment plant in Poznan.

The repression of workers' autonomy was accompanied by a
corresponding retreat in the newly opened 'private sector.' In October 1956, the Central Committee formally resolved to foster small
private factories and retail outlets "in those branches of production
in which they could contribute to increasing the supply of goods on
the market, without at the same time encroaching on the raw
material sources of state and cooperative industries." In the next
month, private business establishments began dropping out of the
trees, in a volume which the Marxist planners had scarcely con-
templated. Within 6 months 10,067 new commercial firms appeared. After a year retail stores increased by 134%, with heavy
increases in the numbers of handicraft shops and small factories.

Although the liberal economists fought hard for them, the Party
men were soon able to show Gomulka and the Central Committee
how unruly this development had become. Their products found
easy markets, since they were of better quality than the government output. And they began inevitably to find their way into lines
of endeavor outside of the rigidly demarked limits which the
Marxist economists had set for them. Their greatest sin, like that of
the workers' councils, was that they were of course not amenable
to Party political control.

As a result, a series of restrictive laws, exorbitant taxes, and enforced materials shortages were visited on emergent Polish businessmen. A vicious circle was put into effect. When a private business man resorted to bribery to get raw materials (after government sources had reneged on their promise to supply them), he
could be caught as a "speculator" and prosecuted, or at least driven

out of business. In September 1957, rents for private businessmen were increased—often quintupled. A tax policy was effected, which increased taxes progressively with the hiring of labor. "In this way," the economic journal *Zycie Warszawy* commented, "the tax system restricts the expansion of artisans' workshops and encourages the establishment of dwarf enterprises which are economically unsound and provide no opportunities for training apprentices."

It did not require any skilled reader of economic auguries to say that by the middle of 1958 the Party economists were far ahead of the liberals in their increasingly back-stage struggles. Gomulka's plan to restore the authority of the political Party had collided with the drive for economic efficiency and won, hands down. The men of the Plan were back at the controls, working at all the magical central levers and push-buttons with which Marxist-Leninist theory pretends an economy can be run. Stimulated by partial victory, they had even announced not a five, or six, but a Fifteen Year Plan, with presumably infinite opportunity for rosy vision, glorious targets and heroic struggles in production fulfillment. So well had the revision to Marxist inefficiency progressed that by 1958 the Soviet press was warmly quoting Gomulka as an economic authority.

Fortunately, the extreme Planners overreached themselves. By the Twelfth Plenum in October, 1958, it was apparent that Gomulka and his favored economist, Jedrychowski, were in favor of a "centrist" position in economics as well as politics. Although Szyr and his friends had come a long way out of the woodwork since 1956, their appeals for a second violent, headlong industrialization were sharply turned down. Although Jedrychowski continued to deserve the label of a Party economist, the Gomulkist program he announced specifically included compromises with the need for housing and consumer goods, a very cautious approach to further capital investment, and even some safeguards for the much-attacked "private sector." The voice of the liberals continued to be heard, although they lost at least for the time being their fight to restore some semblance of fair pricing systems and the early progress towards a market economy.

Only in agriculture did the liberals stay successful. Against all renewed Party criticism Gomulka held firm to his original October

1956 promises. All the Party speakers at the Twelfth Plenum paid lip service to the ultimate goal of collectivization, but the figures told another story. In the second quarter of 1958, for example, 41 collective farm units were formed; 45 were dissolved. Agriculture of course remains the one prosperous area of the economy.

Remembering the golden promises of October 1956, the liberal economists might well mutter to themselves Lenin's old reproach (given in the opposite context) of "one step forward, two steps back." Yet for all of the backward steps taken since 1956 Poland remains many cuts above the level of industrial servitude known in the other Communist countries. Some of the liberals' economic ideas remain in force. The real tragedy of all the current government solutions is that they have become not vital changes, but superficial repairs. With a frankness unmatched anywhere else in modern Marxism, for example, the Poles in 1958 set about a mass pruning of surplus workers, estimated to constitute some 20% of all industrial employment. This was in itself a laudable and necessary reform. Since full employment is regarded by Communist regimes as a political necessity, surplus labor tends to proliferate, whether to keep down local unrest or to insure that the seasonal goals of the Planners can find fulfillment. In trying to rationalize their industry, the Poles took a courageous step.

Yet, without a general economic reform, the reduction of surplus employment only caused trouble. The removal of local factory independence has precluded any plans for expanding production in areas, mainly consumer goods and light industry, that could profitably absorb the excess working population. Similarly, the freeze on private enterprise has obviated the possibility of workers getting employment there. When initiative and independence are thrown out of consideration, mass firings in themselves are not likely to be a very happy solution. Equally unhappy is the announced alternative of the Party economists: more headlong industrialization to give the jobless work.

*   *   *

Za Stalina dyscyplina
Za Bieruta, Nowa Huta
Za Gomulki, Puste polki . . .

This little rhyme, which owes its euphony to the highly inflected structure of Polish nouns, is not quite fair to the present Polish government; but it has a lot to say about the past effect of Communism on the Polish people, and the overriding economic problem today, as seen by the man in the street, looking in at the store window.

> "In Stalin's time, we had discipline;
> In Bierut's time, we had Nowa Huta;
> In Gomulka's time, we have empty showcases."

The transition is in itself a back-handed testimonial to Gomulka's humanity. It is some sign of progress that the country's attention has been directed from getting arrested by the local agents of the M.V.D., through watching a colonial steel mill fastened on their economy by Russian technicians, to the healthier concern of wondering out loud when more consumer goods will appear on the shelves. If the concern is healthy, it is the only healthy thing about the wage-price situation in Poland. The years after the October revolution have brought some improvement. The amount of consumer goods produced in 1957, for instance, was a good ten per cent more than the year before. But the improvement has been only a slight fraction of what is needed. The Polish wage-earner remains angry, tired and half-despairing.

Gomulka's urgent efforts at wage rises and the distribution of consumer goods slowed the rising cost of living, more or less, from a jump to the pace of a steady hop. But it still rises. One-third of the families in the four most important branches of industry still live on a level of bare subsistence. In December 1957, the Swiss newspaper *Neue Zuercher Zeitung* published a detailed break-down of one white-collar worker's expenses, which tells its own story.

"To get a more accurate picture of the living standard of the average Polish citizen, we studied the monthly budget of a young engineer, assistant in a scientific institution. Of his monthly salary of 1,100 zlotys, taxes take 53, the rent of a furnished room (light, gas and use of the kitchen included) 40, trainfare to the office 16, and food between 25 and 30 zlotys per day. Together that makes about 900 zlotys, so that only 200 remain for clothes, books, entertainment, etc. We noted the prices prevailing in various cities and found them as follows, for one kilo each of sugar—12 zlotys; flour—6; butter—75; apples—8; grapes—15; a simple woman's dress, 1,500 zlotys; a man's suit (wool usually mixed with synthetic material) 2,000 to 3,000 zlotys; a pair of shoes of medium quality, 400 to 700 zlotys; a ticket to a movie or theatre show 4 to 18 zlotys.

"Under these circumstances a family can make both ends meet only if all its adult members work for money. Some people have two jobs—a secretary will do translations after hours, a museum attendant play the piano in a night club, others work as representatives for several firms, journalists write for several papers, etc. Needless to say, labor productivity is not improved by this practice."

If the *Neue Zuercher Zeitung*'s engineer wants to marry and have a family, probably his best immediate hope is to live on a farm in the countryside (if he happens to have relatives there). Housing is still in desperate straits. The government's housing program, although steadily increased since the October Revolution, has not been able to keep up even with the annual rise in population, which is, roughly, 500,000 souls. Here again the victory of the Party economists shows its teeth. For all the resolutions about new housing plans, the supply of materials allocated has been pitifully small. The government was and is unwilling to make heavy investments for it on a public scale, and the efforts of private business to substitute have been hamstrung by the growing weight of restrictions upon it.

In Marek Hlasko's short-story "We Take Off For Heaven," the hero renounces a new life with the woman he loves, when her present husband taxes him with the job of finding a roof for her and her child. "How long," says the crushed but curiously sympathetic husband, "will these lots last, these hostels, these five zloty collections for vodka, these lists of malingerers, these crowds in street-cars, these lines for butter? How long will lovers have no place to live, how long will people have to part because of an apartment, washing and trash like that? If I didn't know how things were before, I would think I was in hell now."

Such despair, compounded of utter frustration, is the theme song of the Poland of Economic Reality. So many of the problems of housing, food, and what the recipients of literary awards like to call human dignity, have been rendered virtually beyond the power of an individual to deal with. In conditions of extreme need, the individual worker is denied scope for the initiative by which he shackled by the over-industrialization of the past, Poland is also the prisoner of incidentals like falling world coal prices, or the suspicion of American Congressmen in withholding large-scale loans, the only way by which the country could have got a temporary breathing-space in which to work on its cumulative problems.

In this regard the Lenin Works at Nowa Huta can be seen as a microcosm of an entire country. It produced its first steel in 1954, the crowning glory of the Moscow Polish Planners. It remains the showplace of Polish industry. Foreigners are assiduously invited to view its modern furnaces and its new rolling mill. Visitors can discuss production problems with the hard-working director. It is an impressive experience. Although steel mills, like shipyards, have a certain universality about them, no one can doubt, after a few hours' tour, that the workers are competent, much of the machinery good, the products well worth exporting to a variety of customers that run the gamut from Egypt to France. Yet the very bigness and newness of Nowa Huta is a disaster. Unless iron ore miraculously springs out of the ground at the Shrine of Czestochowa some day soon, Nowa Huta's heaping ore-cars can never be much more than a depressing reminder of Poland's economic dependence on the Soviet Union, its faded poster slogans and thinly smiling workers a memorial to the domestic tragedies of Warsaw's ideological and economic slide-rule merchants.

The entrance to the Lenin Works is broad and impressive, the main headquarters building a shiny structure of stone and marble. Going up the marble stairs into the administration building, curiously, the most distinguishing single feature is the rows of empty holes, where railings presumably were intended. Some Planner's rule had evidently slipped. More spectacular slippage was evident in the ambitious production goals still visible (in mid-1957) on the large posters left over from the pre-October period. They have long since been scaled down to believable levels. The 1957 goal was set at 1,000,000 tons, although it fell short of realization. The

1956 figure was 700,000 (actually produced) as opposed to a fantastic planned target. Yet the constant rise in output is real and to the men on the spot encouraging. The principal gap in the picture is that no one knows what to do with it all.

The steel combine, in common with all pre-Gomulka enterprises, was planned as a part of the Soviet Union's closely integrated system for the satellite economy. Plans were speeded at the time of the Korean War, when the Russians observed the obvious advantages of having their satellites do the work of munitions production for limited wars, leaving the Soviet economy intact for more sophisticated tasks. When in October 1956, the Poles made bold to think of some economic free-lancing, it became plain that Nowa Huta would have a hard time making its way in the non-Communist export market. Its proprietors and their Ministry representatives now do their best to hawk the mills' wares—most of which is simple steel sheets—where they may. The only way they can do this, at a price of $150 a ton for rolled goods—is by persistent government subsidy.

Lest the managers in Nowa Huta and Warsaw think too friskily of their rising export trade, there are always the loaded ore-cars to remind them where their raw materials come from. "Seventy-five per cent of the ore we use we import," one of the plant officials explained, "and of that amount 85% comes from the Soviet Union." To facilitate the flow of raw material, a canal has been planned to connect the Vistula with the Dnieper. This would insure a steady two months' supply of the sandy ore from Krivoi Rog, not judged sufficiently highgrade for the Russians' own uses.

The ore from Nowa Huta, transformed into its steel plates and locomotives, goes off on its way to markets abroad. There is no domestic market for such a quantity. If half the output of steel sheets was exported in 1957, the primary reason was that Polish industry could not possibly use it all. What the West and the underdeveloped Eastern countries do not take, the Soviet economic system finds uses for—although not those of much interest to any Poles seeking the national profit.

There are 17,000 workers in the Lenin Foundry—"the Foundry of Socialism" as the title over the entrance proclaims—not counting some 9,000 building and construction employees. Three thousand of them are Party members, although their Party spirit is no higher here than anywhere else. Among the more incongruous signs left from the pre-October days was one with the legend: "The strength of the Party is its connection with the masses." Noticing it, at least in mid-1957, was good for a sure-fire smirk from any representative of the toiling masses in the vicinity. For Nowa Huta workers, providing the motive power for the planners' show-place, are little better off than wage-earners anywhere else in the country.

They have had, it is true, a barren new town built for them just east of Cracow, which in its aesthetic adornments and friendly neighborhood surroundings is about on a par with some of the slum clearance projects erected in recent years by the City of New York. The average wage for a mechanic is 1800 zlotys a month. Although the men working in the furnaces get up to 3000 zlotys, a good wage by Polish standards, the maximum figure is not too frequent. The average of about 2,000 (the sweepers get only 700) is calculated to keep a family of three barely going in the present state of the economy. But there is a bonus plan. Single workers in the mechanical departments operate on a piecework basis. In most departments, however, bonuses are calculated by production figures. If a department gets its production up over 90% of the set figure, every man in it gets 4% of his salary for each point in excess of 90%. It is complicated, but better, almost everyone agrees, than the rigid system of norms in vogue under the Bierut regime.

In October, 1956, the Nowa Huta workers gathered in the big garage to express their solidarity with the Gomulka Revolution. Like almost everyone else in their position, they have since been disappointed by the consequent lack of pie-in-the-sky, or even a healthy bite. But their morale is higher than in most areas of the economy, as is fitting for a show-place. Most of them have roots in the villages of the immediate area—it was part of the original Nowa Huta scheme ("the sociological motive," as an angry Cracow visitor described it) to settle there surplus farm workers, building a 'workers' community' to counteract the hostility of the conservative Cracow population to the regime. So they are now tied to their new working place, a situation where 90% of them are working for the first time. They are reasonably active in workers' councils and similar activities, but they grow ever more cynical about their powers. They have at least the stimulation of starting something new, a specific enterprise which for all its shortcomings and base original motives, is a testimonial to the zeal that can infect Polish industry.

They are fortunate, also, in that the regulation of their lives by the government at least obviates any worries about the quality of their product, its cheapness, its marketability. "Must this always be dependent on Russia," the foreign visitor asks himself. "Is there any hope for getting ore by boat and barge economically down the Vistula from the Baltic ports? Would it be better to close the whole project down—or is it now too late? At least the Silesian coal is nearby." Such questions can never be far away from either the Ministry in Warsaw, or the hard-pressed director of the plant, an engineer who, like many technicians in the same boat, has been working in steel mills and running them for several different kinds of governments. "There are no privileges connected with this position," said the director to a visitor at the close of a 20 hour day, "Only hard work. There are not many people willing to take it."

*　　　*　　　*

The most distinguishing thing about a Communist economy is waste. It is not the productive waste of a capitalist society, as it is known at least in the Western Hemisphere, where the outmoded products, the faded ideas, the rejected entrepreneurs are themselves turned into ultimately productive forces by the very urgency of competition. In the dead world of planification, waste stagnates. It stimulates nothing, because competition there is none. The end result of the long march from blueprints to finished articles is a litter of defective parts and disgruntled people.

The human element enters only to compound the economic felony. Since the Marxist-Leninist system, and the Party, are by definition perfect, every mistake must be blamed on somebody. In the paper world of ideology, mistakes may cost little. An over-clever editorial in *Trybuna Ludu* or an inquisitive exposé in *Nowa Kultura* can be stopped by the censor, or even forgotten in the general paper welter. But a factory full of defective parts is harder to conceal or forget. An assembly-line of cars with unworkable clutches cannot be erased in somebody's office. That is why the bloodiest personal struggles in the world of Communism, the grossest errors, the blackest purges have their starting points in the economy.

The waste of the Soviet economy has become so ingrown with the entire system that even the most critical commentators often forget about it. The world is too obsessed and disturbed by the news of Khrushchev's intrigues or diplomatic offensives in Central Europe, Asia or the Middle East to make much of the fact, for example, that his gamble on grain production resulted in a staggering loss to the Soviet economy. Yet even in the Soviet Union, dedicated since the agriculture purges of 1928 to sacrificing economy for politics, economic errors are costly—in men, if not in money. For a Khrushchev mistake at the highest level, someone down the line must pay the piper.

The government of Gomulka had a chance to attack this waste, within the limits of its system and the international politics that are both the ultimate and the visible sanction of that System's authority. For a time it did so, often with outstanding success. But through the months it dawned on some of the leadership (it had never escaped others) that the waste of planification, bureaucracy and Party rule was essential to the System. When the two Polands moved together, the Poland of Reality, with its normal instincts for hard work, incentives and simple human efficiency, speedily showed its ability to overthrow the Poland of the Plan. Here, as in politics, the partial honesty of Gomulka's national Communism quickly uncovered the basic fraud of Communism itself.

The battle between efficiency and ideology is not over in Poland; but it has become just that. In shying away from anything like a market economy, in re-imposing restrictions on private enterprise, or the enterprise of individual state factories, Gomulka has shown himself as aware as Khrushchev that Marxist economics are an inverted form of ideology, or, more simply, the central means of keeping the Party in power. But due to the relative freedom of expression existing in Poland, the battle is at least visible, and it is not wholly one-sided. There are many fissures in the monolith of the state's economic control. Lacking the normal Communist secret police force—and not wanting one, either, Gomulka has made compromises with reality that Communists like the neighbor Czechs regard as veritable wild and wooly capitalism.

Yet the reforms of the October Revolution were curbed. They were screened by the verbal gymnastics of "anti-capitalism," "anti-revisionism" or appeals to the sovereignty of that mythical neo-Platonic universal called "the workers." Nothing more clearly illustrates the paradox of modern Poland than the spectacle of this economy partly released from its fetters, but condemned by the political premises of its rulers never really to be free. Whether the paradox is realized, enjoyed, or regretted by Wladyslaw Gomulka and his staff, no one can rightly say.

Epilogue

IN JANUARY, 1959, when this book was finished, the Polish October Revolution was not yet two and a half years old. As it faced the world, it had to admit of many humiliations. Gomulka, who first hoped to weld a new solidarity with the neighboring revolt in Hungary, had been forced to denounce the leaders of this revolt in public, using the same slander of "counter-revolutionary" long since codified by the Soviet Union. When Imre Nagy and the other leaders of Hungary's brief freedom were killed by the Russians in July, 1958, Gomulka kept his silence. His government, which alone among Communist regimes had made peaceful, honest negotiations with the outside world, was reduced to using assembly-line Soviet platitudes against "imperialists" as a substitute for diplomacy.

Inside Poland the Frozen Revolution had justified its name. Its original movers seemed stopped in the act of motion—not killed, or seriously persecuted, but stopped—so that the country's political and social landscape looked like a camp of Arctic explorers trapped by a sudden, killing ice storm. The commander was fixed at his post, taking sightings. The cook stood rigid in his galley, in the act of stirring the now solid food. The scouts were eternally getting out of their sledges, bearing game and good news. The followers in the camp stood, mouths open, cheering. The repairmen were frozen at their posts, tools still in hand. Even the camp conspirators were congealed in the act of plotting.

There was partial retrogression from Gomulka's original advance away from the Russian Communist system. Censorship once more was a force to be reckoned with. The industrial economy was being misshaped by some of the same doctrinaire Communists who had wrecked it once before. Yet the farm economy remained free and consequently prosperous. The truce with the Church creaked and clattered; but the severe efforts of both the First Secretary and the Primate to preserve it showed its necessity. Foreign radio broadcasts were not jammed. The secret police had not been reinstituted, at least in any way which normal Communist standards would call effective.

The forward motion of the Revolution was gone. The roar of press protest against the evils of the Communist System had been tuned down to an angry mutter. The freedoms of the farmers and the Church were subjected to ever-increasing snipings and petty infringements. Hope had died aborning that the workers' councils or the new retail establishments could bring about a new rational kind of economy, socialist but efficient and value-giving. People could still criticize, but they could do increasingly less about correcting the abuses they disliked.

Pressure from the Soviet Union grew steadily heavier. There was no fear of overt action, as long as the Gomulka regime retained its strong popular base. The regime's public chantings against the "American imperialists" (which disturbed Gomulka little) and its public approval of the Hungarian terror and executions (which disturbed him a great deal) were sufficient to appease the Russian demands for solidarity, at the moment. But Poland's constant, corrosive influence on the thinking of Communists elsewhere was responsible for the constant yells for orthodoxy among the other members of the Communist flock. The Poles were accustomed to hearing Walter Ulbricht and the Czechs make disparaging comments about how they fostered and coddled that by now permanent intra-Party menace, "revisionism." When Khrushchev began to state meaningfully that any true Communist state must have complete collectivization this was a more serious matter. So they had made their peace with Khrushchev, and Ulbricht, too.

How long could this Frozen Revolution retain even the half-successes of its October? How long could a recognizable theory of government exist, stabilized only by the balance of its incongruities? Commentators on politics had regularly predicted the fall of Gomulka's government, since the first months after the October Revolution of 1956. The grounds for their predictions were well-reasoned and precise. That is exactly what made the predictions baseless. The reasonable predictions neglected that most unreasonable factor, the people of Poland. The Poles of history were rash and heedless; their descendants, although abundantly capable of the rash act or the senseless statement, had been taught an extraordinary respect for cautious temporizing by 15 years of an existence more horrible than any national experience of modern times—barring small nations like the Kalmucks or the Chechen-Inguish, who were extinguished for their ancestors' indiscretion in settling areas later occupied by the Soviet Union.

The reasonable predictions had consistently undervalued the talents of Wladyslaw Gomulka, as a patriot and as a practical politician. Under consistent pressure, he had yielded step by step to the demands of the Russians that he more closely approximate the parrot behavior of the Czechs and the East Germans. At the same time, in a far less publicized way, he had steadily purged from the Polish Communist Party leadership the "Stalinists"—nowhere else in the Communist world is this term still in fashion—who were either direct agents of the Russians or postulants in this field. Gomulka had stood almost alone in October 1956. By October 1958 he had gained control of the Party apparatus and peopled it with his supporters. The Russians faced an exasperating paradox: the man who daily increased his public protestations of pro-Russianism used the credit gained to speed the political liquidation of the pro-Russians remaining inside his government.

The Primate's efforts continued to be made in the same direction, however distasteful the necessity of collaborating with the Church's plighted enemies. When the tension between Church and state broke into the open, as in the police raid on the monastery shrine of Jasna Gora in July 1958, both principals made every effort to smooth the consequences—after each had made his point. Intellectuals continued to go from Poland to the West—on scholarships, visits or delegations. Although they were discontented with the course events had taken, there was little question in their minds about returning. They left freely. They returned freely. In this regard they were different from the traveling representatives of any other variety of Communism.

The principal error made in estimating the duration of the Frozen Revolution lay in disregarding the times that had engendered it. For the very reason that such a change had been successful, for the same reason that it had not finally succeeded, it was doomed to its state of suspended animation. The international stalemate denied the Russians the chance to repress any national Polish movement, without risk. In January 1959 the American position was not so strong as it was in October 1956; the Russian was not so weak. But over two years after the Revolution, the differences in missile stockpiles or thermonuclear progress were as yet not significant enough to tilt the power balance decisively— nor for a time would they be. It was a special kind of irony that Madam Curie's home country gained and kept what freedoms it had as a result of various radioactive possibilities.

It was in any sharp imbalancing of this tension between two poles that the real danger to the Frozen Revolution was contained. In its more hopeful aspect, the imbalance could come from a steady rise in American power—and wisdom, capable of exerting steady liberalizing pressure on the Communist world. In its less hopeful aspect, imbalance could come from the Russian power. If this happened, the fate of the Revolution was sealed.

In the two years since the October Revolution the shape and size of the Russian power had changed ominously. The October of 1956 had seen it at its weakest since the days when Moscow lacked the Bomb. The satellite empire was in revolt, the new leadership of the Moscow oligarchy not yet fully established, the barely controllable post-Stalin Thaw was melting its way through every corner of society *inside* the Soviet Union, as well as without. In the east its unruly ally, China was about to be torn by a major intellectuals' revolt of its own. Its widespread nature suggested that a number of Chinese, for Mao Tse Tung's purposes uncomfortably large, had mastered the differences between Confucianism, freedom and the closed Communist society. This was temporary.

In one perspiring year, the Russians managed to shore up the foundations of their empire and, for appearance's sake, their ideology. By the end of 1957, after celebrating the Fortieth Anniversary of their October Revolution, they had restored outward order everywhere, and could afford to glare, as in the case of Yugoslavia, where they had previously found it expedient to fawn. The obliging absence of any serious American pressure—diplomatic, economic, or even promotional—on the Soviet empire in this period greatly assisted the Russians in their housecleaning.

But the internal damage done by the events of 1956, the Russians realized, could not be so easily repaired. The successful nationalism of Gomulka, in particular, and the democratizing ideas of the Polish revisionists continued to spread their message behind the Iron Curtain. In late 1957 and 1958 a storm of protests arose among intellectuals in Romania and Bulgaria, previously thought the safest of Soviet strongholds. They were made on lines strikingly similar to the Polish and Hungarian protests of the year before. Such public furores, and the private reactions to them, only stressed the priority of the Soviet offensive against a partially free Poland. The Russian effort to overturn the tense balance in Poland redoubled.

The methods used were only partly in the form of political threat, both inside and outside Poland. More effectively, they included strong economic leverage. After 1956 it would have taken the Poles at least five years to wrench the principals of their economy out of the Soviet orbit. Between *sputnik*-building and new donations of political aid to the Middle East, the Russians found time to extend their economic hold on the Poles, by a judicious combination of carrots and sticks. The Polish threat was directly responsible for the new stress in 1958 on Russian-satellite cooperation and joint economic planning, its terms more generous than those of the former relationship. It was here that the Russians were succeeding. Without answering pressures from the outside no amount of Polish heroism could in the end fend them off.

It is probably easier to see danger than opportunity. Which may explain why the United States, although alerted to the possibilities of the Frozen Revolution's continuance, did little to keep alive the necessary degree of tension. The total amount of U. S. loans made to the Poles came to $193 million in 1957 and 1958. This amount was useful and appreciated. It represented some concessions by the U. S. Congress, which is generally conservative about any loans, the more especially after it has authorized too many foolish ones. (Poland's misfortune was to come in for aid after the gravy train had chugged into a siding.)

Yet the amount was small and inadequate for the purpose it might have accomplished. Rarely has there been a case where U. S. financing could have been used to better purpose. For every dollar wisely given to Poland meant quite literally that the Poles were decreasing by at least that amount their dependence on the Soviet Union. Every piece of mining machinery purchased in the United States meant that the Polish industrial plant was that less susceptible to Soviet economic blackmail. Every student or technical expert educated in the United States was that much more influence against the resumption of Russian cultural and technical hegemony.

It is not pertinent to this book to discuss the broad misshapings of American foreign policy in this period. But the behavior of the Eisenhower administration in the case of Poland justified its comparison to a lazy optimist possessed of spasmodically working fire-drill reflexes. After Washington had finally realized that Gomulka was not just another Communist, it took eight months to get an emergency loan to the Poles, which they wanted immediately in order to forestall Russian economic domination and effect direct, immediate internal reforms. (The surplus American wheat, for example, enabled the Gomulka government to ease up on forcible quotas, thus speeding the return of the farms to free enterprise.) The effect of an instant loan to Poland would have been tremendous. Among other things it would have appreciably diminished the suspicion of Gomulka and his entourage towards American motives. The slow timing and the relatively small amount offered took away a large part of the loan's effectiveness as a gesture and most of its effectiveness in practice.

It is purposeless to argue that Congress balked the loan, or that the U. S. was throwing money away. Witness, in the same year the huge sums given to the rickety kingdom of Laos. In this, as in other activities, the Eisenhower administration failed to transmit any sense of urgency about Polish aid to either the Congress or the country. Similarly, in the summer of 1958, there were senators who tried manfully to amend the Battle Act, so that the Administration could make loans or grants to highly unorthodox "Communist" countries like Poland in the U. S. national interest, if the urgency of a situation warranted it. After originally promising its support, the Administration lifted not a finger to help the bill through. It died in Congress.

In the life of an American newspaper reader, or even of an average Congressman, these lapses in 1957 and 1958 meant little. But the unconcern with which they were greeted was part of a general ignorance that the situation in Poland was an open flank of the Russian position, waiting to be turned. Nothing of the sort was intimated. As a result, the astonishing American inaction of October, 1956, was repeated in some degree through the two years following. A new ambassador was sent to Warsaw, but six months after the real time for maneuvering had passed. U. S. books and magazines were sent to Poland, but after long waiting. Help was given, but in a very routine way.

Not many Americans realize how well regarded their country is in Poland. There the activities of the United States and Russia in recent history have almost fitted into a polar pattern of good versus evil influence. It was Woodrow Wilson who forced the creation of modern Poland in 1919, by holding firmly to this thirteenth of his Fourteen Points. It was Lenin, at the same time, who sent his armies into Poland "to break the crust of the Polish bourgeoisie with the bayonet." Despite the horrendous mistakes of the Roosevelt foreign policy dealings with the Russians in World War II, the Poles retained a traditional admiration for the United States— although they could (and often did) argue that Franklin D. Roosevelt's diplomatic ignorance had undone them as an independent country. Through the post-war Communist decade, American influence had been effectively shut out of Poland, with no opportunity, as the State Department saw it, to reenter.

In 1956 the Russians left a vacuum in this country, when they were virtually expelled from it. The Eisenhower administration, for all its official talk of "power vacuums," lacked the skill or enterprise to introduce effective American influence into the vacuum. In Poland—and of course in Hungary—in 1956, as with the Berlin crisis in late 1958, the men who had preached "liberation" in their election campaigns waited for the Soviet Union to act, so that they might *re*-act. The advantages, even the possibilities of original enterprise in international politics seems to have escaped them. Meanwhile the Russians, like good infantry soldiers, began to crawl back into their old positions, using every available device of bribery, threat and intimidation to enforce their return.

In the long run the Frozen Revolution can only hold its curious half-permanent ground in Poland if a concerted effort is made by the Americans to restore their half of the slipping world power balance. This may involve heavier economic assistance, and increase of the private educational aid so well begun by the Ford and Rockefeller foundations. Above all, it demands a flexible, attentive diplomatic policy, which can realize the Russian pressure behind Gomulka's international party-lining and counter it with tangibles, instead of merely watching it. It goes without saying that the impact of American policy here depends, also, on the overall strength of the U. S. military position.

Poland has acted the role of a pilot-study in Communist decay, although its Communist proprietors would hardly admit it. It has worked out the fulfillment of national aspirations against the imperialism of the Russians. By its very concessions, it has demonstrated the scant worth of a Soviet-exported system when unsupported by cruel police coercion, the hopeless failures of the doctrinaire ideologies and economists when their mistakes can no longer be disguised by harsh "administrative measures." Nothing should be allowed to obscure the importance of these facts to the world political situation.

This importance is not lost on the Poles. The country of the Frozen Revolution reacts with extraordinary quickness to the slightest change in the tension of the two forces that determine its attitude. Even when the domestic struggle seems to abate, when the opposing currents inside Poland are locked in their recurrent temporary truce, the images of the outside remain. As the poet, Adam Mickiewicz noted almost a century before:

> "Within their silent, perfect glass
>   The mirror waters, vast and clear,
>   Reflect the silhouette of rocks,
>   Dark faces brooding on the shore."*

* Translated by Cecil Hemley.

Within their country's limitations the Poles continue to work and fight, however deep their disillusionment. The October was never fulfilled, but it is a monument, perhaps a permanent one, in the history of this century. Its freedoms may be modest, compared to its hopes. It offers the prospect of no dashing victory, no triumph of good over evil, no supremacy of truth. On the contrary it is the living enactment of our strongly Manichean world, where the good must live side by side with the bad, the healthy with crippling in a nuclear intimacy, with hope for breathing space but despair of foreseeable victory.

There is hope for all free men in Poland's living witness to the power of free men and free institutions to force compromises on the leaders of an enslaving society—without a remotely comparable physical force of their own and near the center of Communist world power. With all the disadvantages of the Polish position, the Poles have continued to hold it. Their success is both a demonstration and an augur that the cast-iron Communist System, as we know it, cannot long live in an atmosphere of democratic meeting and mutual honest concession. One can only repeat—and second—the words written by the editors of *Tygodnik Powszechny* on the first anniversary of their revolution: "The defense of October means the defense of a reasonable compromise. We are again undergoing a serious test, but . . . we engage our forces with the belief that the great deed of October will not be wasted."

Index

Agriculture, 28, 176–177, 218, 225, 238–241, 246–247
All-Polish Union of Atheists and Freethinkers, 122, 150
Andrycz, Nina, 78
Andrzejewski, Jerzy, 113–114
Argumenty, 122, 150
Armia Krajowa, see Home Army
Auschwitz, see Oswiecim
Autochthons (of Western Territories), 172, 180–181

Banczyk, Stanislaw, 47
Barth, Karl, 135
Berling, Zygmunt, 208
Berman, Jacob, 7, 37, 54, 193
Bezpieka, see U.B.
Bienkowski, Wladyslaw, 19, 47, 69, 75–76, 120, 148, 150, 227
Bierut, Boleslaw, 5–6, 37, 43, 46, 48, 50, 53, 70, 144, 239
Bismarck, Otto von, 130–131, 202
Bobrowski, Czeslaw, 77, 222, 224, 237
Boleslaw I, 196
Boleslaw III, 196
Bor-Komorowski, Tadeusz, 206–208
Brandys, Kazimierz, 113
Breslaw, 169, 174 (see also Wroclaw)

Bug River, 221
Bukharin, Nikolai, 35, 73–75, 100, 227–228
Bulgaria, 119, 219, 260
Bytom, 218

Calvinist Churches, 125
Captive Mind, The, 100
Caritas, 133, 145, 151
Casimir the Great, 48, 196
Catherine the Great, 198
Catholic Church in Poland, 122–168; historical background, 126–133; piety of members, 125–127; ratio of members to total population, 125; relation of Church to nationalism, 126–131, 164; relations with Orthodox Church, 129–130; semi-isolation from other Catholic peoples, 126–129; under Communist regime, 16–17, 19, 22, 51, 61–62, 67–68, 122–124, 132–168, 258 (see also Wyszynski, Stefan Cardinal)
Cegielski factory, see Poznan riots
Central Committee (Poland), 56, 65, 75–79, 81–82, 107, 223, 244–246
China, 219, 259
Churchill, Winston S., 172, 208

265

Collective farms, 28, 58, 176–177, 178–179, 218, 225, 238–241, 246–247

Communist Party in Poland, 5–9, 33, 38–50, 56–87, 97–99, 132–134, 143–153, 173–174, 215–255

Cyrankiewicz, Joseph, 7, 9–11, 13, 16, 71, 77–78, 188, 231

Czechoslovakia, 119, 219, 228

Czestochowa, Shrine of Our Lady of, 125–127, 151–152

Czuj, Jan. 158

Danzig, see Gdansk

Dibelius, Otto, 136

Djilas, Milovan, 35, 69

Dmowski, Roman, 64fn, 200

Dudintsev, Vladimir, 70–71

Dzierzynski, Feliks, 8

Dzis i Jutro, 155, 158

Eastern Poland, compared to the Western Territories, 220

Economy of Poland, 215–255

Education, Communization of, 97–98

Eighth Day of the Week, The, 30

Eisenhower, Dwight D., 207, 210, 261

Election of January 20, 1957, 61–63, 149

Europa, 84, 109, 166

Fejgin, Anatol, 51–52

Fifteen Year Plan, 246

Finder, Pawel, 43, 44

First Step in the Clouds, The, 115

Frank, Hans, 204, 205

Frederick the Great, 198

Gdansk, 171, 182–184

Germany, historical relations with Poland, 128–129, 130–131, 195–202; occupation of Poland, 125, 154–155, 185–191, 202–208; traditional dislike of Poles, 155, 190, 202–203, 204–205; in Western Territories, 169–172, 174–175

Gero, Erno, 81

Glos Ludu, 97

Gomulka, Wladyslaw, 7–8, 11–19, 32–87, 104–108, 114–117, 123–124, 148–153, 173, 194, 218–219, 231–234, 240–248, 254–258; associates, 75–78; career, 7, 38, 42–48; character, 35–37; defiance of Russians, 11–13, 33, 46–47, 53; fall from power (1948–1951), 7, 53–55; relations with Catholic Church, 122–123, 144, 148–153, 165–168; relations with intellectuals, 18–19, 84–85, 104–108, 114–117; speech of October 20, 1956, 56–59, 87, 231–232, 240; struggle to stay in power, 19, 61–64, 71–73, 78–87, 211, 256–263

Gomulka, Zofia, 37, 55

Hertz, Pawel, 109

Hlasko, Marek, 30, 114–115, 166, 249

Hlond, August Cardinal, 132, 137, 138, 155, 174–175

Hochfeld, Julian, 60

Home Army of Warsaw, 43–45, 205–209

Hungary, XI-XIV, 15–16, 80–81, 220, 256

Inco (Pax organization), 156–157

Industry in Poland, 215–227, 231–233, 241–243, 247, 250–253

Intellectuals, 13–14, 18–19, 60, 88–121

Internal Security Corps, 10, 13

I Saw Poland Betrayed, 47, 222

Jagiello, Duke of Lithuania, 196–197

Jasna Gora, 125, 258 (see also Czestochowa, Shrine of Our Lady of)

Jastrun, Mieczyslaw, 113–114, 117

Jazz in Poland, 29

Jedrychowski, Stefan, 72, 236, 246

Jelenski, K. A., 167fn

Jews in Poland, 125, 188–194

Kaczmarek, Czeslaw, 147, 148

Kadar, Janos, 87, 220

Karski, Jan, 202
Katyn Forest massacre, 96
K.B.W. (Internal Security Corps),
    10, 13
Khrushchev, Nikita, and October
    1956 crisis in Poland, 11–13, 14–
    15; speech at Twentieth Party
    Congress, 5, 56–57, 63, 86, 100;
    mentioned, 72, 74, 119–120, 254,
    257
Khrushchev and Stalin's Ghost, 72
Kisielewski, Stefan, 161, 204
Kliszko, Zenon, 47, 75
Klosciewicz, Wiktor, 81
Kolakowski, Leszek, 19, 79, 108–
    113
Komar, Waclaw, 10, 13
Konev, Ivan, 11, 12, 13
Korbonski, Stefan, 52
Kosciuszko, Thaddeus, 198–199
Kott, Jan, 94, 103–104, 109
Kruczkowski, Leon, 109
Kulturkampf, German, 131, 142
Kuznica, 98, 101

Labor in Poland, 13–14, 241–245,
    247–248, 251–253
Lane, Arthur Bliss, 47, 222
Lange, Oscar, 77, 235–237, 243
Lassota, Eligiusz, 62, 98, 104, 108
Lechon, Jan, 25
Lektorat (Communist Party lecture
    agency), 66
Lenin, Nikolai, 38, 42, 262
Lenin Works, see Nowa Huta
Living standards in Poland, 217–
    218, 226, 241–242, 248–250
Loga-Sowinski, Ignacy, 77
Lutheran Church, 135–136
Luxemburg, Rosa, 38

Majdanek (German concentration
    and extermination camp), 189–
    190
Mao Tse Tung, 22, 57fn, 259
Mazur, Franciszek, 13, 71, 80, 81,
    155
Mickiewicz, Adam, 24, 263
Mijal, Kazimierz, 19, 80

Mikolajczk, Stanislaw, 46, 47, 53,
    172fn
Mikoyan, Anastas, 11, 12
Milosz, Czeslaw, 100
Minc, Hilary, 37, 48, 193, 223–224,
    226
Mindszenty, Joseph Cardinal, 136,
    141–142, 168
Montini, Cardinal, 142–143
Mother of the Krols, The, 113

Nagy, Imre, 256
Napoleon, 199
National Council of Culture and
    Art, 103–104
Natolin Group, 33, 80
Nazis (National Socialist Party),
    154–155, 170, 185–191, 200
New Class, The, 69, 220
N.K.V.D., 155
Not by Bread Alone, 70–71
Nowa Huta (steel town), 215–216,
    243, 250–253
Nowa Kultura, 94, 97, 101–103,
    104, 109, 115–116, 235
Nowak, Zenon, 80
Nowe Drogi, 67, 71
Nowotko, Marceli, 43–45

Ochab, Edward, 7–8, 54, 146, 241
Oder River, 221
Opiela, Eryk, 67
Opole, 181–182
Ordass, Lajos, 135–136
Orechwo, Nikolai, 49, 50
Orthodox Church in Poland, 125,
    128, 129–130, 132, 134–135
Osmanczyk, Edward, 82
Ostapczuk, Bronislaw, 175–177
Oswiecim (German concentration
    and extermination camp), 185–
    190

Parliament, see Sejm
Pasternak, Boris, 57, 109–110, 118
Pax movement, 153, 155–160
Peasant Party, 33, 60
Peasantry, 28, 172, 238–241 (see
    also Agriculture, Collective farms)
Piasecki, Boleslaw, 19, 153–160

Piast kings, 195–196
Pilsen riots, 228
Pilsudski, Jozef, 38, 39, 132, 199–202, 220
Plenum, Eighth (October, 1956), 4–5, 56–59
Plenum, Eleventh (April, 1958), 244–245
Plenum, Ninth (May, 1957), 19, 79–81, 244
Plenum, Tenth (October, 1957, 82
Plenum, Twelfth (October, 1958), 246–247
Poem for Adults, 101–103
Poland, Agriculture, 28, 176–177, 218, 225, 238–241, 246–247; army, 9, 10–11, 15, 48, 202–204; boundary changes, 195–200, 205; Catholic Church, 122–168; Communist Party, 56–87, 215–255; disillusionment since 1939, 22–23, 210–214; economy, 215–255; election of January 20, 1957, 61–63, 149; German occupation, 125, 154–155, 185–191, 202–208; historical background, 128–131, 195–202; industry, 215–227, 231–233, 241–243, 247, 250–253; intellectuals, 13–14, 18–19, 60, 88–121; Jews, 190–194; labor, 13–14, 241–245, 247–248, 251–253; language, 26, 182, October 1956 crisis, 3–31; population changes, 125, 171, 200, 210; Russian occupation, 45–46, 172, 205–209; underground (World War II), 205–206 (see also Home Army); Western Territories, 46–47, 169–184, 220–222; World War II, 202–210
Polanians, 196
Polish Communist Party, see Communist Party in Poland
Polish Corridor, 200
Polish Parliament, see Sejm
Polish people, character traits, 19–22, 28–29, 211–214
Polish United Workers Party, 4–5, 43, 46, 47, 62, 65–68, 82–83, 223 (see also Communist Party in Poland)

Politburo, and Poland, 7, 8–10, 15, 41, 50, 53, 55, 65 (see also Communist Party in Poland)
Polityka, 108–109
Ponomarenko, Panteleimon, 13, 48
Po Prostu, 29, 94, 103, 104–105, 107, 108–109, 118–119, 166, 167, 235
Population, makeup of Polish, 125, 171, 200, 210
Poznan riots, 6, 18, 228–230
Protestant churches, 125, 135–136
Protestant Reformation, 129
Putrament, Jerzy, 119

Radio Free Europe, 118, 193
Radkiewicz, Stanislaw, 50–51
Rajk, Laszlo, 55
Rakosi, Matyas, 81, 193
Rape of Poland, The, 47
Rokossowski, Konstanty, 9, 12–13, 14–15, 94, 206
Roman Catholic Church, see Catholic Church in Poland
Romania, 119, 260
Romkowski, Roman, 51
Roosevelt, Franklin D., 172, 208, 209, 210, 262
Rozansky, Josef, 51
Russia, 195–202 (see also U.S.S.R.)

Sapieha, Adam Cardinal, 137, 140–141
Sejm (Parliament), 23–24, 161–162, 218
Serov, Ivan A., 52–53
Shrine of Our Lady of Czestochowa, 125–127, 151–152
Sikorski, Wladyslaw, 44, 205–206
Silesia, 171, 181, 202
Six Year Plan, 58, 223–227, 231–232
Slansky, Rudolph, 55
Slonimski, Antoni, 94, 103, 113–114
Slowo Powszechny, 156
Smigly-Rydz, 201, 203–204
Sobieski, John, 198
Social Democrats, 33, 60, 71
Socialists, 33, 47, 223
Spychalski, Marian, 47, 55, 76

Stalin, Josef, 5, 41–42, 56, 72–73, 100, 119, 172
State Commission of Economic Planning, 224
Stettin, see Szczecin
Stomma, Stanislaw, 31
Story of a Secret State, 202
Strikes, 40, 244–245
Students, 13–14, 29, 92–93, 94
Swiatlo, Joseph, 8, 54–55, 193
Szambierki mine, 218
Szczecin, 171, 182, 221
Szczepanski, Jan, 86–87
Szpilki, 68
Sztandar Mlodych, 94
Szyr, Eugeniusz, 232–233, 236, 238, 246

Teutonic Knights, 128, 196
Tito (Joseph Broz), 53, 73, 98, 123
Tokarski, Julian, 228
Trybuna Ludu, 65–66, 86, 103, 146
Twentieth Party Congress (U.S.S. R.), 5, 56–57, 59, 63, 86, 100
Tygodnik Powszechny, 150, 161, 162–163, 264
Tyrmand, Leopold, 113–114, 157

U.B., 8–9, 48–53, 229–230
Ulbricht, Walter, 257
Uniate Church, 125, 130
Union of Patriotic Priests, 158
Union of Socialist Youth, 120–121
Union of Soviet Socialist Republics, economic control of Poland, 215–216, 232–233, 242, 250–251, 253; increasing pressure on Poland, 19, 61–64, 80–81, 85–87, 211, 215–216, 250–251, 257, 259–260; occupation and control of Poland, 45–46, 48–49, 172, 205, 206; Warsaw uprising, 43–45, 206–209; mentioned, 9–10, 39, 219–220

United States, 20, 173, 222, 260–263
University of Lublin, 150, 162
Urzad Bezpieczenstwa, see U.B.

Vatican, 137fn, 142–143, 144, 145–146, 149, 152, 158, 174
Veritas (Pax organization), 156–157

Warsaw, 25–27, 43–45, 88–89, 191, 206–209
Warsaw Ghetto, 191
Warsaw Uprising, 43–45, 206–209
Wazyk, Adam, 101–103, 109
Werblan, Andrzej, 85
Western Territories, 46–47, 169–184, 220–222
We Take Off For Heaven, 249
Wilson, Woodrow, 200, 262
Wolfe, Bertram, 72fn
Woroszylski, Wiktor, 15, 97–98, 99, 100
Writers' Union, 117–118
Wroclaw, 169–170, 174, 175
Wyszynski, Stefan Cardinal, 16–17, 122–168, 258; career, 138–139; character, 124; election of January 20, 1957, 61–62, 149; relations with Communists, 141–168; relations with Gomulka regime, 148–153, 165–168

Yagoda, G., 239
Yalta Conference, 172
Yugoslavia, 17, 73, 123

Zeran auto factory, 232
Zimand, Roman, 20–21fn
Znak, 23, 153, 161
Zolkiewski, Stefan, 107
Zvezda, 86
Zycie Warszawy, 94, 235